The Discourse of Advertising

Advertising is an important topic which focuses issues from a range of disciplines. In keeping with recent developments in the study of language and advertisements, this comprehensive introduction to advertising discourse examines the language of contemporary advertising, seeing it not as an isolated object, but in complex interaction with the texts around it, with music and pictures and, importantly, with the people who make and experience it. Clearly explaining relevant theories of linguistics and poetics, each chapter ends with a series of stimulating exercises, and theoretical discussion is accompanied by examples of literary and sub-literary texts and recent advertisements.

Putting forward the controversial view that adverts answer a need for play and display in contemporary society, Guy Cook explores the social function of advertising, moving from the uses of sound and sight, through creativity and word play in the poetic intricacies of the text, to assess the effect of these on the people who receive adverts every day, and whose identity is partly constructed by them.

Guy Cook is Senior Lecturer in Applied Linguistics at the London University Institute of Education.

The INTERFACE Series

A linguist deaf to the poetic function of language and a literary scholar indifferent to linguistic problems and unconversant with linguistic methods, are equally flagrant anachronisms.   (Roman Jakobson)

This statement, made over twenty-five years ago, is no less relevant today, and 'flagrant anachronisms' still abound. The aim of the INTERFACE series is to examine topics at the 'interface' of language studies and literary criticism and in so doing to build bridges between these traditionally divided disciplines.

Already published in the series:

NARRATIVE
A Critical Linguistic Introduction
Michael J. Toolan

LANGUAGE, LITERATURE AND CRITICAL PRACTICE
Ways of Analysing Text
David Birch   •

LITERATURE, LANGUAGE AND CHANGE
Ruth Waterhouse and John Stephens

LITERARY STUDIES IN ACTION
Alan Durant and Nigel Fabb

LANGUAGE IN POPULAR FICTION
Walter Nash

THE LANGUAGE OF JOKES
Analysing verbal play
Delia Chiaro

LANGUAGE, TEXT AND CONTEXT
Essays in stylistics
Edited by Michael Toolan

The series editor
Ronald Carter is Professor of Modern English Language at the University of Nottingham and was National Coordinator of the 'Language in the National Curriculum' Project (LINC) from 1989 to 1992.

The Discourse of Advertising

Guy Cook

London and New York

First published in 1992
by Routledge
11 New Fetter Lane, London EC4P 4EE

Simultaneously published in the USA and Canada
by Routledge
a division of Routledge, Chapman and Hall, Inc.
29 West 35th Street, New York, NY 10001

Typeset in 10/12 pt Times by
Florencetype Ltd, Kewstoke, Avon
Printed in Great Britain by
TJ Press (Padstow) Ltd, Padstow, Cornwall

British Library Cataloguing in Publication Data
Cook, Guy
  Discourse of Advertising. – (Interface
  Series)
  I. Title II. Series
  302.23

Library of Congress Cataloging in Publication Data
Cook, Guy.
    Discourse of advertising / Guy Cook.
      p.   cm.
    Includes bibliographical references and index.
    1. Discourse analysis. 2. Advertising. 3. Applied linguistics.
  I. Title.
  P302.C625   1992
  659.1′014—dc20   92–2778

ISBN 0 415 04170 8
    0 415 04171 6 paperback

To Roxana

Роксане – ровеснице этой книги

Contents

Series editor's introduction to the Interface series

There have been many books published this century which have been devoted to the interface of language and literary studies. This is the first series of books devoted to this area commissioned by a major international publisher; it is the first time a group of writers have addressed themselves to issues at the interface of language and literature; and it is the first time an international professional association has worked closely with a publisher to establish such a venture. It is the purpose of this general introduction to the series to outline some of the main guiding principles underlying the books in the series.

The first principle adopted is one of not foreclosing on the many possibilities for the integration of language and literature studies. There are many ways in which the study of language and literature can be combined and many different theoretical, practical and curricular objectives to be realized. Obviously, a close relationship with the aims and methods of descriptive linguistics will play a prominent part, so readers will encounter some detailed analysis of language in places. In keeping with a goal of much work in this field, writers will try to make their analysis sufficiently replicable for other analysts to see how they have arrived at the interpretative decisions they have reached and to allow others to reproduce their methods on the same or on other texts. But linguistic science does not have a monopoly in methodology and description any more than linguists can have sole possession of insights into language and its workings. Some contributors to the series adopt quite rigorous linguistic procedures; others proceed less rigorously but no less revealingly. All are, however, united by a belief that detailed scrutiny of the role of language in literary texts can be mutually enriching to language and literary studies.

Series of books are usually written to an overall formula or design. In the case of the Interface series this was considered to be not entirely appropriate. This is for the reasons given above, but also because, as the first series of its kind, it would be wrong to suggest that there are formulaic modes by which integration can be achieved. The fact that all the books address themselves to the integration of language and literature in any case imparts a natural and organic unity to the series. Thus, some of the books in this series will provide descriptive overviews, others will offer detailed case studies of a particular topic, others will involve single author studies, and some will be more pedagogically oriented.

This range of design and procedure means that a wide variety of audiences is envisaged for the series as a whole, though, of course, individual books are necessarily quite specifically targeted. The general level of exposition presumes quite advanced students of language and literature. Approximately, this level covers students of English language and literature (though not exclusively English) at senior high-school/upper sixth form level to university students in their first or second year of study. Many of the books in the series are designed to be used by students. Some may serve as course books – these will normally contain exercises and suggestions for further work as well as glossaries and graded bibliographies which point the student towards further reading. Some books are also designed to be used by teachers for their own reading and updating, and to supplement courses; in some cases, specific questions of pedagogic theory, teaching procedure and methodology at the interface of language and literature are addressed.

From a pedagogic point of view it is the case in many parts of the world that students focus on literary texts, especially in the mother tongue, before undertaking any formal study of the language. With this fact in mind, contributors to the series have attempted to gloss all new technical terms and to assume on the part of their readers little or no previous knowledge of linguistics or formal language studies. They see no merit in not being detailed and explicit about what they describe in the linguistic properties of texts; but they recognize that formal language study can seem forbidding if it is not properly introduced.

A further characteristic of the series is that the authors engage in a direct relationship with their readers. The overall style of writing is informal and there is above all an attempt to lighten the usual style of academic discourse. In some cases this extends to the way in which notes and guidance for further work are presented. In all cases, the style adopted by authors is judged to be that most appropriate to the mediation of their chosen subject matter.

We now come to two major points of principle which underlie the conceptual scheme for the series. One is that the term 'literature' cannot be defined in isolation from an expression of ideology. In fact, no academic study, and certainly no description of the language of texts, can be neutral and objective, for the sociocultural positioning of the analyst will mean that the description is unavoidably political. Contributors to the series recognize and, in so far as this accords with the aims of each book, attempt to explore the role of ideology at the interface of language and literature. Second, most writers also prefer the term 'literatures' to a singular notion of literature. Some replace 'literature' altogether with the neutral term 'text'. It is for this reason that readers will not find exclusive discussions of the literary language of canonical literary texts; instead the linguistic heterogeneity of literature and the permeation of many discourses with what is conventionally thought of as poetic or literary language will be a focus. This means that in places as much space can be devoted to examples of word-play in jokes, newspaper editorials, advertisements, historical writing, or a popular thriller as to a sonnet by Shakespeare or a passage from Jane Austen. It is also important to stress how the term 'literature' itself is historically variable and how different social and cultural assumptions can condition what is regarded as literature. In this respect the role of linguistic and literary theory is vital. It is an aim of the series to be constantly alert to new developments in the description and theory of texts.

Finally, as series editor, I have to underline the partnership and co-operation of the whole enterprise of the Interface series and acknowledge the advice and assistance received at many stages from the PALA Committee and from Routledge. In turn, we are all fortunate to have the benefit of three associate editors with considerable collective depth of experience in this field in different parts of the world: Professor Roger Fowler, Professor Mary Louise Pratt, Professor Michael Halliday. In spite of their own individual orientations, I am sure that all concerned with the series would want to endorse the statement by Ròman Jakobson made over twenty-five years ago but which is no less relevant today:

> A linguist deaf to the poetic function of language and a literary scholar indifferent to linguistic problems and unconversant with linguistic methods, are equally flagrant anachronisms.

The Discourse of Advertising supports a major aim of the series by analysing discourses which are not normally understood as literary, but which reveal much which may be of interest to students of literature, when analysed from a linguistic point of view. Guy Cook also draws explicit attention to analogies between literary representation and the kinds of representation found in advertisements. However, the book also goes beyond any straightforward integrated approach to language and literary studies. Guy Cook explores the relationship between language and ideology, language and gender, and language and persuasion, areas which, as he demonstrates, can be illuminated by taking advertising discourse as a main textual source. The book should be useful to students and teachers working not only in language and literature departments, but also in the rapidly developing areas of cultural and media studies.

Figures

Foreword

0.0 SUBJECT MATTER

This book is primarily concerned with contemporary British ads from tv, magazines, posters and (to a lesser extent) direct mail. It avoids ads aimed at small children, as they raise different issues. It calls advertisements 'ads' to save space and effort (both yours and mine).

Defined very generally, advertising is 'the promotion of goods or services for sale through impersonal media',[1] but in this book the term is interpreted both more broadly and more narrowly: more broadly because it includes ads which do not offer a product at all; more narrowly because, with the advent of tv advertising in the 1950s, advertising was transformed in character, and the word 'advertisement', out of context, is no longer associated equally with everything which falls under this dictionary definition. The fact that such a definition will encompass a seventeenth-century shop notice, a classified ad, a 1950s hard-sell tv commercial, and a sophisticated contemporary thirty-second tv mini-drama indicates that our vocabulary has not kept pace with change. The advertising of the 1990s is radically different from that of the 1950s and 1960s, though also in a direct line of descent from it. There is no clear point of change, but the recognition that there have been changes is essential.

0.1 PROBLEMS

Writing on advertising is difficult. The reasons are partly formal, arising from its ever-changing uses and combinations of language, pictures and music. They are also social and moral, for advertising arouses a greater strength of condemnation or support than most other contemporary discourses. I comfort (or deceive) myself that twenty years ago, both formally and morally, the task of description and commentary was much easier. Twenty years hence it may be easier again. Ads now are at a point of transition, making the present confused, the future uncertain, and the past not always relevant. Whatever is said can date as rapidly as the ads on which it is based.

The once vibrant issue of whether advertising is purely commercial or belongs to the category of 'art' seems now rather dated. A study of current ads may lead us[2] to the conclusion that many such long-standing binary divisions – art/trade, art/science, pictures/writing, content/form, aesthetic/pragmatic, fact/fiction, public/private – are not adequate to describe the current state of our culture and its discourse. Current ads reflect radical changes in our technologies and media, our social and economic relations, our sense of personal and group identity. For the insights they provide into the nature of these changes, and for the way they prepare us for further changes to come, they are a particularly valuable field of study.

Their fictions, verbal play, compressed story-telling, stylized acting, photography, cartoons, puns and rhythms are often memorable, enjoyable and amusing. New ads cause comment. I have invariably found, while teaching, that the words and details of ads come to students' minds more readily than those of novels and poems and plays, and that they are often recalled with more laughter and enthusiasm. Yet enjoyment frequently causes unease, and is often denied. With some ads, we suffer a split, contradictory reaction: involuntary spontaneous enjoyment, conscious reflective rejection. With other discourses we usually know where our loyalties lie; with ads we are just confused.

But these are generalizations, both about ads and about people, and although advertising seems to be homogenous and increasingly inter-national and cross-cultural, such generalizations about its nature or recep-tion immediately run into trouble. The ads in this book are almost all from Britain; there are also a few from the USA. Reading, discussion and personal experience suggest that the reception and function of advertising in these two countries is very different. In Britain in 1992, where ads are both fewer and more indirect, there is some admiration for them, or at least a lull in the criticism; in the USA, where ads are more pervasive and intrusive, socially concerned opposition remains strong, and opinion polar-ized. If Europe continues to follow directions initiated in the USA, per-haps a change of mood is to come. But if Europe (including Britain) takes its own directions, then the divergence may continue, or increase. Seeing how fast some critiques of advertising have become dated and irrelevant, I shall avoid the assumption that the status quo will last, or that I or anyone else can predict how it will change. If this book reflects a particularly British or 1992 attitude to ads, I hope it may yet stimulate readers in other places and later times to reflect on their own advertising.

0.2 ADS AND LITERATURE

One of the aims of this book is to compare advertising with literature. But there is as little consensus about what constitutes literature as there is about the status and morality of advertising. Though people use the term 'literature' quite successfully, and know what kinds of text they will find in the 'literature section' of a book shop or the reading list of a 'literature course', attempts to define the term have been notoriously unsuccessful. Whatever criteria are used – whether linguistic, semantic, functional, social or psychological – there are too many exceptions: works classed as literature which do not display the cited characteristics, and works not classed as literature which do. New 'sub-literary' genres, as they are patronizingly called, have intensified the problem, for they share a great deal with 'literature'. There are fictional worlds in sitcoms and soap operas, verbal play in ads, social and personal significance in pop songs. These genres have proliferated with the increased output of tv, video and sound recording. They use not only language – as literature does – but also music and/or film. The easy solution is to say that this mixing of modes disqualifies these genres from comparison with literature, and that advertising is obviously different from literature, as its language is almost always used in conjunction with music, pictures or film. But as most theorists who seek to characterize literature have scorned purely formal aspects – such as the fact that it is written – and preferred to rely on its wider social and psychological significance, this sudden retreat to formal criteria seems evasive.

Yet literature – despite disputes over individual works – undoubtedly is a recognizable category of discourse. As I need to talk about it, I shall adopt three circular, reductive and easily deconstructed working hypotheses as a starting point: the first is that literature is what people say is literature; the second that it is a group of written texts not fully accounted for by any other category; the third that it is accorded considerable acclaim and value by individuals or by a society as a whole.

One explanation of the acclaim of literary texts, especially in schools and universities, is their supposed social and psychological insight. The value attached to them, moreover, is not solely utilitarian or ideological. For most people, literary texts are neither useful texts, nor texts with which they necessarily agree. A different source of value is the literary use of language – though for most people this is valued as a vehicle for social and psychological insight. And, indeed, this subordination of language to other criteria has in its favour the fact that the alternative formalist view – that literary language is both distinctive and valuable in itself – runs into severe difficulties when it tries to posit linguistic characteristics of literariness. There are too many exceptions, of which advertising is a leading example. We are stuck, it seems, with imprecision, circularity and the indefinable.

0.3 ADS AND LINGUISTICS

In the analysis of ads, general theories of language and literature are not always helpful. Paradoxically, many schools of linguistics and literary study, like our culture in general, are reluctant ever to value language processing and production for itself. They seek within it something else. Words are referred to disparagingly as 'surface forms' and their importance is ephemeral; what matters is their 'deep' meanings or structures. In recent years there has been a move away from analysing texts for their underlying meaning or structure, to analysing texts for their function, but in both approaches there is an unwillingness to accept language as having any value unless we can be sure that it 'contains' information or emotion, or has a practical or social purpose. Even poetry is valued for something other than its language: a social or psychological insight, a place in tradition, an intertextual connection, a clue to the poet's biography.

Most theories, moreover, concentrate on communication through speech in face-to-face interaction, or through writing on paper. Ads, however, are representative of a kind of discourse which arises from new technologies, and which creates new kinds of relationship between participants. Such discourse should make linguistics, discourse analysis and literary studies rethink many of the methods, assumptions and categories on which they have relied in the past.

0.4 TERMS, ANALYSES, EXERCISES

Despite these reservations, and the relatively uncharted discourse type with which it deals, the theoretical basis of this book, and its terminology and approach, does derive from linguistics and discourse analysis. The book does, however, aim to be accessible to a reader who is a newcomer to these disciplines. For this reason, technical terms are in bold type on or near their first mention, and a brief explanation of them is given. All emboldened terms together with the page reference of this explanation will be found in the index.

There is also grammatical notation. For this I use the convention of marking off phrases with round brackets ( ), clauses with square brackets [ ] and co-ordinated constructions with angle brackets < >. The following abbreviations are used for grammatical functions:

S = subject; Od = direct object; Oi = indirect object;
P = predicator; C = complement; A = adjunct; o = object of a preposition; VOC = vocative.

The following abbreviations are used for forms:

For clauses: MCl = main clause; NCl = noun clause; ACl = adverb clause; RCl = relative clause

For phrases: NP = noun phrase; VP = verb phrase; AjP = adjective phrase; PP = prepositional phrase; AvP = adverb phrase; cj = conjunction.

The symbol Ø indicates an ellipted word.

At the end of each chapter, there are exercises and suggestions for further reading. Some of the exercises deal with the chapter they finish, others look forward to the issues in the following chapter. If you want to use this book in an active way, and explore your own opinion on each topic before being exposed to mine, then I suggest that you do each set of exercises before reading the chapter.

Acknowledgements

Ron Carter, the editor of this series, deserves especial thanks for his unfailing energy, enthusiasm and help with this project, which is only a small part of his continuing contribution to the study of language and literature.

I should also like to thank the following people for having shared with me, while I was writing this book, their own considerable insights into advertising and the discourses of the contemporary world: Tony Cowie, Charles Forceville, Val Gough, Paul Hammond, Maisie Langridge, David Peck, Tony Smith, Rita Walsh, Henry Widdowson, Malcolm Williams. Mostly, however, I thank Elena Poptsova Cook for her sustained support, help and inspiration.

There are many ads reproduced and quoted in this book. Some manufacturers were friendly and helpful; others were obstructive. For her patience and efficiency in dealing with the latter, I am particularly grateful to Louise Snell at Routledge.

Kyoko Yoshino and Tong Yan translated and commented upon, respectively, the ads in Japanese and using Mandarin Chinese.

The publishers and I would also like to acknowledge gratefully the use of copyright material in the illustrations and text from the following people and organizations:

Figure 4 Eighteenth-century ad: *The Spectator*: The Brotherton Collection, Leeds University Library; *Figure 10* London Fire Service ad: Duckworth, Finn, Grubb, Waters; *Figure 12* Uniroyal tyres ad: Leeds Postcards; *Figure 13* Hamlet cigars ad: Gallaher Limited, Surrey; *Figure 14b* Allied Dunbar seminar invitation: Martyn Hopson, Financial Planning Consultant, Allied Dunbar; *Figure 15* Coca-Cola's Sprite soft drink ad: Coca-Cola Great Britain. 'Sprite' is a registered trademark of the Coca-Cola Company; *Figure 16* Wrigley's chewing gum ad: stills by courtesy of The Wrigley Company Ltd; *Figure 18* Persil/Electrolux washday ad: Marcus J.R. Bleasdale, Brand Manager Electrolux, and Lever Brothers; *Figure 19* Kodak, Ford and Kellogg's logos: Ford Motor Company Limited; Eastman Kodak Company; Kellogg Company of Great Britain Limited; *Figure 20*

Maxwell House coffee, AA Insurance, Kelloggs Special K cereal, Kattomeat catfood ads: Nick Howarth, Account Executive on Maxwell House; AA Financial Services; Kellogg Company of Great Britain Limited; Bill Ward, Account Manager of Kattomeat; *Figure 25*: Lypsyl lip-salve slogo or strapline: Aisling Cloonan, Group Brand Manager of CIBA Consumer Pharmaceuticals; *Figure 27*: Elizabeth Taylor's Passion perfume ad: Edwina Bradshaw, Product Manager of Parfums International Limited; *Figure 28* Sun Alliance Insurance ad: Andrew C. Melvin, Regional Customer Services Division Manager, Scotland and N. Ireland Region, Sun Alliance Assurance, UK; *Figure 30* Black Heart Rum ad: Scott Hill, Senior Brand Manager, URM Agency Limited; *Figure 31* Revlon's X'ia Xi'ang perfume logo: Anne Cafferty of Revlon International Corporation; *Figure 32a* Van Cleef & Arpels' Tsar eau de toilette for men ad: B. Gunther, Sanofi Beauté; *Figure 34* P & O Ferries ads: S. Colegate, Marketing and Commercial director of P & O Scottish Ferries Limited; *Figure 35b* Gianni Versace perfume ad: Charles of the Ritz Limited; *Figure 36* Eau Perrier ad: *Cosmopolitan* magazine spine: Mark Blears, Account Supervisor of Leo Burnett Advertising; *Figure 37* Subaru car ad: Edwin W. Swatman, Managing Director of Subaru (UK) Limited; *Figure 38* Volkswagen Seat car ad: Ayer Ltd, London; *Figure 39* Armitage Shanks bathrooms ad: Patrick K.J. Plant, Group Publicity Services Manager, Armitage Shanks; *Figure 40 SHE* magazine ad: Karen Pusey, Associate Publisher of *SHE*; *Figure 42* Charnos lingerie ad: Tony Hodges, Managing Director – Brand; *Figure 43* Heinz Spicy Pepper Sauce ad: M. Cook, Company Secretary of H.J. Heinz Company Limited; *Figure 44* Harrison Drape Superstyle curtain track ad: Jonathan Hawley, Marketing Manager of Harrison Drape; *Figure 47* Pretty Polly nylons ad: F.K. Bond, Marketing Director of Pretty Polly Limited; *Figure 53* Sharp Lager ad: I.D. Grieg, Brand Manager of Guinness Brewing G.B.; *Figure 54a* Southern Comfort Bourbon ad: John J. Davis III of the Brown-Forman Corporation; Kentucky Fried Chicken (Great Britain) Limited for the Colonel Sanders text; Kwik-Fit (G.B.) Limited for using the words 'A Kwik-Fit Fitter'; Nicki Jones, Market Co-ordinator, Mars Confectionery for use of 'Galaxy Minstrels'; C.J. Edwards, Manager – National Advertising Peugeot Talbot Motor Company Ltd for use of 'Takes Your Breath Away' text; Tony Walters, Senior Brand Manager Confiserie Suchard, for use of the end line from the commerical Milka LilaPause.

Four lines from 'Stopping by Woods on a Snowy Evening' in *The Poetry of Robert Frost*, edited by Edward Connery Lathem, copyright 1923 © 1969 by Holt, Rinehart & Winston. Copyright 1951 by Robert Frost. Reprinted by permission of Henry Holt and Company, Inc.; 'In a Station of the Metro', Ezra Pound: *Personae*. Copyright 1926 by Ezra Pound. Reprinted by permission of New Directions Publishing Corporation: also by permission of Faber & Faber; excerpt from *The Great Gatsby* by F. Scott

Fitzgerald, reprinted with permission of Charles Scribner's Sons, an imprint of Macmillan Publishing Company. Copyright 1925 by Charles Scribner's Sons; renewal copyright 1953 by Frances Scott Fitzgerald Lanahan; 'This Just to Say' by William Carlos Williams in *Collected Poems*, published by Carcanet Press Limited. Reprinted by kind permission of Carcanet Press Limited; 'I Shall Be Free' and 'It's Alright Ma', both songs written by Bob Dylan. Copyright Warner Chappell Music Ltd. Reproduced by kind permission of Warner Chappell Music Ltd; excerpt from *Bliss* by Peter Carey, published by Faber & Faber, reproduced by kind permission of Rogers, Coleridge & White Ltd; excerpt from *The Whitsun Weddings* by Philip Larkin, reproduced by kind permission of Faber & Faber.

Every attempt has been made to obtain permission to reproduce copyright material. If any proper acknowledgement has not been made, we would invite copyright holders to inform us of the oversight.

1 Introduction:
ads as a discourse type

1.0 ADVERTISING AS DISCOURSE

The purpose of this book is to analyse ads as **discourse**. Although the main focus of **discourse analysis** is on language, it is not concerned with language alone. It also examines the context of communication: who is communicating with whom and why; in what kind of society and situation; through what medium; how different types and acts of communication evolved, and their relationship to each other. When music and pictures combine with language to alter or add to its meaning, then discourse analysis must consider these modes of communication too.

The breadth of this approach is justified by the belief that neither specific acts of communication nor the internal mechanisms of language can be well understood in any other way. Contrary to the theory and practice of some schools of linguistics, which treat language as a neatly isolated object, discourse analysis views language and context holistically.

As there is a good deal of dispute over the terms 'context', 'text' and 'discourse', I shall need to say more precisely how I am going to use them here.

Text is used to mean linguistic forms, temporarily and artificially separated from context for the purposes of analysis.

Context includes all of the following:

1 **substance**: the physical material which carries or relays text
2 music and pictures
3 **paralanguage**: meaningful behaviour accompanying language, such as voice quality, gestures, facial expressions and touch (in speech), and choice of typeface and letter sizes (in writing)
4 **situation**: the properties and relations of objects and people in the vicinity of the text, as perceived by the participants
5 **co-text**: text which precedes or follows that under analysis, and which participants judge to belong to the same discourse
6 **intertext**: text which the participants perceive as belonging to other discourse, but which they associate with the text under consideration, and which affects their interpretation

7 **participants**: their intentions and interpretations, knowledge and beliefs, interpersonal attitudes, affiliations and feelings. Each participant
is simultaneously a part of the context and an observer of it.
Participants are usually described as **senders**, **addressers**, **addressees**
and **receivers**. (The 'sender' of a message is not always the same as the
'addresser', the person who originates it. Neither is the 'receiver'
always the 'addressee', the person for whom it is intended. In a tv ad,
for example, the addresser may be an actor, though the sender is an
advertising agency; the addressee may be a specific target group, but
the receiver is anyone who sees the ad. In advertising and other types of
fiction, this model is complicated by the presence of other personae –
narrators and characters into which participants project themselves –
and we shall need more elaborate categories at a later stage.)

8 **function**: what the text is intended to do by the senders and addressers,
or perceived to do by the receivers and addressees.

Discourse is text and context together, interacting in a way which is
perceived as meaningful and unified by the participants (who are both
part of the context and observers of it). The task of discourse analysis is
to describe both this phenomenon in general and particular instances of
it, and to say how participants distinguish one type of discourse from
another. To do this, it needs to pay close attention not only to human
cognitive processes in general, but also to features specific to a given
culture.

Understandably, discourse analysis is sometimes accused of being large
and rather messy, for it cannot bring to analysis the precision of approaches which isolate one facet of communication from others. It is a
premise of this book, however, that the precision of such methods is
bought at the price of misrepresenting the complexity of human communication. The study of language must take context into account, because
language is always in context, and there are no acts of communication
without participants, intertexts, situations, paralanguage and substance.
Denial of this may yield tidy descriptions and theories with pretensions to
explain comprehensively 'how language works'. But unless such approaches are an intermediate stage of description, a temporary tactic
preceding a reintegration of this fabricated object with context, it is not
clear what is being analysed. Language does not exist on its own outside
the purpose-made illustrative examples in linguistics textbooks, and there
seems little point to a theory which cleanly describes something it created
for itself. Its conclusions are circular and illusory.

By refusing to ignore context, discourse analysis embarks upon a journey
with no destination. Yet this is a necessary condition of its subject.
Discourse – especially discourse as complex as advertising or literature –
always holds out more to be analysed, leaves more to be said. But this
need not be a cause for despair. It would be both depressing and self-

deceptive to believe that one could exhaust a discourse type and present an answer to all the problems it poses.

Many studies of advertising do separate out components of ads, concentrate on one or a few, and ignore the others. Thus there are studies of the language of advertising which have little or nothing to say about its pictures and music or the people who create it, but there are also studies which describe the pictures of advertising without paying any attention to language. Research within the advertising business often concentrates solely upon receivers of ads, endlessly debating how best to divide them, inventing ever more delicate categories (given names like 'trendies', 'cowboys', 'puritans', 'drifters', 'utopians', 'traditionalists', etc.),[1] and assessing their reactions with ever more sophisticated techniques. Describing advertising as discourse is both more complete and more difficult than any of these approaches, for it means trying to describe all these elements, and their effects on each other. As a starting point, the approach may be summed up by Figure 1. An ad is an interaction of elements.

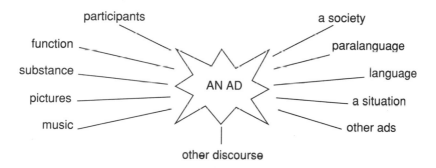

Figure 1 Interaction of elements in ads

A problem is to decide whether we should put any of these factors at the centre of the diagram, and thus, by implication, at the *centre* of our approach. (In the diagram, the centre is the interaction of all the elements around, and in a sense there is nothing there.) One possibility, for example, would be to put the text of the ad (its words, and perhaps its music and pictures) at the centre, making a stable point to which all the other elements relate. This book attempts not to do this. Though the focus is on language, I shall try always to see language in relation to the other elements, remembering that a change in any one element usually entails a change in the whole. An ad is not a tangible or stable entity; it is the dynamic synthesis of many components, and comes into being through them.

This interdependence of elements is not peculiar to the element at the centre of Figure 1 – 'an ad'; it is true of all the other elements in the figure too; each comes into existence through the interaction of the others. A society is its senders, receivers, discourses and situations. A participant is identified by his or her language, paralanguage, position in society, and knowledge of other discourses.

In addition to its existence in the here and now, each element of communication which makes up an ad or any other act of communication has a history. Figure 1 does not take this into account, but presents a **synchronic** snapshot of a moment in time and ignores the **diachronic** history of each part.

Although it is sometimes said that there have been ads at least since classical times – the earliest known ad supposedly being for a brothel in Ephesus (D. White 1988) – advertising in the era of tv and colour magazines is a new phenomenon, both in nature, quantity and effect. Yet, although advertising in its contemporary form is relatively young, it has already established a considerable tradition. Each new ad is encountered through knowledge of thousands of earlier ads. The effect of reading in the context of tradition is well known in the study of literary discourse, and is what most university literature courses devote themselves to developing in their students, but it is often overlooked in discussions of ads, perhaps because a time when advertising seemed new and tradition-free is still well within living memory. Nowadays, we do not experience advertising as a new phenomenon, as was perhaps the case in the 1950s and 1960s. Many academic studies have been slow to realize this. They read each ad in isolation, discounting the effect of the growing tradition, and participants' detailed knowledge of it.

1.1 DISCOURSE TYPES

Both individuals and societies pour out discourse all the time, but it is not, for them, an amorphous and undistinguished stream. It is part of a person's cultural competence to divide the discourse of their society into units, to give those units names, and to assign them to categories. Some discourses are perceived to be conversations, for example, others are consultations, lessons, prescriptions, news bulletins, brochures, prayers, squabbles, gossip, stories, jokes, plays, reprimands, standing orders, printouts, handouts, operas, soap operas, games, stories, films. There are hundreds of such categories (Dimter 1985), or **discourse types**, which merge into each other and defy exact definition. There are also many different ways of categorizing discourse types: by situation, by function, by participants, by text, by substance, or by a combination of these factors. Consequently, a given discourse may be several types at once. There is nothing mutually exclusive, for example, in the terms 'story', 'gossip', 'joke' and 'cartoon', and a discourse could be all four at once. Discourse types also stray into non-verbal forms of communication, and merge with them to varying degrees. Films usually have dialogue, but not always, and even when they do the relative importance of words and pictures varies considerably, not only from film to film, but also from spectator to spectator. The same is true of ads. There are ads without language – or in which language plays a subordinate part.

The importance of discourse types in a theory of communication, and of the way participants recognize them, is another reason why discourse analysis cannot be limited to descriptions of abstracted parts of discourses like single sentences, but needs to describe both text and context, including physical form. In speech, identification of discourse types may be influenced by whether the language is shouted or sung, whether it is beamed down from a satellite on to millions of tv screens, or whispered in darkness to one person through the grille in a confessional. In writing, it may be influenced by whether the communication is scribbled in pencil, embossed in gold, word-processed, or flashed from giant neon tubes.

1.2 ADVERTISING AS A DISCOURSE TYPE

Advertising is a prominent discourse type in virtually all contemporary societies, and I shall assume that you, the reader, like me, the writer, live in a society where it is already well established – or rapidly gaining ground. (It is this assumption which motivates my use of 'us'.) Because of this prominence, advertising can tell us a good deal about our own society and our own psychology.

Many people decide, when faced with the problem of defining the word 'ad', and trying to distinguish ads from similar discourse types, that the crucial distinguishing feature is function, because this is always to persuade people to buy a particular product. They may add that, whatever else it may say, an ad must always contain the name of a product. Yet there are a number of reasons to reject these popular definitions. Firstly, there are discourses described as 'ad', which do not sell anything, but plead or warn or seek support. (As I write this chapter, on 15 January 1991, there are 'commercials' appearing on US network tv, urging Americans to support their President and troops in Iraq.) Secondly, there are discourses such as poems or songs, which become ads by being used in a particular way (a process which may be reversible, allowing an ad to become a poem). Thirdly, even if the majority of ads have the function of persuading their addressees to buy, this is not their only function. They may also amuse, inform, misinform, worry or warn. It can be argued that these other functions are all in the service of a main function which is usually to sell; alternatively, even selling ads perform multiple functions which are more or less autonomous (whatever manufacturers may believe). Moreover, if an ad is defined by its selling function alone, then one might wonder what it becomes when the product is no longer available, or when the receiver is someone who can not or will not buy the product. I can receive ads for cigarettes, bubble gum, tampons, denture cleaners and holidays in the Bahamas, though as a non-smoking adult male with all my teeth and limited funds, I know that these are not for me. I look at an ad for 'Galco International Miami Classic Handguns' showing a handsome young male executive and his blonde female leather-mini-skirted secretary, leaning very close to each other across a desk, both wearing guns in shoulder holsters – his heavy and masculine, hers lightweight and feminine (*Peter-sen's handguns*, September 1990), but I have neither the intention (nor the legal right) to buy the product. This does not mean that the ad says nothing to me.

The issue is further complicated by the fact that the term 'function' can be understood from two perspectives. The function which the sender intends the discourse to have may not be the same as the function it actually does have for the receiver. The sender may intend the gun ad to persuade people to buy Galco guns (I do not flatter myself that I am one), but the reader may use it in a discussion of gun laws, or as an example in a book. With ads, as with certain other discourse types, there is the further complication that there is no single sender, because ads are not the creation of an individual. There are, rather, many strata of senders, ranging from the manufacturer through the agency and its creative depart-ment, to the actors and camera crews who produce it. For each stratum, the intended function may be different. Though the manufacturer may seek only to persuade to buy, the writer may seek to impress other colleagues, or realize an aesthetic aim. For these reasons we shall need to distinguish different kinds of function, such as **addresser-function**, **sender-function**, **addressee-function** and **receiver-function**.

One way out of this definitional quagmire would be to insist that, despite awkward cases, the overriding defining factor is nevertheless the function of persuading to buy, and that discourse described as advertising which does not do this is misclassified. This seems wrong for two reasons. Firstly, the term *is* used more broadly. Secondly, to be satisfied with this simple characterization distracts from the variety of ads, and from the points of contact they have with other discourse types such as political propaganda, conversation, songs, films, myths, poems, soap operas, sitcoms, plays, novels, graffiti, jokes, cartoons.

1.2.1 Defining definition

Attempts to define ads as a discourse type run into severe trouble when they look for textual or contextual features, or combinations of features, which all ads have in common, but are not present in other discourse types. The problem here, however, may be the kind of definition we are looking for: the definition of 'definition' itself.

One way of defining a word or set phrase is to look for 'components' of meaning which it brings together and which describe properties of the entities or concepts to which it refers. Thus, for example, the word 'stallion' has the components 'adult', 'male' and 'horse', and all adult male horses can be described by this word. If meaning is a statement of equivalence, then the meaning of the word is its equivalence to these components, and this, in one sense, is 'what the word means'. **Semantics** is the study of equivalences between linguistic units and entities or events in the world. (Some people may prefer to say that it deals with equivalences between linguistic units and people's concepts of entities and events in the world, because these may or may not correspond to what is actually there: words like 'hassle' or 'hero' reflect culturally determined ways of categorizing reality rather than anything in reality itself; other words like 'water' or 'birth' may be seen as corresponding to entities or events in the world which are independent of cultural determination, or culturally universal – though this too is disputable.) Another kind of meaning equivalence is translation: we can say the Russian word *zherebets* means 'stallion' – although translation often appeals to semantics in justification of its choices.

Broken down into components, words can be described as entering into various **sense relations** with each other according to components they do or do not have in common, and these relations can be described hierarchically. Going upwards through the hierarchy, we can say that 'a stallion' is a kind of 'horse', which is a kind of 'mammal', which is a kind of 'animal'; going down, we can say a 'palomino stallion' is a type of 'stallion'; going sideways, we can say that a 'mare' is another kind of 'horse', though female rather than male (see Figure 2). 'Horse' is described as the **supernym** (name above) of 'mare'. Conversely, 'mare' is a **hyponym** (name below) of 'horse', because the latter has all the components of the former, plus one more ('female') which makes it more specific. 'Horse' is the **co-hyponym** of 'dog' because, although the two share components ('warm blooded' 'hairy', etc.) of a mutual supernym 'mammal', each also has a distinctive component which is mutually exclusive ('equine' and 'canine').

While this approach to definition systematizes the meaning of certain words, it has a number of severe drawbacks. It cannot deal with grammati-

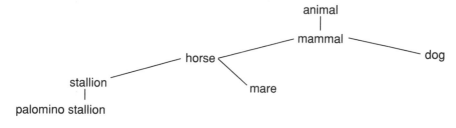

Figure 2 Semantic relations: horse and dog

cal function words like 'of' or 'the', but only with the open-set content words: nouns, verbs, adjectives and adverbs. Even there, it can describe only a portion of meaning, for it cannot cope with **connotations** (the vaguer associations of a word for a group or individual) or metaphorical uses, both of which are particularly important in ads. (Imagine a perfume called 'Stallion', as opposed to one called 'Gelding' or 'Bull'.) Although componential analysis works well enough with a word like 'stallion', and differentiates it from related words, it is less successful with words whose meanings are different to different individuals or groups, and merge into related words in a fuzzy intermediate area. The components of words denoting political creeds ('fascism', 'communism', 'parliamentary democracy'), for example, are very different to their supporters and their opponents. There are also apparent co-hyponyms whose boundaries merge, even for an individual. What are the components of the word 'love', for example, and how do they differ from those of 'like'? Other words, though reasonably fixed, do not lend themselves to this kind of definition at all. 'Game' may refer to activities as diverse as a toddler throwing pebbles into a puddle, and a world championship chess match. These two instances have only what Wittgenstein ([1953] 1968: 32) described as a 'family resemblance', a connection which needs tracing through several intermediate instances, rather than any shared components.

A more satisfactory approach to meaning, which may help us to define 'ad', is that of **prototype theory** (Rosch 1977), which suggests that we choose or understand a word by reference to a mental representation of a typical instance.[2] Whether a given entity is a bird, for example, will depend on its resemblance to our prototype of a bird. This will vary from person to person and culture to culture. For most Europeans a typical bird may be a sparrow, for most North Americans perhaps an American Robin. The less like our prototype an instance is, the less likely we are to identify it with the word for that category, but we are still willing to tolerate fuzzy, borderline and dubious cases.

If we apply this approach to the problem of defining 'ad', then discourses which are described as 'ads', but do not share the components of a typical ad, need no longer trouble us. The prototypical ad will vary between individuals, cultures and periods, but probably, for most British people in the 1990s, it is a soap-powder commercial in which a housewife praises the product for making her family's clothes so white. In the USA it is likely to be an ad showing a satisfied family eating an instant dessert. Like most prototypes, this is likely to be derived from a specific instance (a Persil ad in the UK,[3] a Jell-O ad in the USA) and also to be slightly out-of-date. The further a given discourse moves from this yardstick, the less likely it is to be classified as an ad (though even ads for political parties have something in common with eulogies of soap-suds). Because it tolerates fuzzy and indeterminate areas between concepts, prototype theory is also very helpful when dealing with the hybrid discourse types created by advertisers' frequent and ingenious attempts to disguise their ads as something else.

A weakness of both componential analysis and prototype theory is their concentration on a word or what it refers to, rather than its environment. Yet with an 'ad' (as with 'stallions' and 'birds') it is sometimes nothing intrinsic which helps us in identification, but rather the immediate sur-roundings (Beezer et al. 1986; K. Myers 1983). We tend to view anything which occurs at a given position in a tv schedule, or in a certain position in a magazine, as an ad, quite irrespective of components which can be ticked off on a checklist, or the way it can be related to a prototype.

1.3 CATEGORIES OF AD: MEDIUM, PRODUCT, TECHNIQUE, CONSUMER

The issue of defining 'ad' is closely linked to that of defining categories of ad. But here again the issue is anything but simple.

One might reasonably claim that the medium in which an ad appears is an important parameter of difference, and that ads in magazines are quite different from those on tv or roadside hoardings. (I use the term **medium** as the singular of the term (mass) media, to refer to such different means of mass communication as the printed book, tv, radio, newspapers, maga-zines. As such, a medium is partly but not wholly distinguished from others by its use of a particular technology, such as radio waves, print or photography, which in turn limits the modes of communication available to it (see 3.0). Yet the distinction between one medium and another is not always so concrete, and can also be situational or functional, as in the difference between books, newspapers and magazines.) Many ads are affected by, or take advantage of a particular medium. Ads on subway trains and platforms, for example, often have longer copy, or demand reflection, on the assumption that their receivers, in the enforced idleness of awaiting or riding on a train, are likely to scrutinize the ad more carefully. (An example from the London Underground is an ad for Clinomyn Toothpaste which shows Humphrey Bogart holding a tube of toothpaste and saying: 'If this gives smokers gleaming white teeth then I'm not Ingrid Bergman'.) TV ads rely on music and moving pictures in ways that magazine ads cannot. Yet many campaigns cut across media by running the 'same ad' concurrently in many media: though their professed intention may be to use one medium to remind addressees of a campaign in another (R. White 1988: 101–2), keeping, let us say, some part of the words and images of a tv ad in front of people, even when they are away from home.

Another way of categorizing ads is by product (or service). Luxuries like spirits, perfume and chocolate demand (and get) different techniques from household necessities like soap and eggs, and both of these categories have expensive counterparts: holidays and hi-fis (perceived as luxuries), or cars, houses and fridges (perceived as necessities). Not all ads, however, sell products or services: as well as **product ads**, there are also **non-product ads**, including, for example, those for charities and political parties.

Another possible means of categorization is by technique. One well-worn and long-established distinction is between the **hard sell** and the **soft sell**. Hard selling makes a direct appeal. My prototype of a hard-sell ad involves a man in a suit, standing in front of a pile of carpets, talking loudly and directly to the camera about low cost, limited availability and guaranteed reliability. Soft selling relies more on mood than on exhortation, and on the implication that life will be better with the product. The possessor reflects the possessed: this is a major unspoken premise of all soft-selling ads. A typical soft sell is a cinema ad for Bacardi rum, in which slim and athletic young men and women in revealing swim-wear dive from a yacht into blue water and bask happily on a tropical beach. The implications hardly need spelling out, though perhaps their extraordinary reversal of the effect of possession does, because it is so complete that it may pass unnoticed. Drinking spirits makes people fatter, less fit, less sexually potent, and poorer; in direct sunlight it also gives people headaches; it is not typically the activity of muscular young men or slim young women in cutaway swim-wear, but rather of fat, stressed middle-aged men in suits!

Another classification of technique is that between **reason** and **tickle** (Bernstein 1974: 118). Reason ads suggest motives for purchase. Fairy Liquid, for example, is said to be a better buy than other washing-up liquids because – squirt for squirt – it washes more dishes. Tickle ads, on the other hand, appeal to emotion, humour and mood. Cigarette ads (with the exception of those stressing a low tar content) are of necessity ticklers. (What reasons could they give?) But the reason/tickle distinction is not just the hard/soft distinction with a new name. A soft sell often implies reasons for purchase without a direct appeal. An ad for Audi cars shows a prosperous and conventionally handsome man receiving an urgent phone call during the night, waking his small son, wrapping him in a blanket and putting him in the car, then driving swiftly but carefully through dawn streets to a maternity hospital where his wife has just given birth. In the early-morning half-light, a milk float, whose driver presumably expects the streets to be empty, emerges suddenly from a side street. The Audi responds quickly and swerves efficiently without skidding. The implication is that this manoeuvrability is a reason for purchase – though there is no direct statement of this. The ad also implies (softly) that possession affects the possessor, for the driver is good-looking, loving, responsible and alert.

The techniques of **slow drip** and **sudden burst** refer not to the content of an ad, but to the frequency of its release (R. White 1988: 93–5). Another important and self-explanatory difference is that between **short copy** and **long copy**.

Choice of technique, however, clearly relates to product, to media, and to copy length. It is easier to reason in the long copy of a magazine ad than in the twenty or thirty seconds of a tv commercial. Luxuries lend themselves to soft, tickle selling. More expensive items, whose purchase merits longer consideration, are prone to reason selling, and therefore to longer written copy. Similarly, there is an aura of respectability about slow-drip campaigns which suggest product reliability and durability, and for this reason they are commonly used both with big buys like cars and for cheaper domestic purchases like baked beans, whose markets are less susceptible to seasonal variation than, say, toys and perfumes, both of which scramble wildly for attention before Christmas and then diminish in January.

As far as advertisers themselves are concerned, the most important categorization of ads is by consumer. The advertising industry expends enormous effort on attempts both to categorize people effectively and then to target the categories. Fashions change as fast as ads themselves and there is endless discussion about whether the best divisions are those of lifestyle, socio-economic class, point in the life cycle, neighbourhood, personality type, or of something else altogether. Again, there is overlap with the other types of categorization suggested above. Certain products are more likely to be bought by men than by women, by the rich, by a certain age group and so on. Tickle may work better on one group than on another.

None of these modes of categorization allows us to separate off one kind of ad distinctly from another. The factors of medium, product, technique and copy length all interact. There is also an additional hazard. The chronic frustration of all attempts to typologize ads is the advertisers' striving to grab attention through surprise. The fact that a particular targeted group, or a particular product, associates with a particular medium or technique is in itself often a good reason for change.

Advertising has become too various and vast an activity for any study to be comprehensive. This book is primarily concerned with the cryptic subterfuges of soft selling, as inherently more interesting than louder and more transparent hard selling (a decision which eliminates what is, numerically, the largest group: small ads in newspapers). It is also primarily concerned with advertising to adults rather than to children, as the latter raises some different moral issues. It has more to say about tv and magazine advertising than about direct mail, despite the fact that many advertisers, apparently oblivious to the colossal waste of paper involved, are increasingly shifting their efforts in that direction. Yet despite these limitations I shall attempt to cover ads for different media, different people and different products. Not everything can be included, and I have found it most instructive to look at ads which occupy extreme points in this multi-dimensional classifying grid. Thus I have tried to pay particular attention to ads which are very much of their medium and not easily lifted to another; to products which are at the extremes of the cost spectrum (chewing gum and cars) or of the luxury/necessity continuum (perfumes and washing-up liquid); to ads which target particular groups (women/ men, young/old, working/middle class) in particular roles (friends, lovers, parents, employees). Whatever ad one looks at, it is always worth categorizing it in the ways I have outlined here: by medium, product, technique, consumer.

1.4 THE STRUCTURE OF THIS BOOK

Despite the difficulty of definition, this book is structured around the notion of ads as a discourse type. It rejects the dismissive characterization of ads as 'acts of communication whose primary purpose is to sell a given product'. This is too simple – whether we are in love with ads or hate them. It is a way of closing down the analysis before it begins. It ignores the complexity of ads, trying to analyse them away, to reduce them to silence.

There are three parts to this book, each one divided into three chapters. They examine the textual and contextual features of ads one by one and **bottom-up**, though without seeking determinate definition.

Part I deals with the materials of ads.
Chapter 2 examines their substance and surroundings.
Chapter 3 examines choices of music and pictures, writing and speech, and the combination of all four.
Chapter 4, entering the interface between substance and linguistic form, examines paralanguage, and the uses of phonology and graphology.

Part II deals with the texts of ads.
Chapter 5 examines the connotations of words and phrases on their own and in context.
Chapter 6 describes and evaluates linguistic parallelism in ads and its relationship to poetry.
Chapter 7 examines the linguistic features which create cohesion in the texts of ads,[4] and their communicative effect.

Part III focuses upon the participants in advertising communication, and tackles problem of evaluating and assessing advertising as a whole.
Chapter 8 discusses the senders of ads and the stance they take up towards their addressees. (The three categories of people in this part of the book are not separate: the senders and observers of ads are also its addressees, like everybody else.)
Chapter 9 examines ways of hearing ads; it discusses the observers of ads and their judgements upon them.
Chapter 10 returns to the issue of defining ads as a discourse type (the subject of this introductory chapter) and discusses their psychological and social function.

Using the metaphor of discourse as a series of layers with a top and a bottom, this structure can be represented diagrammatically, as in Figure 3.

Part III	(PEOPLE)	social/psychological function	'TOP'
		observers and addressees	
		senders and narrators	
Part II	(TEXT)	connected text	
		grammar and prosody	
		words and phrases	
Part I	(MATERIALS)	paralanguage	
		music and pictures	
		substance	'BOTTOM'

Figure 3 Hierarchy of discourse and chapters in this book

1.5 LOCATING ADVERTISING IN TIME AND SPACE

Advertising is not unique to Western late-twentieth-century high-tech capitalist societies (see Figures 4, 5 and 6), but in these societies it is different, and more prominent, than it is in others.

In contemporary capitalist society, advertising is everywhere. We cannot walk down the street, shop, watch television, go through our mail, read a newspaper or take a train without encountering it. Whether we are alone, with our friends or family, or in a crowd, advertising is always with us, if only on the label of something we are using. Given this ubiquity, it is strange that many people are reluctant to pay attention to ads. An ad is never the programme they are watching, never the letter they are waiting for, never the part of the newspaper they are reading. Despite all the care and skill in their creation, ads are flicked past, put in the bin, **zipped** (fast-forwarded on a VTR) or **zapped** (avoided by remote-control channel switching). People pay to see films and read books; they put paintings in galleries and sculptures in museums; but advertising is often regarded as a peripheral creation – except by those directly involved in it. This is odd, because a stranger to our society (the proverbial Martian anthropologist?) would probably be struck by the prominence and quantity of advertising, and pay more attention to it than to those discourse types, like literature, law, science and journalism, which we say we value more highly. Advertising is everywhere but nowhere. A major aim of this book is to explore the reasons for this paradoxical and ambivalent status.

Discourse types may be described in terms of their social function, but equally societies may be categorized in terms of the types of discourse they use. Foucault (1971) argues that a culture is the sum of its **orders of discourse**. In this interplay of social systems and discourse types, advertising occupies a salient position, exactly because it is both colonizing new territories and becoming ever more prominent in its homelands. Yet, although it is both part of, and helps to create, a new global culture which

> renciniver, that I do incress enter my Caveat against
> this Piece of Raillery.
>
> *ADVERTISEMENTS.*
>
> The Number of Silk Gowns that are weekly
> Sold at Mrs. Roge:s's in Exchange-Ally (though not much above a
> Month since she has undertaken it) makes it very evident that her
> Gowns are very cheap as well as the nicest Fancies, for she doth not
> heap a great deal of Rubbish together, but chooses the most proper silks
> and suitable Linings : And for the future will keep such Choice, that
> all Persons of Quality and others may be furnish'd with Variety of
> Fancies and all Sizes. Note, There will be a Parcel of new Vene-
> rian Gowns made up, to be seen next Wednesday.
>   At Sutton in Surrey, on the Edge of Bansted:

(By courtesy of The Brotherton Collection, Leeds University Library.)
The number of Silk Gowns that are weekly sold at Mrs. Rogers' in Exchange Alley (though not much above a month since she has undertaken it) makes it very evident that her Gowns are very cheap as well as nice Fancies, for she does not heap a great deal of rubbish together, but chooses the most proper silks and suitable Linings: And for the future will keep such Choice, that all Persons of quality and other may be furnished with varieties of Fancies and all Sizes.

Figure 4 Eighteenth-century ad: *The Spectator*, 12 March 1711

Translation: Retro Eau de Cologne Lotion for Men. An aroma which compliments your style. Retro! The freshness and warmth in the fragrance of the eau de Cologne, the medicinal and rejuvenating action of the lotion, cannot escape the attention of a modern man. The New Dawn Factory.

Figure 5 A Soviet ad for eau de Cologne

In this ad the woman is saying: 'As I would like to have a bright child, maybe I could meet a graduate of Tokyo University. . . .' The columns on the left list men already registered with the agency: their age, height, company, hobby and university.

Figure 6 A Japanese ad for a marriage agency

ignores national boundaries, it can also reflect differences between cultures, even among the advanced industrialized capitalist societies – as the Japanese ad for a marriage agency reveals (Figure 6).

The late 1980s and early 1990s have produced a striking example of advertising as an index of cultural change and difference in Eastern Europe, where centralized socialist states are changing into pluralist capitalist societies. In this transition, certain discourse types (definable in the terms we have suggested above) are disappearing. (Precisely because these types belong to a different kind of society, they often have no translation equivalent in the languages of societies which do not use them.) In the pre-glasnost Soviet Union, the *lozung* was a hoarding, neon sign or strip of red material bearing a communist slogan, put in place by the authorities and addressed to the population in general. In the post-glasnost Soviet Union, the *lozung* ceased to exist. Similarly, the *anekdot*, a satirical political story, more thought-provoking and serious than a 'joke' (the word by which it is often translated), declined with the system it mocked. Advertising, though not altogether unknown in Eastern Europe under communism, was strikingly rare. Its absence struck visitors from capitalist countries very forcibly: bare walls in metro stations, unbroken print in newspapers, mail deliveries without circulars. Conversely, visitors to the West from Eastern Europe were often overwhelmed by the quantity of advertising, and quite inexperienced in dealing with it, finding it difficult to ignore or interpret. (Ironically the reception of the *lozung* in socialist societies and of the hard-selling ad in capitalist countries have certain features in common; both are treated with indifference and distrust by their target audience, but with interest by outsiders.) As the Eastern European societies change, new, capitalist discourse types become more prominent. Pre-eminent among these is advertising.

1.6 ATTITUDES TO ADVERTISING

Our attitude to a discourse type can be indicative of our personality, or social and ideological position. This is not equally true of all discourse types, many of which are relatively uncontroversial. Few people, if any, have strong views about the need for recipes or car number plates. Other types arouse stronger feelings. Some people feel that a university lecture is an authoritarian way of teaching, that Christmas cards are an unnecessary waste of paper and time, and that census forms are an intrusion upon privacy. In this respect, advertising is one of the most controversial of all contemporary discourse types, partly because it is relatively new, but also because it is closely associated with the values of the competitive high-growth market economy in which it thrives. In a world beset by social and ecological problems, advertising can be seen as urging people to consume more by making them feel dissatisfied or inadequate, by appealing to greed, worry and ambition. On the other hand, it may be argued that many ads are skilful, clever and amusing, and that it is unjust to make them a scapegoat for all the sorrows of the modern world. Thus to ask someone their opinion of advertising in general, or of a particular ad, can be to embark upon an emotionally and ideologically charged discussion, revealing their political and social position, and their acceptance of, or alienation from, the status quo. (This argument is complicated by the confusing effect of ads which attempt to appeal to an urge to rebel or dissent, such as a Wranglers ad which shows a young man abandoning a taxi in New York without paying the fare.)

I have sometimes felt, teaching courses on the language of advertising to undergraduates, that students choosing the course have fallen – broadly speaking – into two categories. In crude and unsympathetic terms I might caricature one category as amoral aesthetes mesmerized by the decadent beauty of advertising, and the other as over-serious moralists, interpreting everything in the terms of some fixed political or social creed. The first category toy with ideas of working in a big ad agency, the latter believe that by understanding advertising they will neutralize its effects and improve the world. This simple dichotomy is clumsy and exaggerated. There are certainly many more delicate categories within these two bands (as well as an apathetic group who don't choose courses on advertising at all) but it has a degree of truth. Advertising is a topic which both causes and reveals existing social divisions. In an educational setting, advertising can be a stimulus – vying with the claims made for literature in a liberal education – for discussion of the most urgent issues of our time: the destruction of the environment, the wealth gap (both within and between countries), the choice between socialism and capitalism, the growth of a world culture, the struggle of feminism and patriarchy, the status of art and popular culture, the consequences of mass communication and high technology. Few discourse types can generate so much.

In the wider world, the same kind of division of opinion also exists, though the sharpness of earlier differences may be softening with the growth of a general acceptance that advertising is now well established and not likely, in the near future, to be swept away by either revolution or reaction. Intense large-scale advertising now has a history. People grow up with it and grow used to it, so that even when it is perceived as an evil it is also perceived as inevitable and unremarkable. In addition, advertising itself has changed, becoming more subtle and more entertaining than the crude hard selling of the 1950s and 1960s (though this very subtlety can be seen as more pernicious). Many people also feel confused by advertising's apparent change of attitude towards contemporary problems. Some ads make a show of ecological concern, of support for women's rights, of recommending a healthy diet to prevent disease. This apparent social conscience may give rise to three very different judgements. According to the first, advanced by some leading advertisers, it is possible for advertising to influence society: for good as well as for bad. In the second view, advertising is amoral, and merely reflects states and changes in society, whether good or bad (R. White 1988: 176–83). In the third view, the apparent social concern and progress professed in some ads is simply fraudulent, and ads are always bad: a veneer of feminism masks deeper sexism; superficial environmental concern still cynically sells pollution. In its strongest form, this last view may argue that a growth economy, social exploitation and inequality, violence and the destruction of the planet are all inextricably linked to each other, and that advertising is both an expression of this apocalyptic unity and dependent upon it.

EXERCISES

1 Try to characterize the discourse types (written down the side of Figure 7), by identifying the features of context (written across the top) which are peculiar to them. The first one has already been done.
   Add some more discourse types of your own in spaces 8, 9, 10.

   Are the features you identify essential or optional to the discourse type? Could a road sign, for example, be any of the following: whispered (physical form); to a doll (addressee); by a six-year-old child (sender/addresser); as an expression of love (function); in a bus queue (situation)?

Context	Participants		Function	Intertexts	Co-texts	Situation	Paralanguage	Substances
	sender	receiver						
Type			warn	other	none			
1 Road signs: transport			inform	road		roadside	large	metal
	ministry	motorist		signs			letters	board
2 Catholic mass:								
3 Bank statement:								
4 University exam:								
5 Driving licence:								
6 Love letter:								
7 Poem:								
8 ———————								
9 ———————								
10———————								

Figure 7 Features of discourse types

2 Is it possible to characterize the discourse type 'ad' by features or combinations of features? Who or what are the

    participants ....
    function ....
    intertexts ....
    co-texts ....
    situation ....
    paralanguage ....
    substance ....

3 Consider the following. Do they fit the description of ads you have given in Exercise 2?

a   'CAPE TOWN (Reuter) – President F.W. de Klerk placed full-page advertisements in newspapers yesterday urging blacks and whites to "listen to the dreams of others" and build a united post-apartheid South Africa. The advertisements showed a soaring dove of peace and the slogan: "Politicians can work out a new South Africa, but they can't make it work – only you can do that." '(*The Independent* 4 February 1991)

b   A poster displays the words:

    'Your best friend is the one
    who won't buy you a drink –
    when you're driving.'

c *To a Haggis*
Fair fa' your honest, sonsie face,
Great chieftain o' the puddin'-race!
Aboon them a' ye tak your place,
    Painch, tripe or thairm:
Weel arc ye wordy o' a grace
    As lang's my arm.

Paper bags used by a haggis-making butchers' firm in Edinburgh (McSweens) reproduce all eight stanzas of this poem by Robert Burns.

d A tv programme about an expedition to the Arctic showed explorers with the brand name GORE-TEX written on their coats. This was not *just* an endorsement. The explorers had chosen Gore-Tex as the best clothing for their purposes.

e 'Friends and relatives of the British journalist John McCarthy will tomorrow mark his 33rd birthday – his fourth in captivity – by placing an emotional advertisement in a Beirut newspaper, published in the city where he is believed to be held prisoner' (*The Observer* 26 November 1989).

f Leech (1990) analyses a poster in a Kentucky Fried Chicken restaurant which was positioned in such a way that it was visible to the staff serving behind the counter, not to the customers.

There was a man who had
a dream . . . a dream that
involved hard work,
dedication and integrity.
Where other men would
have given up, this man
made that dream a reality.
His dream was
Kentucky Fried Chicken . . .
and his name was
Colonel Harland D. Sanders
    1890–1980

g In December 1989 a Pepsi ad showed Tina Turner and Rod Stewart singing the song *It Takes Two, Baby*. A record of the song was released at the same time.

4 Note some differences between the ads in Figures 4–6 and those of

a contemporary society
b capitalist society
c occidental society.

FURTHER READING

(Full references to further reading suggestions can be found in the bibliography at the end of the book.)

On advertising in general

Non-academic

There is a good deal to read and watch on ads *apart from* academic analyses and textbooks:

1 The journals of the advertising trade, such as *Advertising Age* (in the USA) and *Marketing* and *Campaign* (in the UK).
2 Tv programmes on ads, both serious and humorous. Two outstanding series of programmes in the UK were
   • *The Marketing Mix* Yorkshire TV and Channel 4 (UK) Spring 1986
   • *Washes Whiter* BBC2 (UK) April 1990
3 Codes of advertising practice such as the *British Code of Advertising Practice* (available from the Committee of Advertising Practice in London).
4 Books by advertisers; two excellent introductions are:
   White, R. (1988) *Advertising: What It Is and How to Do It*
   Douglas, T. (1984) *The Complete Guide to Advertising*.
5 Frequent items and articles about advertising in the daily press.

Academic

1 Among academic books and articles, some of the earliest are still the best. Particularly recommended are:
   Goffman, E. [1976] (1979) *Gender Advertisements*
   Leech, G.N. (1966) *English in Advertising*
   McLuhan, M. (1964) 'Keeping upset with the Joneses', in *Understanding Media*.
2 More recently, there are excellent sections on advertising in Alvarado and Thompson (1990) *The Media Reader* and Davis and Walton (1983) *Language, Image, Media*. Good general introductions are Vestergaard and Schroder (1985) *The Language of Advertising*, Myers (1986) *Understains . . . the Sense and Seduction of Advertising* and Dyer (1988) *Advertising as Communication*); there are many interesting papers in Umiker-Sebeok (ed.) (1987) *Marketing and Semiotics*.

Further reading on this chapter

General introductions to discourse analysis are Brown and Yule (1983) *Discourse Analysis*, Stubbs (1983) *Discourse Analysis* and Part I of Cook (1989) *Discourse*. For a discussion of discourse type, see Dimter (1985) 'On text classification' and Swales (1990) *Genre Analysis*.

Part I
Materials

2 Substance and surroundings

2.0 THE SUBSTANCE OF ADS

All communication relies on physical substance. Communication involving language uses a number of different kinds. Spoken language is carried by sound waves originating from the human vocal tract (or occasionally a speech synthesizer). Written language is carried by marks on a prepared surface such as paper or painted metal, by points of light on a screen, or by three-dimensional letters, such as those used in neon signs. The sign languages used by the deaf (which are as complex as any spoken language) are carried by movements and configurations of the hands. These **primary substances** of language can be relayed by **secondary substances** such as celluloid film, computer disc, electric cable, magnetic tape or radio waves. Discourse types are often associated with particular choices and combinations of substance. A 'chat', for example, is carried by sound waves and may be relayed by telephone, but is not printed on expensive paper or carved in stone. A 'letter' is typed or written on paper. A 'tv news broadcast' is first written, then relayed by auto-cue, then spoken, then relayed by cable or by radio waves.

Choices of substance matter. In a broad sense, they affect the 'meaning' of the discourse, though the impact of particular choices varies between cultures. The significance of the choice of primary substance – sound waves, paper, slate, screen – will depend on the state of literacy and technology. All languages use speech (or signing), and only later, if at all, develop writing. As the use of writing spreads in a society, it comes to be associated with public, formal and commissive communication. The spoken undertakings of orality give way to the signed documents of literacy. Literate societies generally accord more status to writing than to speech, though there are some notable exceptions – such as liturgies, lectures, marriage ceremonies, inaugurations and legal proceedings – which have survived the shift and are still communicated orally, though they are in fact likely to be read, learned from, or prompted by writing. Within a culture which uses both handwriting and print, it is the latter which usually carries more status, while typewriting is somewhere between the two.

Even more distinctions accompany the advent of sound recording and broadcasting, which effect a new transition, sometimes referred to as a 'secondary orality' (Ong 1982). In some ways, these new media seem to return us to orality, while preserving the advantages of writing. Language is preserved in time and disseminated across space, but comes to us as sound, in the voice of an individual. Word-processing introduces yet more changes, and again seems to mix the features of both speech and writing. On screen, a good deal of writing, like speech, disappears without trace. It has none of the finality of print, for what is written can be endlessly altered. People converse in writing through E-mail (electronic mail). So, strangely, the computer reintroduces behaviour reminiscent of an oral culture. Promises are again made without signatures.

Advertising is very much a child of this secondary orality. Even when printed it affects the style of personal spoken communication. Most ads are short tv and radio broadcasts, magazine pages, roadside hoardings or junk mail. As such they use a wide array of primary and secondary substances. The choice of substance affects the nature of the ad and is an integral part of its identity, although the variety of substances in ads means that the discourse type of advertising cannot be identified with any one. (It is looser, for example, than the connection between 'road sign' and paint on a metal board, or between 'credit card' and embossed plastic.) Yet the choice of substance in a particular ad is an essential part of its identity. This intimate relationship of an ad with its substance presents a marked contrast with literary discourse, for although literature, like ads, is carried in a variety of substances it is usually described as though it were independent of them, existing in some incorporeal region of the mind. Some essence of *Hamlet* is felt to remain the same, whether it is a tv production, a live performance, the quarto manuscript, a dog-eared paperback, or a calf-bound gold-tooled edition, and no imperfection in any of these substances would alter opinion of this essence. People talk about such different instances as though they were essentially the same work. This is not so much the case with advertising.

Choices of advertising substance are limited only by the advertiser's ingenuity. In December 1989, at the cost of $4 an issue, Texas Instruments placed a talking micro-chip in the US magazine *Business Week*:

> a plastic card holding an all-in-one solid state chip containing micropro-cessor, memory, filter, and signal converter, three aspirin-sized batter-ies and a one-inch piezo electric speaker. On lifting a flap, a male voice (it could have been female, with a choice of accent, language – even a recognizable individual) recited a 42-word 15-second speech . . . to promote Texas-Instrument's MegaChip Technology.
>
> (*Electric Word* 17 1990)

The trick was repeated by Absolut Vodka, who placed a chip which said 'Merry Christmas' in four languages in every copy of the same month's

Vanity Fair, at a total cost of $1.4 million. Araldite have advertised their glue by sticking a complete car to a roadside hoarding, and in Britain, rather less expensively, there have been ads written on the side of cows grazing alongside the London to Brighton railway line (R. White 1988: 96–8). Magazines carry samples of perfume to be released by the lifting or peeling of odour-impregnated paper. Scratch-and-smell food ads use a similar device, and at least one also gave the time of a tv commercial for the same product, enabling the reader to watch and sniff simultaneously. Ads are relayed by telephone ('The time sponsored by Accurist will be . . .') and vicariously by the grooved black plastic of re-released or purpose-recorded pop records and their covers (see Figure 8). There are ads on book matches, milk cartons, t-shirts and – less commonly – on vapour trails and firework patterns in the sky. There are also ads which, though printed on paper, make that paper appear ripped (Figure 9) or burned (Figure 10).

At Grand Slam tennis tournaments, the bottles and cans seen on the umpire's stand between games, though rarely used by the resting players, *become* ads for the products. This raises the issue of whether every product has a dual and ambiguous identity. By having its own brand-name written on it, every product is both itself and an ad for itself. Nor can this issue be dodged by drawing a distinction between contents and wrapping. In many products, such as chocolate and soap, the brand name is not only written on the wrapping, but also cut into the object, making the substance which carries the name the same as the substance to which it refers. If we assume, as seems likely, that the drinks displayed in tennis tournaments are not those actually drunk by the players, but are there only as ads, then there is justification in saying that their existence as ads outweighs their existence as themselves. It is almost impossible to separate the advertising from the advertised. This morning, through my letter box, I received a miniature bottle of *Vidal Sassoon Wash-and-Go Salon Shampoo and Conditioner All in One*. Even if not used, it is still an ad: for itself.

A list of all the different substances of ads would be vast, and is no doubt growing every day. Ads use any of the substances available to language – and adapt new ones such as soap or vapour.

Such variety fulfils several purposes. Firstly and most obviously it is attention-getting, and can compensate for an intrinsic lack of interest in the message itself. Talking micro-chips are novel and memorable (as the existence of an article about them reveals), but the linguistic message of such ads ('Merry Christmas', etc.) is in itself banal. The appeal of novel substance, unlike that of novel text, is intrinsically short lived. With every repetition, effectiveness diminishes.

Secondly, certain choices of substance, or combinations of them, help to fix the product more firmly in the memory by actively involving the reader. This is particularly the case with the exhortation to scratch-and-smell while watching tv. The talking chip, activated by opening and closing the pages

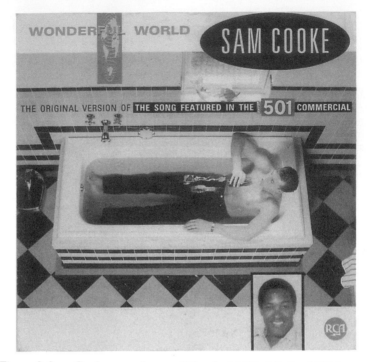

Figure 8 Sam Cooke record cover 'Wonderful World': Levi 501 jeans

Figure 9 A Dutch ad for Burger King hamburgers

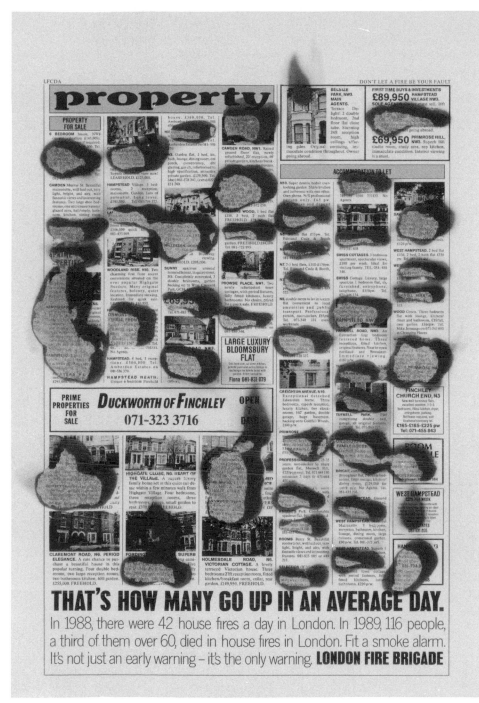

Figure 10 London Fire Brigade ad for smoke alarms

of the publication, is also likely to stimulate repetitions of this action in the reader. Toys in cereal packets make children rummage. People buy records of pop-songs from ads (often bringing them commercial success).

Lastly, an innovative use of substance may poach some of the intrinsic interest and prestige associated with another discourse, medium or event: firework displays, tennis matches, quality clothing, pop concerts or computers.

2.1 THE SITUATION OF ADS

When an ad appears on a wall or a shirt, it is not the substance of this environment which matters, but its social meaning. The buildings in Times Square are not just bricks and mortar; the shirt of an Olympic champion is not just cloth. The substance of an ad which is a vehicle for its own linguistic and pictorial messages exists in a situation composed of other substances which carry other meanings of their own, and the interaction of ad and situation can create a third meaning which is quite different from either. This third meaning may undermine or enhance the advertiser's intention. It may derive from contrasts between the world of the ad and the world around it, as in Figure 11.

Figure 11 Street scene: an ad and a passer-by

2.2 ACCOMPANYING DISCOURSES

In many ways, at every level, ads are **parasitic** upon their situation and other discourses. Just as the substance of an ad is often stuck to some other significant substance, so its discourse both occurs within other discourse and also imitates it. I use the term 'parasitic' rather than 'symbiotic', because even though many magazines and tv channels depend on ads economically, ads are not needed in the communication effected by the situation or discourse to which they attach themselves.

Many discourses are parasitic. Literary criticism is parasitic upon literature, sports commentary upon sport. Just as many parasitic organisms may be beneficial if not necessary to their hosts, the same may be true of parasitic discourses.

Among the elements of context listed in Chapter 1 are situation and intertext. Although these categories adequately describe the linguistic and non-linguistic environment of most discourse types, they are not sufficient for a description of ads. This is because ads typically occur together with, or embedded in, other discourses, to which they make no direct reference. An ad may occur in the middle of a tv news broadcast, together with, yet isolated from, other ads. A printed ad occurs in the middle of a magazine article to which it makes no reference. These other discourses are not covered by the term 'situation' which applies to the non-linguistic environment, nor by the term 'intertext' which implies texts which are related, in intention or interpretation, to that under consideration. Consequently, we need another term, and I shall refer to them as **accompanying discourses**. As with situation, the interaction between ads and accompanying discourses creates new meanings, either by chance, through manipulation by the advertiser, or, more rarely, through subversive intervention against ads from outside.

Thus it was presumably by chance that an ad showing a Vauxhall car dodging through collapsing construction work gained an unpleasant and unforeseen overtone when, on 18 October 1989, it appeared immediately after news coverage of the car-crushing collapse of a two-tier freeway during the San Francisco earthquake. In the *Observer* magazine, an ad for *Birds-Eye Menu-Master Tandoori Chicken Masala* appeared on the page before a photograph of emaciated children in Auschwitz; an ad for *Rapport parfum pour homme* appeared with a photograph of dirty, emaciated prisoners emerging from eleven years in a Soviet gulag.

Yet chance may also work to an ad's advantage. I have seen ads interspersing a magazine article about photography awards, and felt my attention drawn to the excellence of the ads' photography, which I preferred to that of the winning entries.

There are times when such contrasts are not accidental, but deliberately intended to subvert. The wittier graffiti on ads fall into this category. The ad (Figure 12) showing a Mexican urchin, crouching by tyre tracks in the desert and listening to a cassette recorder,

He only knows three words of English – Boy George and Uniroyal

prompted someone to cross out these three words and substitute another three:

Yankee Go Home.

Such detrimental additions need not always be the hurried and illegal work of the graffiti writer; they are also used openly by well-established organizations. Essentially the same technique was used by the Anti-Apartheid movement when, campaigning against the involvement of British Leyland in South Africa, it produced its own 'ads', juxtaposing the Leyland **slogo**[1] 'Forward with Leyland' with photographs of the South African security forces using Leyland LandRovers as prison vans and armoured vehicles from which to harass and terrorize the black population. It is an effective technique with a degree of poetic justice. By imitating an ad, it uses advertising's own penchant for raiding another discourse type, but against the ad itself. Paradoxically, by so doing, it both criticizes a particular ad and pays implicit tribute to the techniques of advertising in general.

One of the strangest aspects of the relationship between ads and their accompanying discourses is the rarity of any cross-reference between the two.[2] Tv programmes pause with euphemisms such as 'We'll take a break'

Figure 12 A graffito on an ad, by courtesy of Leeds Postcards

or 'See you in a minute'. Magazines interleaf ads and articles without comment. Deliberate exploitation of this alternation is so rare that it suggests publishing and broadcasting guidelines which forbid cross-reference. Occasional transgressions of these written or unwritten rules only emphasize their force, as when the comedian Clive Anderson says

> We've got to stop for a bit now while people try to sell you things you don't want.

Such interventions are rare: hardly surprisingly, given the financial dependency of most accompanying discourses on the ads which live within them. It is for this reason that, while programme producers do not even see the ads which punctuate their shows, advertising agencies can buy space in specific programmes, and exercise considerable control over the interaction of one discourse with another.[3] Usually, this amounts to no more than an attempt to match an audience of an ad with the market for a product, or exploitation of desires aroused by a programme or article, but it may also extend to imitation of the accompanying discourse in an attempt to blur the boundary between the two. This not only attracts attention to the ad, but also tries to invest it with some of the authority of the accompanying discourses. In newspapers, some ads are presented in the print and format of the news around them, a tendency which is sometimes combated by explicit editorial labelling with the word 'advertisement'. On tv, in the USA (though not in Britain) celebrities appear in ads punctuating their own shows, in settings very like those of the show itself. Bill Cosby for example appears in ads for Jell-O and Polaroid in the middle of his own *The Cosby Show*, causing momentary confusion in the mind of the spectator, who initially perceives the ad as part of the comedy – which, as they have chosen to watch it, they presumably like. (This tendency is accentuated in countries where the screen does not go blank for a fraction of a second between each ad as it does in Britain.) There are also tv commercials which fake the beginning of another programme, such as a Hamlet cigar ad in Britain which uses the **logo**[4] and music of its host, Channel 4, as though the advertising break were over, then rearranges the strokes of the numeral '4' to form a face which starts smoking a cigar (see Figure 13). Another ad, for Kellogg's Corn Flakes, appears to be a news broadcast, until the camera draws back to show a couple watching it, and the newscaster remarks on their odd habit of eating breakfast cereal in the evening. An old Birds Eye ad showed an actual weather forecaster, standing in front of a map of Britain on which the clouds were all fish fingers.

On tv, such imitation is often humorous and unconvincing. Real confusion, however, is sought by junk mail, which, mindful of its unopened destiny in the rubbish bin, frequently poses as something else. Thus there are circulars which look like postcards, telegrams, newspapers and invitations (see Figure 14). Such discourses are more than parasitic, attempting

Figure 13 Hamlet cigars ad: 'Channel 4 logo'

to take on, and take over, the features of another type. Only one or two of the identifying parameters of the imitated discourse type are different. The sender of the postcard is not a friend but a firm; its function is not to greet but to sell. In every other respect it is a regular postcard. The trick may backfire, not only on the public, who may overlook important communications, but also on the firms themselves, as it is more likely to annoy than to persuade.

A different kind of merger with accompanying discourses occurs in sponsored tv programmes (common in North America and legalized in Britain in the late 1980s) and **advertorials**: lengthy entries in magazines and newspapers which attempt to combine article and ad, using the publication's house style, and providing the reader with information or discussion which is more substantial and less single-minded than that in the majority of ads. As both of these intermediate genres cut the costs of broadcasters, publishers and agencies, they bloom in periods of economic recession. In these sub-genres of the ad, the expansion of the limited span of time and space usually available can be quite catastrophic to the interest and effectiveness of the ad. It is a relationship in which the parasite destroys its own host. The best ads are successful bandits, raiding the borders of their accompanying discourses, but with the sense not to stay too long.

2.3 PARASITE DISCOURSE

This chapter has emphasized the way ads exist through other discourses and culturally significant artefacts, either by attaching themselves to them (sometimes quite literally), by co-occurring with them, or by imitation.

Figure 14a Junk mail: Sol Holidays postcard

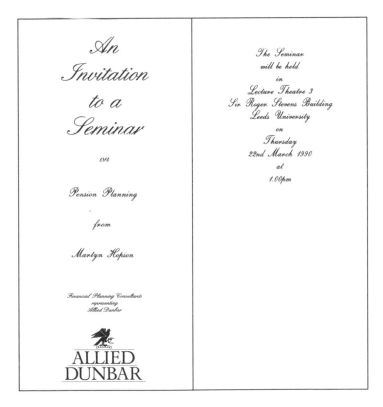

Figure 14b Junk mail: Allied Dunbar financial planning seminar

Ads make use of substance which is already being used for some other purpose, including the substance and wrappings of their own subject matter; they find a place in the time and space of other discourses, and are seldom alone (magazines and programmes consisting only of ads are both rare and unsuccessful); they borrow so many features of other discourses that they are in danger of having no separable identity of their own. Yet, as already remarked, this notion of the parasite discourse need not in itself be negative, nor is it true that it applies to advertising alone. It is rather that advertising is an extreme example of a tendency apparent in all discourse. Though the attachment to occupied substances and discourse spaces may indeed be peculiar to ads, its imitation to the point of self-destruction is not. Many literary texts, and especially modernist ones, achieve effect through **bricolage**, the borrowing and inter-weaving of other discourse types, to the extent where they too, like the collage painting which is their pictorial equivalent, have no existence independent of the sources they have plundered. Joyce's *Ulysses*, for example, is an assembly of a range of styles – newspaper, romance, catechism – none of which, in isolation, can be identified as the voice of either the author or the book. Dos Passos's *U.S.A.* uses various discourse types in the same manner. To denigrate such techniques as inferior to their sources implies a belief in both the possibility and the virtue of original and autonomous discourse. This disputable idea, like many others in contemporary attitudes to literature, derives from the Romantic stress on literary discourse as the vehicle of an isolated and extraordinary individual identity. An alternative view regards all discourse as to some degree the reworking of others, and in this perspective finds virtue in the complexity of writing which can tolerate many voices and influences at once, without seeking to simplify by silencing some at the expense of others. In this view it is no longer the self-assertiveness of the writer which is admired but, rather, his or her receptiveness and lack of individuality. Discourses such as parody and comedy thrive on such tolerance and imitation, and many literary works regarded as classics re-work existing plots, while allowing the voices of other discourses to enter into them with an accompanying potential to subvert the ideology which the original enshrined. Thus *Hamlet* may be seen as a revenge tragedy invaded by philosophy, *Crime and Punishment* as a detective story mixed in with a parable of religious salvation. Their stature comes not from originality, in the narrow and impossible sense, but from a deeper originality of selection, combination and tolerance of contradiction. If advertising is parasitic in this positive sense, drawing blood from virtually every discoursal source from which it is not legally barred, then it is not this which disqualifies it from the acclaim accorded to literature, but some other features. The task which we must set ourselves is to understand what these differentiating features may be.

EXERCISES

1 Consider the effect of the following places for ads:

    a facing the lanes of a swimming pool
    b on the cover of a record (see Figure 8)
    c on a t-shirt
    d on the side of a truck
    e on the side of a bus

Do they enhance or diminish the effect of an ad?
Make a list of unusual situations in which you have encountered ads.

2 'TV ads intrude into classroom. American teachers are aghast at the intrusion of television ads into the schoolroom as Channel One, a news show designed for teenagers, was broadcast in 400 schools across the country this week' (*Guardian* 7 March 1990).

    a Are there television programmes in which the appearance of ads is undesirable?
    b Are there tv programmes in which astute advertisers would not want their ads to appear?
    c Consider the positioning of ads in tv broadcasts of live sport, religious worship, news of major disasters and state funerals. What is the policy of tv networks on this?

3 Is an ad still an ad when it is away from its accompanying discourses, or when it is sought out and bought by the receiver? Consider the following cases.

    a 'Hamlet cigars commercials, which have run on television since 1984, are being made into a video for sale and rental' (*Observer* 16 June 1991.)
    b There are postcards whose picture is an ad.
    c Many people have genuine or imitation bar mirrors with old ads on the glass.
    d 'Go on, Flake my day. Our hungry lady readers are hungry for the chance to be telly ad stars and their motto is: 'if you've got it flake it!' We asked if YOU could be the girl Cadbury's are seeking to replace mouth-watering model Deborah Leng, who is quitting the sexy Flake ads' (*Sun* 30 November 1990)

The article shows five contestants inserting Cadbury's Flakes into their mouths.

4 'If tv companies are incapable of delivering the sorts of audience that advertisers require – why shouldn't the advertisers have a crack at

making some suitable programmes themselves?' (*Campaign* 3 May 1991: 32).

What is your answer to this question?

FURTHER READING

Chapters 10–14 in R. White (1988) *How Advertising Works* provide a sensible and pragmatic view of different media from the advertiser's point of view.

The effects of unusual substance and of accompanying discourses are often neglected both in general discourse analysis, and, more surprisingly, in analysis of ads. See, however, the article by Beezer, Grimshaw and Barker in Punter (1986) *Contemporary Cultural Studies*.

3 Pictures, music, speech and writing

3.0 INTRODUCTION

The term **mode** is used in this book to refer to the choice between three means of communication: music, pictures and language.[1] All may be further subdivided in various overlapping ways. Music may be orchestral or solo, amplified or acoustic; pictures may be still or motion, cartoon or photographic; language may be sung (in which case it overlaps with music), spoken, written or signed – and each of these divisions may be further subdivided. I shall refer to these further subdivisions as **sub-modes**. This chapter examines the effect of the selection and combination of the different modes in ads, and of three sub-modes of language: song, speech and writing.

Any analysis of the language of ads immediately encounters the paradox that it both must and cannot take the musical and pictorial modes into account as well. It must do this, because there are many ads in which picture and music are the essence of the communication: creating mood, imparting information, persuading and making claims so strongly that, if language features at all – and there are many ads in which it does not – it is often only in a peripheral or auxiliary way. Even in those ads where language is the dominant mode of communication (perhaps a minority), it is still deceptive to look at it in isolation, because it rebounds against both picture and music, gaining and giving new meanings and connections. Yet analysis cannot adequately cope with music and pictures, because they are different from the mode of the analysis itself, which is language. While the words of this book can put the words of an ad on the page, they can only hint at the nature of its music and pictures, for these cannot be written down 'as themselves' but only as something else – words. This problem is more serious with tv than with printed ads, for on paper pictures stand still (and can even be reproduced), and there is no sound. Yet even in analyses of printed ads the problems are legion. To use too many accompanying reproductions alters the character of a written analysis, leaving the writing dwarfed and swamped by the ads themselves. Reproduction, moreover, is unlikely to do justice to such factors as size, colour and position within accompanying discourses. In considering tv ads, where pictures move, music plays, and language comes in changing combinations of speech, song and writing, reproduction is virtually impossible, and a video, to be watched while reading, would transform a written analysis even more than companion illustrations.

Many analyses of advertising solve this problem by ignoring it. When they analyse pictures, they limit themselves to printed ads where the pictures can be reproduced, and ignore tv; alternatively, if they select from both print and tv, they ignore the pictures, or relegate them to a secondary role, even when in the original it was the language which was secondary. With music, the situation is even worse. Few linguistic analyses make mention of the effect of music and song.[2] It is just too difficult to include.

I do not see a way of overcoming these problems – but neither do I believe they should be ignored. The obstacle which they pose enables advertising to keep analysis at bay, for it can shift its ground constantly, emphasizing now one mode and now another. There is a danger of dilution in an analysis which attempts to tackle too much, and no individual analyst will feel equally at home in all modes and all media; but I believe that the converse fault – of fragmentation and incompleteness – is worse. Advertising, unlike analysis, operates in all modes and media at once, and must be treated accordingly. Therefore, though the focus of this book is on language, it also considers the effect on language of the other modes. Music and pictures are part of the discourse of ads, and to ignore or downplay them is a serious distortion.

3.1 AN EXAMPLE: 'THE PERFECT COMBINATION'

These problems and pitfalls are best illustrated by an example. Let us take a fairly ordinary tv ad, firstly as words only, and secondly as words in interaction with music and pictures. The example raises two quite separate problems: how to transcribe music and pictures on the page; and how to analyse their interaction with each other and with language. The ad is a tv commercial for the soft drink Sprite[3] (screened in Britain in 1990). The words are:

> When the heat is on,
> And the pace is slow,
> There's a cool fresh world
> Where you can go:
> Clear, crisp and light,
> It tastes of Sprite.
>
> A twist of lemon
> For a taste sensation;
> A squeeze of lime
> Is the perfect combination:
> Clear, crisp and light,

Sheer taste of Sprite;
Clear, crisp and light,
Sheer taste of Sprite.

During the course of the ad two small written texts appear very briefly at the bottom of the screen. The first says

Sprite and Diet Sprite are registered trademarks of the Coca-Cola Company

and the second

Diet Sprite can help slimming or weight control only as part of a calorie controlled diet.

In addition, the words 'Sprite' and 'Diet Sprite' are visible on the product itself. The jingle, the small print, and the brand names are the only language. Along with these words go twenty camera shots of four separate locations (see Figure 15); and the words are sung – rather than spoken – by a man's voice (with inevitable cheerfulness!).

The music and the singing voice pass through four phases, distinguished by marked changes in speed and beat. The first phase conveys a sense of urgency building to a climax; the second phase releases the tension of the first with a bouncy and regular rhythm; in the third phase this rhythm disappears, there is an absence of percussion, and sound effects creating an air of magic and mystery; finally the fourth phase repeats the second, confident and animated as before.

The relation of the words to accompanying pictures and to these phases of the music is set out, approximately, below:

Words	Pictures

SCENE ONE: THE TRAFFIC JAM
MUSIC BUILDING TO A CLIMAX

Words		Pictures
When the heat is on	1	Couple in an open car in a traffic jam at the entrance to coastal (Mediterranean?) road tunnel. The driver of a truck behind has left his cab to try to see ahead.
And the pace is slow		Everyone is very hot and frustrated.
There's a cool fresh world	2	Close-up of hands reaching into a cool-box containing ice, Sprite and Diet Sprite.
Where you can go	3	Close-up of the couple in the car. The man (the driver) looks at the woman.
	4	Both swig from their cans.
	5	Camera's 'eye' moves through the opening in the top of the can, into the Sprite inside!

Figure 15 Sprite soft drink ad: 'The perfect combination'

SCENE TWO: THE TOBOGGAN RUN
MUSIC INTENSIFIES, SPEEDS UP, LOOSENS

Clear, crisp and light	6	A professional toboggan run as seen from a high-speed toboggan emerging from a tunnel.
It tastes of Sprite	7	Close-up of the yellow helmet of the tobogganer.
	8	Toboggan run as seen by the tobogganer. (9/10 Repeat 7/8)
A twist of lemon	11	The track is blocked by a giant slice of lemon.
For a taste sensation	12	We see the lemon reflected in the visor of the approaching tobogganer.
	13	Close-up of the slice of lemon: drops of juice are oozing out of it.
	14	We now see there are two people on the toboggan, one holding tightly to the other. The toboggan smashes through the lemon.

SCENE THREE: IN THE TUNNEL
MUSIC SLOWS, LOSES BEAT, GROWS WHIMSICAL

	15	An underwater shot inside the toboggan tunnel and/or the can of Sprite. We are moving through ice cubes towards the surface.
A squeeze of lime	16	Camera comes to a slice of lime at the other end of the tunnel, and breaks through.
Is the perfect combination	17	The two tobogganers are out in the open again. Their toboggan is approaching another tunnel.

SCENE FOUR: MOVING TRAFFIC
MUSIC RETURNS TO REGULAR CONFIDENT BEAT

Clear, crisp and light	18	The toboggan enters the tunnel.
Sheer taste of Sprite	19	Close-up of the couple back in
Clear, crisp and light		the car, moving fast. The woman is drinking from a can of Sprite
Sheer taste of Sprite	20	The car emerges from a tunnel on a coastal road. The man and woman are cool, happy and relaxed.

Taken together with the pictures of these four scenes, and the four corresponding phases of the music, the words of the jingle, which are so one-dimensional in isolation, take on new meanings, and contribute to a complex set of visual metaphors and parallels. A number of words, phrases and clauses become puns. Thus

When the heat is on,

no longer has only its dead-metaphorical sense of

When life is difficult

it also refers to the uncomfortable heat experienced in the waiting vehicles. By the same process

And the pace is slow,

refers specifically to the traffic jam, as well as, idiomatically, to a dull period of life. Alternatively, or additionally, the pictures reinstate the lost force of the dead metaphor from which the idiomatic sense of these phrases derives. In the line

There's a cool fresh world

'world' in the context of Scene Two refers to the fantasy world of the toboggan run which is apparently inside the can; the words

Where you can go

accompany the transition shot in which we see the can from the point of view of the drinker, and seem to enter into it. In this fantasy world, inside the Sprite, all the undesirable qualities of the world in the opening scene are reversed. There is cool snow and fast movement. In the lines of the bouncy chorus which accompany these new pictures, 'it' refers both to this fantasy world, and to the Sprite itself.

Clear, crisp and light,
It tastes of Sprite.

The visually created puns continue.

A twist of lemon

is also on a twist (a bend) in the toboggan run, and a twist in the tale – for who would expect to find either a toboggan run inside a soft-drink can, or a slice of lemon on a toboggan run? The lemon, appearing on the track, is both a fantasy within a fantasy (and thus at an even further remove) but also, because Sprite tastes of lemon, the beginning of a transition back to the opening scene, for on the other side of the lemon we are back in the can, and as we emerge from it the car emerges from the tunnel in Scene Four. Perhaps it is far-fetched to say that

A squeeze of lime

refers punningly to the squeezing of the front rider by the pillion rider, but I have no doubt that the words

Is the perfect combination

occurring with the picture of the two tobogganers, refer to their athletic teamwork, to the relationship of the couple in the car (who are presumably also the tobogganers), to the combination of Sprite with a hot day, and to the combination of flavours in the Sprite itself.

These complex interrelationships between the three worlds (traffic jam, toboggan run, Sprite can) are all aided by the image of the tunnel, which occurs in each one, and whose darkness effects the transition from one world to the next. Connections between the worlds are reinforced by the puns, but separated in mood by changes in the music, allowing the ad to make two suggestions – both frequent in ads – that

The product is a panacea, the product is a bond of love.

In this ad, the couple (good-looking, young, affluent, happy, heterosexual) have a problem: they are stuck in a traffic jam on a hot day. Perhaps this is a symbol of a difficult or colourless life 'the heat is on . . . the pace is slow'. They drink Sprite and enter its magic world. Within that world, the problems of heat and inertia do not exist; but when they return from that world these problems have ceased to exist in their everyday world too. We do not see what started the traffic moving, but we feel it was the Sprite.

The young man and woman are, like the flavours in Sprite, 'The perfect combination'. They are also dressed in the Sprite can colours of yellow and green – both in the car, and on the toboggan. As they drink they look at each other. The product appears to contribute to their compatibility.

What I have tried to show by this analysis is that the effect of the ad is not to be found in any of the three major modes alone, but only in their combination. Each mode gains from the other. In this ad, the message is distributed fairly evenly between music, pictures and (sung) language. (The least powerful sub-mode of language in this ad is writing, used in the reminder of trademark registration and the caveat imposed by the IBA code of advertising practice, neither of which is part of the 'story', and both of which are emasculated by their small print and brief duration – see 3.4 below.) Not all ads distribute their attention so evenly between modes, and in the remainder of this chapter we shall examine the varying degree of emphasis on music, pictures, speech and writing.

3.2 MUSIC AND CONNOTATION

Music has been described as a 'syntax without semantics'. Like language, it has a formal structure, but unlike language this structure cannot be related with any degree of consensus either to the world or to any conceptual representation of it. Arguably, music is also greater in its combinatory power than a language.[4] For, though music moves forward in time, it can also combine notes at any instant on that line as harmonies, and additionally vary those harmonies by using different combinations of instruments and voices. In addition, the degree to which music can vary the pace and duration of notes, and exploit pitch variation, far exceeds that of language.

The formal structure of a piece of music can be transcribed in music's own notational system (as a score) with enough accuracy for one interpretation of the transcription to yield results very much like another. Yet the formal structures of a piece of music – the timing, melody, harmony, rhythm and combination of instruments – are not what matters in the use of music in advertising and other films. For, although music may have no semantics, in the sense of making reference to the world in a way which will be understood in a similar way by all members of a community, it does have, as language also has, connotations. For an individual, or for a group, a given piece of music may evoke a certain mood, or associate with quite specific places, events and images. Such connotations are at once both predictable and also vague and variable. A certain type of music might, for example, be described in the broadest terms as signifying or creating 'cheerfulness' or 'gloominess'. (The degree to which such perceptions are culturally conditioned or universal is a largely untapped area for empirical research.) More specific reactions will vary not only between social groups, but also between and within individuals. To give an example of a group-specific connotation, one which is much exploited by advertisers, it is likely in contemporary Western society that indulgent nostalgia can be induced by playing middle-aged people the pop music of their youth.

A further problem is that connotations in music, as in language, are indeterminate even to a particular individual in a particular situation. They cannot be paraphrased into language with any precision. A piece of music has an effect on me, and means something to me, of that I am sure: but what it is is beyond words – a truism whose triteness is itself verbal, and self-reflexive, for my retreat into this cliché is an illustration of the very limitation of language which I am trying to describe.

These aspects of music endear it to most film-makers, and especially to advertisers. The connotation of music can create or overshadow both pictures and words. (There is simple experiment in illustration of this. Watch a section of film with different musical soundtracks and you transform its mood completely. The menace and foreboding of a horror film, for example, is generally musical, and can be destroyed by an inappropriate choice.)

Advertising favours any mode of communication which is simultaneously powerful but indeterminate in this way. This also applies to its use of language (see Chapter 5); for, although there are semantic meanings on which a certain agreement can be reached, any discourse also has connotations as elusive and as personal as those of music, and it is on the manipulation of these that advertising concentrates. To search advertising for fixed meanings and then to challenge them, as most critics and litigants do, is quite to miss the point, and to treat the discourse of advertising as though it were law, business or science – all of which aspire to more precise meanings. Like poetry, advertising thrives on meaning which is both predictable but unprovable. The effect achieved, and its appeal to the advertiser, can be illustrated by analogy with sexual suggestiveness in pictures. Suppose that a picture of a young woman picking up a milk bottle makes one person think of oral sex, but someone else says that this meaning says more about the observer than it does about the picture. This kind of dispute, with its assumption that meaning resides in a text quite independently of individual and group preconceptions, is depressingly common in discussions of advertising. As the picture does not in fact depict oral sex, but something else, what the dispute comes down to is whether everyone, a substantial number of people, a few obsessed individuals, or one particular person, understand it in this way. Without an opinion poll, the dispute is unresolvable, but it is really quite improbable that such an interpretation will be individual. It is more likely to be the interpretation of a sizeable group, and, if the ad is well prepared, this will have been predicted and assessed as an interpretation which will happen in, and be likely to increase sales among, a target audience. Yet the fact that it is unprovable on a personal level, that each addressee may consider it as possibly an individual rather than a group interpretation, and that members of this group may thus be unwilling to express it either to each other or to another group, will make it more powerful.

Music makes its impact in a similar way. It is not, in this case, an unwillingness to express its effect which keeps people silent but, rather, an inability to formulate the impression in words. Its formal structure ('the score') is quite beside the point (as irrelevant as the literal behaviour of the woman with the milk bottle). What matters is connotation, a vague and indeterminate world of associations quite alien to any description with pretensions to scientific rigour. Yet if such descriptions have to leave music aside because they cannot reduce it to precise formulation they are avoiding a mode with a power extreme enough to overbalance those of both pictures and language. I have no answer to this problem, but I intend to describe the music of ads, where relevant, in impressionistic terms (as I did for the Sprite ad) always remembering that such descriptions may be idiosyncratic, peculiar to a limited section of the audience, or attempts to describe the indescribable.

3.3 PICTURES WITH MUSIC AND LANGUAGE

3.3.1 Two tales of soccer and sex

1.   A man is decorating an empty flat. He has come by bicycle. He opens a can of lager and sits down in front of the tv to watch a soccer match. The tv has only an indoor aerial and he can't receive the picture. He tries to adjust it. He looks at his watch in desperation. The match is about to begin. Suddenly he has an idea. He goes to the window (without curtains) and looks out. In a flat opposite a woman is cleaning a window. He mouthes a message to her ('watch the tele') but she ignores him. He tries again, mouthing the word 'football', but again without success. He mimes a soccer match, kicking and heading a ball of newspaper (from the floor of the empty house) and scoring a goal. The woman finally understands and beckons him over. He goes to the fridge and takes a can of Tennent's lager. On second thoughts he takes two. He goes next door. One of the woman's female flat-mates (presented as grumpy and unattractive) is watching tv and eating crisps on the sofa. He changes the channel without asking and sits down to watch the soccer. He is joined by a third flat-mate, a conventionally pretty blonde with bare feet who seems quite happy to squeeze in close beside him.

2.   A teenage boy has gone to see a small local soccer match, but it is pouring with rain. A teenage girl is standing with her mother and sister in the small crowd under a large umbrella. She joins the boy. Her mother and sister look at each other knowingly. The boy's umbrella is very small, so she has to stand close to him to keep dry. Her father comes and tells her they are going home. She takes the boy's umbrella with her. As she leaves, she looks back at the boy with regret. He arrives back at his home, soaked and depressed. He puts on the gas fire. The artificial coals glow warmly. He takes off his shoes and wiggles his feet in front of the fire. The doorbell rings. He opens the door. It is the girl. She has brought back his umbrella. She takes off her coat and joins him on the sofa. He turns up the fire, and sits down very close to her. He starts to put his arm around her. A soccer match begins on tv. His mood changes and he loses interest in the girl. She is annoyed. She hits him on the head with a cushion and leaves. (The ad is for British Gas heating. As it was released at the time of the privatization of this company, it could also be regarded as, indirectly, for the sale of shares.)

These stories have more in common than being about insensitive males who prefer watching soccer on television to developing a relationship with a female. They are both told in forty-five seconds, through the pictorial mode alone. As such they are typical of a particular kind of tv ad. These are mini-dramas which compress a large number of narrative events into a very short space of time, through the highly stylized gestures and facial expressions of extremely skilful actors. Though these two stories include both language and music, neither of these modes contribute to the development of the plot. In the first, the background Country and Western music creates a mood of humour and frivolity. Language plays hardly any part at all. In fact, the failure of the man to communicate through speech, and his successful substitution of mime, seem to symbolize the primacy of the picture over the word in this and similar ads. The only language is the product name (Tennent's Lager) and slogo (I've goT mine) which appear at the end. And, even in this, writing is used in a pictorial way, because the red 'T' of 'goT' is the logo of Tennent's (for further discussion of logos, see Chapter 4).

In the second story, the music is played on a rich romantic and nostalgic saxophone (as though this is what life was like for the adult viewer, who is the target of this ad, when he or she was young). In this ad language is more prominent. The pictures are accompanied by both speech and writing throughout, but the language creates messages in parallel to the story, rather than forwarding its action. In the second half, after the return home, there is a continuous voice-over, in a benevolent and complacent male voice, extolling the virtues of gas heating: its economy, reliability, effectiveness and long tradition. It finishes with the words:

If only your feelings were as easy to control as gas . . . if only.

(Rather unfairly, these words occur together with a shot of the face of the departing girl, as though she, who has come out in the rain to return the umbrella, and been spurned in favour of a tv programme, were to blame!) On screen, throughout the story, and superimposed on the pictures, there appear a number of punning phrases, which allude to both the relationship and football, or to the relationship and gas heating. They are

1 THE KICK OFF: beginning of the match, the relationship, the story
2 THE MISS (over girl's face): the young woman, missed goal, missed fixture
3 THE NEAR MISS (as she leaves with her father): the girl next door, almost a goal, failed attempt to talk to girl
4 THE NIFTY FOOTWORK (as he warms his feet): skilful play, wiggling toes in front of the fire
5 THE HOME MATCH (as they sit): the match on tv, the lighting of the fire, the domestic setting, their compatibility, the contest between them
6 THE HEADER (as she hits him with the cushion): propelling the ball with the head, her blow
7 THE HEAT OF THE MOMENT (as she leaves): her temper, the up-to-dateness of gas heating.

Yet these phrases are not essential to the story in any way. Coming together with the story, and quite fast, they create for the viewer a considerable processing load whose function may be to distract from the main subject of gas heating, on an assumption – widely if mistakenly believed among advertisers and their critics – that the best learning takes place subconsciously, when attention is not directly on input.[5] Only at the end of the ad, when the pictures, writing and speech all refer to gas heating simultaneously, is the product likely to come to the forefront of attention:

pictures:		the departing girl/the gas fire
music:		climactic crescendo
language:	speech:	if only gas were as easy to control
	writing:	THE HEAT OF THE MOMENT

This final convergence of the three modes, and, within the language mode, of the two sub-modes of writing and speech, is a common feature of tv ads. A typical pattern in tv ads is for each mode and sub-mode to wend its own way for the first two-thirds or more of the time, creating its own meanings; then, in the final seconds, these tributaries suddenly flow together into a single message. This suggests that advertisers, whatever the strength of their faith in pictures, feel it safer to hedge their bets at the end.

This gas ad plays it safe in another way too. Most probably aimed at middle-aged men on the assumption that it is they who usually take big-buy decisions (like the choice of heating), it both attaches the final multi-modal focus on the product to the picture of a conventionally attractive teenage girl (simultaneously inviting identification with her boyfriend by seeing her from his angle), but also introduces, as a compensation for the unattainable nature of this object of desire, a new notion: that the product is preferable to love – like soccer!

3.3.2 Pictures alone

Pictures, however, do far more than carry a story. In what is still one of the best essays on advertising, 'Keeping upset with the Joneses', Marshall McLuhan wrote

> The copy is merely a punning gag to distract the critical faculties while the picture . . . goes to work on the hypnotised viewer. Those who have spent their lives protesting about 'false and misleading ad copy' are godsends to advertisers, as teetotallers are to brewers, and moral censors are to books and films. The protestors are the best acclaimers and accelerators. Since the advent of pictures, the job of the ad copy is as incidental and latent as the meaning of a poem is to a poem, or the words of a song are to a song. Highly literate people cannot cope with the nonverbal art of the pictorial, so they dance impatiently up and down to express a pointless disapproval that renders them futile and gives new power and authority to the ads. The unconscious depth-

messages of ads are never attacked by the literate, because of their incapacity to notice or discuss nonverbal forms of arrangement and meaning. They have not the art to argue with pictures.

(McLuhan 1964: 246)

The foresight of these remarks, published at a time when both ads and analyses of them tended to be quite rudimentary, is striking. Advertisers rely more and more upon pictures, while their critics still harp upon the 'literal' meaning of copy. (Even a quick glance through the *British Code of Advertising Practice*, or the case reports of successful complaints against ads, reveals that a great deal of official criticism in the UK centres upon wording, despite its demonstrably subsidiary role in many cases; the same is true of Federal Trade Commission Reports in the USA.)

McLuhan, publishing at a time when tv advertising was still in its infancy, and ads were far more reliant upon words and literal meanings than now, might have been excused for misjudging the relative power of different modes. Thirty years later, not only have pictures gained ground, but also language, where it is used, leans further and further towards the meanings it derives from interaction with pictures. In addition, many ads create powerful and complex messages entirely – or almost entirely – through pictures and music, and are virtually language-free. In illustration of this, I shall examine one such ad in detail.

This is 'Last stick', a tv and cinema ad from 1990–1 for the internationally best-selling chewing gum Wrigley's Spearmint (Figure 16).[6] It too is a narrative, using thirty-six frames in sixty seconds,[7] but it is not for its skill in compressed story-telling that I wish to analyse it here. The tale unfolds to the music of 'All Right Now' by Free, a pounding pop song of 1970 (successfully re-released at the same time as the ad). Though the words of this song also concern a meeting between two strangers, I shall treat this ad, its message and its methods as fundamentally non-verbal, as I believe they are, though I also briefly refer to the mood of the song in the analysis. In order to discuss the significance of the different images used, I shall first need to give an outline of the story.

The ad begins with a broad panoramic shot of a bus – 'The Westerner' – making its way in bright sunlight past high mountains through prairies full of ripe wheat (Figure 16a). The camera shifts to the interior of the bus where a young man and a young woman sit across the aisle from each other, on the inner seats (see Figure 16b). Both are blond, white, conventionally good-looking. They are clearly attracted to each other, but shy. She glances at him, but as he looks back she looks away. Behind the couple, we glimpse the other passengers: a Hispanic couple (the woman holding a bunch of flowers), another white couple, an older 'country couple' (the man wearing a cowboy hat). There are alternating close-up shots of the young man and young woman (Figure 16c). She is reading a magazine. She looks at the young man again. He looks away, out of the

Figure 16 Wrigley's chewing gum ad: 'Last stick'

window, but seems pleased. The scene shifts back to the prairie outside: telegraph wires along the road, distant mountains, a heat haze. The next shots are extreme close-ups – just the eyes and nose of each main character in turn (see Figures 16d and 16e). He glances sideways; she looks back. The scene changes back to the exterior again: a combine harvester, a man on a horse riding past in the other direction. Back inside, the young woman is fanning herself with her magazine. The young man reaches into the pocket of his shirt. We see a close-up of his hand taking out a packet of Wrigley's Spearmint Gum. He takes out a stick of gum and then looks back into the packet. It was the last stick. He hesitates – then offers it to her and she accepts. From the seat in front, a small boy looks round curiously, until the hand of the invisible adult beside him descends firmly on to his head and twists him back towards the front. We return to the young woman who is reading the Wrigley's wrapping paper. The camera shows her hand in close-up as she breaks the stick in half, and offers one half back to the young man. There are alternating shots – again very close – of the two main characters looking affectionately towards each other. In a longer shot of the interior of the bus, she shifts her body closer towards him. He does the same.

The bus stops outside a building called 'The Rosebud'. Outside, there is a van parked and a horse tethered, a cartwheel leaning against the wall. An 'old-timer' with a large white beard is sitting on the porch whittling a piece of wood. The young man is leaving the bus. He turns and raises his hands in a gesture of resignation. We see the young woman's face close up. She looks down sadly. Inside, the young man sits down, while outside the bus pulls away. As the young man sits dejected, the young woman enters behind him. She has got off the bus to be with him.

The final shots show his hand with half a stick of Wrigley's gum, and her hand with the other half. The two halves join and fit perfectly; they merge into one, then transform into a whole, full packet. Words appear on the screen:

GREAT TO CHEW. EVEN BETTER TO SHARE.

A male voice says: 'Cool, refreshing Wrigley's Spearmint Gum. Great to chew. Even better to share.' The hands disappear, and we see the packet on its own.

In this ad, there are four distinct pictorial perspectives. There is the broad sweep of the outside world of nature – sunlight, corn, mountains – a benign, fertile, agricultural world at harvest time, in which the traditional (horses) and the new (combine harvesters) are in harmony. Moving in more closely, there is the social world of the bus and the bus station. This too is harmonious, with a cross-section of American society: the old man and the little boy, the rural couple, different races. Moving in even more closely, there are shots in which we see the young man and woman, within this social context, forming a relationship. Lastly, closest in of all, we see their faces from so short a distance that the image is one of complete intimacy. Only in an embrace would one see someone so close. The most dominant image is the middle perspective: the young man and young woman forming their relationship in a social context.

The overriding impression, then, is of a young man and woman meeting in a beautiful landscape, as part of a harmonious and approving society. It is also a very American world: the prairie, the old-timer, 'The Rosebud' (the same name as the sled which symbolizes lost childhood in *Citizen Kane*). It centres upon the monogamous heterosexual relationship of a man and a woman, which in turn centres upon the product – chewing gum. The bus, the social world, moves through the world of nature. A further harmony between the human and natural world is effected by the echo of the colour of the corn in the colour of the young woman's hair. In the shots of the interior of the bus, the couple are at the middle, moving, but apparently still, with the agricultural world visible outside the window. Like any couple, they have both a social identity (as they appear to, and with, the other passengers) and a private identity, as they appear to each other (the close-ups). At the very heart of this image is the stick of gum, passed from hand to hand, which brings them together and forms the bond between them. These concentric levels of detail are best represented diagrammatically (Figure 17):

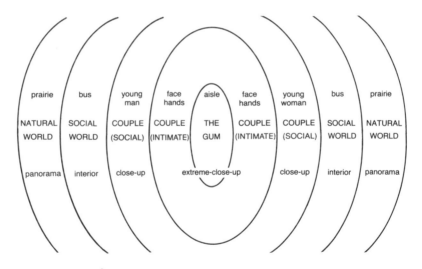

Figure 17 Concentric worlds in 'Last stick' ad

I have been using the word 'aisle' deliberately. The view of the bus is reminiscent of a wedding viewed from the altar: a young man and woman coyly sitting on either side of the aisle, the guests in the pews behind them. (Only the little ·boy – like a choirboy – is in front of them.) The woman immediately behind the young woman is holding a bunch of flowers like a bridesmaid. There are other parallels too. The young man reaches in his pocket for the gum as a groom reaches for the ring. He gives it to her, and it is a symbol of their union. In the final shots, we see an image of joined hands (another symbol of marriage) and also – in the only merged shot of the whole sequence – a transformation in which two become one. (The slow and significant placing of the gum in the mouth suggests both oral sex and the communion service.) There is a tension between this image of holy matrimony and the story of a casual pick-up, between a sexual union sanctified by society and one quite outside its institutionalized constraints. The casual nature of the encounter is emphasized by both the words and the period of the song. This clash of the matrimonial and the extra-marital is an image of fascination to the 1980s and 1990s; it is frequently used, for example, in the stage and video performances of Madonna.

This ad is another classic example of the product as the bond of love, presented at the centre of a sweeping view of the cosmic, social and sexual world, drawing to it the most powerful American ideological images: the Midwest wheat fields, the plural society, the marriage ceremony, and (if the wheaten-haired woman symbolizes fertility) a marriage of man and harvest, man and mother. All this in one minute! If it creates, as I have suggested, a vignette of the American ideology of marriage, then it is interesting to note that the young woman is the one who initiates every stage of the relationship but one. It is she who looks first, who returns half the stick, who shifts her body towards him, who breaks her journey to be with him, while the young man (apart from the one crucial step of offering the gum) is passive.

3.4 SPEECH AND WRITING

The drift away from language towards music and pictures is paralleled by a preference within the language of tv ads for the sub-modes of song and speech over writing. Both tendencies reflect a general return to orality; sound and vision are the vehicles of face-to-face interaction, while in writing we neither see nor hear our interlocutor. The British Gas ad analysed in this chapter provides an example of the relegation of the written word, for it uses speech to deliver its message about the product, and writing only to carry peripheral meanings which are utterly dependent on the pictures.

Further evidence of advertisers' belief in the greater power of speech is provided by the universal tendency in tv ads to use writing for those parts of the message which are thrust upon it from outside. In Britain, control is theoretically voluntary. Two regulative bodies, the Advertising Standards Authority (financed by advertisers themselves) and the Independent Broadcasting Authority, lean heavily on advertisers to comply with codes of practice. In the USA and the rest of Europe control is more often enforced by law. One of the results of regulation, whether legal or voluntary, is the appearance on screen or page of disclaimers such as

1 Investment in Eurotunnel involves a significant degree of risk.
2 Offers apply to inclusive overseas summer 88 holidays booked with Lunn Poly. (UK only)
3 All products and services available at most stores.
4 Cards normally replaced in 24 hours, or less in exceptional circumstances.
5 Some studies suggest that a high-fibre low-fat diet may reduce the risk of cancer. (USA only)

In theory the purpose of such caveats is to rectify, unambiguously, any false impression which might have been given by the ad, or provide factual information which it has not mentioned, but which the consumer might require. In practice, this is often not the case. It is anything but clear in (4) quite how long one has to wait for a credit card to be replaced, in (5) whether there are other studies expressing the opposite opinion, while (3) is a considerable conundrum. The assumption that the viewers' attention is on the pictures and sound is almost certainly correct, and is borne out by empirical research using 'eye trackers' which monitor a subject's attention to different parts of a screen at any given point during an ad.[8] In children's ads this knowing camouflage of the disadvantages of purchase can be particularly deceptive and cruel, for pictures which show lavishly detailed smoothly functioning toys and games are belied by such unnoticed reservations as

6 Some assembly needed.
7 Vehicles sold separately.

3.5 LANGUAGE IN THE SERVICE OF PICTURES

Visual puns and metaphors such as those of the British Gas ad have become a common and complex feature of much contemporary advertising (Forceville 1990). This is as true in magazine ads as on tv. A bottle of J&B whisky which might be described in words as 'fine grain' stands on a table-top whose wood has a visible fine grain, in a different sense. A bottle of Gordon's gin and a glass in which it has been poured 'over jaffa' (i.e. orange) stands on a balcony with a view over Jaffa; in another ad in this series, gin 'over ginger' stands on a piano next to a musical score by Fred Astaire. A joint ad for Persil washing powder and Electrolux showing a woman relaxing next to a washing machine has the copy: 'Take a load off your mind' (Figure 18). In these cases, the phrase is written and its two senses illustrated. In other cases a phrase can be evoked wholly pictorially, without any use of writing at all. Many dead metaphors are revitalized by this technique. Thus an ad for Ultra Bold washing powder shows money pouring down the drain; an ad for one insurance firm shows another literally stealing the shirt from someone's back.

This last type of visual metaphor (the drain and the shirt) have dispensed with both speech and writing, though they do evoke exact idiomatic phrases. In this they manifest an atavistic tendency in ads to return to pre- or quasi-literate forms of communication, and particularly to a stage in the evolution of writing between the use of pictures and the first logograms (a written sign which signifies a whole word – see Bolinger 1975: 469). Though pictures may refer to an event in the world, they cannot be sure to evoke the same words in every speaker. A representation of a man hunting a deer 🏹🦌 may yield many different sentences, such as 'the deer died', 'the man killed an animal', etc. The first 'real' writing may be said to occur when a picture or combination of pictures is linked not to an entity or event in the world – and thus to all of the many linguistic signs and sign-combinations which may refer to it – but to a word. This reverses the previous relationship of one sign to many words, and makes one sign now refer to one word, which may in turn refer to more than one entity in the world.

Limited by the very strict controls of the *British Code of Advertising Practice* (1988: 81–8) on cigarette advertising, a series of ads for Silk Cut cigarettes use pictures only, each of which shows silk and a cut (for example a piece of silk which has been cut by scissors, a silk cloth and a poodle which has just been trimmed, an iron with spikes near a piece of silk on an ironing board.[9] This essentially, despite the use of photography, is the primitive technique of rebus writing in which each syllable of a compound word is evoked by a picture relating to a homophonic word,[10] so that

> In a modern rebus, 'Fancy' can be created by a fan and then the sea, or 'mumble' by a chrysanthemum and then a bull.
>
> (Bolinger 1975: 485)

The Silk Cut ads also use a distinctive colour (in this case purple) to signify the product itself. This technique, which we have already encountered in the Sprite ad, is another means of wordless reference to a product, which is widespread in the marketing of major brands.

There is no writing *in* the Silk Cut ad, but there is writing *with* it. In Britain, it must have one of a number of statutory health warnings, written large and occupying a substantial space, such as

SMOKING CAN CAUSE HEART DISEASE

Nothing could testify more strikingly to the advertiser's faith in the superior power of pictures over words than their evident belief that it is still worth advertising in these conditions. The advertisers even use the warning to identify the ad as one for cigarettes.

Figure 18 Persil/Electrolux washday ad: 'Take a load off your mind'

EXERCISES

1 Try to visualize the typeface of the logos for McDonalds, Marlboro, Coca-Cola. If you can do so, what makes the lettering so memorable? Why was it chosen?

2 What is suggested by Figure 19?

Figure 19 Kodak, Ford and Kellogg's logos

3 A 1970s ad for Rothman's cigarettes analysed by Williamson (1978) showed only a forearm resting on a car door. The following elements in the picture might be interpreted as meaningful:
   - gold braid stripes of a naval officer on the sleeve
   - a muscular hand and hairy wrist
   - an expensive watch
   - a helicopter in the wing mirror
   - the Rothman's coat of arms
   - the word 'Rothman's' imposed on the picture
   - a packet of Rothman cigarettes imposed on the picture.

   What do these elements mean, how do they achieve this meaning, and is the kind of meaning the same in each case?

4 Consider how writing and pictures are used in Figure 20. What is their effect, and does this strengthen the advertisement? Do they use writing and pictures in the same way as each other? List other ads which use the same technique.

   a Maxwell House roof
   b 'When my daddy was ill for a long time mummy said there wouldn't be enough money for us to live on. But daddy told mummy not to worry because he had a special plan with the AA. eleanor age 7.'
   c As the slim young woman climbs out of the pool, the shape of her body merges to the shape of the initial letter of Kellogg's which is also the name of the cereal.
   d A cat tiptoes along the letters of Kattomeat.

FURTHER READING

Interesting general writings on music and words are Roland Barthes (1972) 'The grain of the voice', in *Image, Music, Text*; Leonard Bernstein (1976) *The Unanswered Question* and Robert Hodge's essay (1985) 'Song'.

When my daddy was ill
for a long time mummy said
there wouldnt be enough money
for us to live on. But daddy
told mummy not to worry because
he had a special plan with
the AA.

eleanor age 7

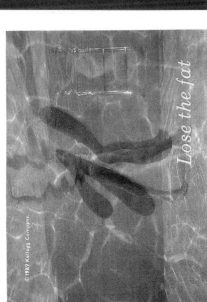

Figure 20 Maxwell House coffee, AA Insurance, Kellogg's Special K cereal and Kattomeat catfood ads

On the pictures of ads, the last chapters of Goffman (1976) *Gender Advertisements*, Chapter 7 of Berger (1972) *Ways of Seeing* and Durand (1987) 'Rhetorical figures in the advertising image' are all thought-provoking and entertaining, making their points by the juxtaposition and correlation of images with the minimum of commentary.

Kress (1990) *Reading Images* is a study of pictures in discourse, and contains many insights of relevance to advertising.

Good analyses of pictures in individual ads are Charles Forceville (1990) 'Verbo-pictorial metaphor in advertisements'; Bonney and Wilson (1990) 'Advertising and the manufacture of difference'; Chapman and Egger's (1983) 'Myth in cigarette advertising and health promotion'.

For those interested in the psychological effects of literacy, Ong (1982) *Orality and Literacy* is a fascinating introduction, as is Chapter 14 of Bolinger (1975) *Aspects of Language* (2nd edn).

4 Language and paralanguage

4.0 LANGUAGE AND PARALANGUAGE: DIMENSIONS OF THE SIGN

Language is usually carried by marks on a surface or sounds in air: **graphetic** and **phonetic** substance. Each of these give rise to two kinds of meaning simultaneously. On the one hand, the substance is perceived as the sounds or letters of a particular language (the **phonology** or **graphology**) which in turn[1] form words and word combinations (the **morphology** and **grammar**) which are in turn perceived as meaningful (the **semantics**). But the substance which carries language is also the vehicle of another kind of meaning, conveyed simultaneously by voice quality, or choice of script, letter size and so on. This latter kind of meaning, occurring together with linguistic meaning, is paralinguistic (see section 1.0) – a term which also embraces other meaningful behaviour which accompanies language but does not carry it, such as gesturing, facial expression, body posture, eye contact, or the way writing is bound or displayed.

Paralanguage has been neglected in twentieth-century linguistics, largely because of the influence of the semiology of Saussure (1857–1913). The next section critically examines some categories of Saussurean theory, partly because they *are* useful in the study of both advertising and literature, but also as a way of approaching the many types of paralinguistic and discoursal meaning which they neglect. From there the discussion moves on to the semiotic theory of the American philosopher Peirce (1839–1914), and a critique of semiotics in general. The description of these theories in the first half of this chapter will involve some digression from the analysis of ads, but one which I believe is important, and whose relevance will be clear in the second half.

4.1 SEMIOLOGY AND SEMIOTICS

The word '**semiology**' (which translates the French '*sémiologie*') is associated with Saussure. The word '**semiotics**' was used by Peirce (see section 4.1.3). Both refer to the study of signs, but a difference is sometimes drawn between the approaches of these two leading theorists. I shall use the term 'semiotics' to cover both, but when talking specifically of Saussure's theory refer to 'semiology'.

4.1.1 Saussurean semiology

In his theory of **semiology** (the study of signs), Saussure ([1915] 1974) described a language as a system of signs which have meaning by virtue of their relationships to each other. Each sign comprises a **signifier** (a word) and a **signified** (a concept). Each sign has meaning only by virtue of its place in the system, and the fact that this system is known and shared by its users. A language is a 'social fact', a convention. Within larger linguistic units such as sentences, meanings are created by choices and relationships of signs. A sentence – a combination of signs – is itself thus a complex signifier for a complex signified, and may be treated as a complex sign. Saussure was primarily interested in speech, regarding writing as derived from it. As speech unfolds in time, with only one sign occurring at each moment, there are two ways of creating meaning. The first is the **syntagm**, in which signs create meaning by their relationships to the signs before or after them – by their order – so that

I see what I eat

is not the same as

I eat what I see

(as the Mad Hatter observes in *Alice's Adventures in Wonderland*). The second is the **paradigm**, in which a given sign creates meaning by virtue of its relationship to other signs which might have occupied the same slot, but did not.

I adore Pepsi

does not have the same meanings as

I adore you.

There is a set of words which can fill each slot in this sentence, and substitution of one for another will change its meaning. This idea of meaning through combination or choice is not limited to language. If we consider clothing, for example, as the expression of a semiotic system with social meaning (Barthes 1967) – rather than just a means of keeping warm – then we can say that, paradigmatically, the meaning of a top hat is different from that of a baseball cap. This meaning created by choice will be effected by meaning created by combination. A top hat has a different signification when worn with evening dress than it has when worn with a swimsuit.

These notions of paradigm and syntagm may be extended to the pictures of ads. In 'Last stick', for example, a blond, white, young man is chosen instead of a black man, or a woman, or an old man (i.e. paradigmatically) and placed in combination with (i.e. syntagmatically) a blonde, white young woman, in a bus (not a Cadillac) in a prairie (not the Bronx). Different choices and combinations yield different meanings.

Paradigmatic and syntagmatic choice also have a particular relevance to marketing and distribution. The layout of shops and the grouping of products within them are generally paradigmatic rather than syntagmatic (Kehret-Ward 1988). In a supermarket, we encounter all the types of cheese in one place, of canned tomato in another, of pizza base in another, of wine in another and so on. We select one of each to fill a particular slot. If, however, the shop was arranged so that mozzarella cheese, and one kind only of canned tomatoes, one kind of pizza base and one kind of wine occurred together, forming the combination 'pizza margherita with chianti' this would be syntagmatic. Recent experiments with syntagmatic marketing include manufacturers' attempts to set up 'product clusters' – for example pre-shave lotion + razor + shaving soap + after-shave lotion. Some stores are experimenting with a syntagmatic layout (Kehret-Ward 1988). Yet the approach of both advertising and distribution as a whole remains paradigmatic. Products are presented as alternatives to their competitors, rather than as complements to their accompaniments.

In Saussure's view, linguistic signs are arbitrary. There is a connection, of meaning, between a signifier and a signified, but it is not motivated by any resemblance between the two;[2] it holds only because it is known to hold by people who use the system. Though the meanings of signs change over time, it is not within the power of any individual to change them: they are both mutable and immutable. The history of a sign, its diachronic development, is not part of its meaning; all that matters is its present position in the system, and the synchronic relationships it enters into with other signs.

Saussure's description of the sign as

$$\frac{\text{SIGNIFIED}}{\text{signifier}}$$

can be extended to describe such figures as metaphor, in which one signifier refers to two signifieds by virtue of a shared component in the signifieds,[3] though not in the signifiers, and puns, where by chance one signifier relates to two signifieds. Figure 21 gives examples from the Sprite ad and the Gas ad in Chapter 3.

In metaphor the sign used illustratively (HEAT/'heat') is called the **vehicle**, the signified with which it associates (DIFFICULTY) is the **topic** (Cameron 1991). Further figures which can be summarized through the S over s equation are **metonymy**, **synecdoche** and **symbol**. In metonymy an entity is referred to by the name of an attribute, or of an entity semantically related to it. The common practice of referring to an object by the name of its producer ('I like that Picasso' or 'That's a Ford') are instances of

metaphor:
e.g.
'when the heat is on'

pun:
e.g.
'the miss'

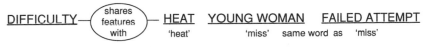

Figure 21 Metaphor and pun

metonymy used in both art and commerce (G. Lakoff and Johnson 1980: 38). In **synecdoche** (which is a special case of metonymy) the name of the referent is replaced by the name of a part of it (see Figure 22).

I shall use the word 'symbol'[4] to refer to a relationship in which, like metaphor, one signifier refers to two signifieds, although the connection is effected more by convention than by any perceived similarity, allowing reference to be made directly from the signifier of one entity to the signified of another. Distinctions between symbol, metaphor and metonymy are often difficult to make, and the three are not mutually exclusive, for a symbol may originally have been motivated by a metaphorical or metonymic relationship which has since weakened. In advertising the problem is compounded by the fact that signifiers may be either verbal or pictorial and the two modes constantly cross-refer. The fire in the gas ad, for example, represented by the pictures, is not only a symbol and a metonym of home, but also a metaphor of the girl's temper, expressed both pictorially and verbally as a pun. An advertiser's aim is often to make the product into a symbol of something positive.

In Saussure's semiology, meaning is a matter of encoding and decoding. By making appropriate choices and combinations, a person who knows the system (the langue) encodes his or her thoughts into words and transmits them to another person (in possession of the same langue) who decodes them, thus recovering the original meaning. This view of language is sometimes referred to as the **conduit metaphor** (Reddy 1978) – or more bluntly as the 'drainpipe view' – because it views language as a kind of pipe through which encoded meanings flow from one mind to another, like water. The conduit metaphor presents language and thought as quite separate, and this – despite some protestations to the contrary (Saussure [1915] (1974): 112) – is what Saussure does. Thought is locked in the head of each individual, to be moved from one head to another by words (see Figure 23 – Saussure [1915] (1974): 11)!

The idea of communication as a simple decoding process is prevalent in a semiotic approach to advertising. The popular phrase *Decoding Advertisements* was first used by Judith Williamson as the title of a book published in 1978, and it has been echoed widely in courses and publications ever since (Umiker-Sebeok 1987: 249–335). The essence of Williamson's approach is to unveil through analysis what she calls the 'real'

synecdoche: (a type of metonymy):   **symbol:**

Figure 22 Synecdoche and symbol

Figure 23 Saussure's talking heads

meaning of the words and images of an ad, and the 'real world' to which the 'unreal' images of the ad refer (1978: 47). In this there is a clear assumption that 'reality' is not only quite distinct from 'fiction' but also morally superior. Thus, for example, at the outset of her book, while examining two ads for two varieties of Chanel perfume (Chanel No. 5 and Chanel No. 19), one showing Catherine Deneuve, the other Margaux Hemingway, she 'discovers' that both women are signifiers, the former signifying 'flawless French beauty', the latter the essence of being 'young, American, way out' (1978: 26). Though the decoding approach on occasion yields interesting insights (in practice often rather obvious ones), a drawback of the approach is its hasty satisfaction that such equivalences constitute a complete analysis. This leads it to jettison all consideration of what is particular to the surface of discourse, or of a particular signifier, and thus miss much of complexity, skill and humour.

The influence of Saussure's theory of language has been immense. Even rejections or modifications (like this one) remain dominated by it, defining themselves in opposition. Despite their shortcomings, Saussure's categories provide a useful starting point, a way of coming to grips with the complex and elusive nature of human communication. Though linguistic communication is not effected solely through a code, it does involve knowledge of a code, and the Saussurean approach provides a way of describing how that code works.

Yet if the study of a message involves three areas – the psychological, the textual and the physical (a tripartite division which itself owes much to Saussure), and the relationship between these areas, then it is fair to say that Saussure deals well with the textual area, but badly with the other two. His description of the psychological status of language relies too heavily on a dubious division between thought and language ([1915] 1974: 111–14), and on the assumption that the thought (concepts) of all who use the same code are sufficiently similar for the meaning of a text to be substantially the same for each person. An alternative view is that thought, especially thought about the kind of messages handled by language, is too closely conditioned by that language to be separated from it. And if internalized meaning is inseparable from the language which handles it, then it can hardly be said to be internal at all, for language is realized outside the individual in interaction with others. Our very identity may be outside ourselves, in our interactions with others. (For further discussion see Chapter 8.)

Nor is thought (or language) so uniform among the speakers of a language that it will allow the kind of straightforward decoding procedure described by Saussure. Speakers of English, receiving the same ad, may interpret it in substantially different ways, depending on whether they are children or adults, women or men, rich or poor, and so on. A combination of linguistic decoding with non-linguistic knowledge creates an interpretation, perhaps *resembling* the intention of the sender, but by no means *identical to* it.

Though language, in Saussure's view, depends upon substance for transmission, his interest in this substance is very limited. He even proposed that linguistics should not concern itself with particular utterances (parole) or acts of communication at all, but only with the code (langue)! In Saussure's semiology, and many other schools of linguistics, the role of substance is only to provide enough clues to identify a particular sign, and other aspects of it can be disregarded. Each word – each sign – is identified by a particular combination of **phonemes** or **graphemes** derived from the stream of sound or the marks of writing. The word 'rat', for example, is a succession of three phonemes /r/ /æ/ /t/ in speech, or three graphemes R-A-T in writing.[5] It is important that the shapes or sounds are such that they will be assigned to a particular grapheme or phoneme and not cause confusion with other phonemes or graphemes; but, other than that, it matters neither what they are made of, nor what their exact shape or sound is. The English phoneme /r/ may be trilled by a Scottish speaker or lateralized by someone from England or the United States, or pronounced as a voiced labiodental approximant (a lippy w) by speakers who cannot make either of these; it may have a higher pitch in a child's speech than in an adult's; but from the Saussurean point of view none of these variations alters its semiotic function. All that matters is that it be recognized as a token of the phoneme /r/ and thus contribute to the composition of the signifier 'rat'. Similarly, in writing, a ꞃ or ꞅ or ꞃ or ꞵ , written or printed, on gold or paper or chocolate, needs only to make a shape which will enable a receiver to perceive it as the letter R. From this perspective, letters and sounds have no intrinsic importance. Their function is only, through syntagmatic combination, to realize the signifier, which, once realized, can start entering into meaningful syntagmatic combinations with other signs.

4.1.2 Language and paralanguage

The Saussurean approach, in dealing with the relationship between language and substance, leaves a great deal out of account. In communication, language always has physical substance of some kind, and though this substance – sound waves or marks on paper – serves as a trigger for the assignation of phonemes or graphemes by the receiver, allowing him or her to build the signs which create linguistic meanings, it carries other kinds of meaning too. In face-to-face communication, important meanings may be conveyed by eye contact, gesture, body movement, clothing, touch, body position, physical proximity, voice quality, volume, pitch range and laughter; in writing, the same is true of page and letter sizes, typefaces and handwriting styles. These and many other factors also carry meaning which may reinforce or contradict the linguistic meaning of the signs which they accompany. They are examples of paralanguage.

It is not enough to say, as some linguists do, that such behaviour is best understood as a manifestation of separate semiotic systems to that of language. Firstly, the two modes of meaning are not separate. Paralanguage interacts with language and on occasion outweighs it. To see that this is true, one has only to imagine the effect of someone sobbing while saying: 'I am not upset.' There is a good deal of psychological experimental evidence to justify this view. In one study (Argyle et al. 1970; 1971) undergraduate subjects, under the false impression that they were taking part in a quite different experiment, were told one of two things after the experiment: to leave quickly so as not to waste the researchers' time, or to stay and chat, as the researchers were always pleased to meet students. These two linguistic messages were combined with two paralinguistic messages, with a similar polarity of meaning. Either the experimenters shook the subjects' hands, smiled, and looked them in the eye while speaking; or they avoided eye contact and touch, and wore unfriendly facial expressions. Each subject thus experienced one of four possible combinations of behaviour (Figure 24). When subjects were asked, some time later, to recall whether they had been treated

Verbal behaviour	Paralinguistic behaviour	Overall effect
+	+	+
+	−	−
−	+	+
−	−	−

(+ =friendly, − = unfriendly)

Figure 24 Paralinguistic and linguistic effects

in friendly or unfriendly manner, their replies correlated only with the paralinguistic behaviour. It did not matter what had been said to them, but only what had been done.[6]

Secondly, although paralinguistic behaviour signifies, and is thus in a broad sense semiotic, the nature of its signification is quite different from that of language. The linguistic sign, as we have seen above, is a discrete phenomenon, a case of being *either* one thing *or* another. In linguistic terms, a sound is perceived as one phoneme or another; there are no intermediate cases. (Though one could create a continuum of sounds between, say, /b/ and /p/, in a stream of speech a speaker of a language with this distinction would perceive a sound along that continuum as one or the other.) Words, composed of phonemes, inherit this absolute quality of their components: a word is either 'bat' or 'pat' or another word, but there are no intermediate cases. A similar either/or quality pertains with letters. Many paralinguistic phenomena, on the other hand, are graded. They are a case of more or less, not either/or. If I smile at you while speaking, squeeze your hand, or laugh, I may increase or decrease the breadth of my smile, the strength of my squeeze, or the loudness of my laugh, thus signifying more or less of whatever it is I mean by these actions. This has two important consequences. Firstly, there are an infinity of different degrees in any paralinguistic phenomenon. One cannot specify the number of different smiles and squeezes and laughs available in one person's repertoire. Secondly, one cannot equate graded paralinguistic phenomena with language by translating or paraphrasing it into words. Paralanguage is literally beyond complete description *in* language, because it belongs to a different kind of communication *from* language (Cook 1990a). That is why, when talking about these acts, I had to use the vague phrase 'whatever it is I mean by them'. This is not to say that one cannot describe something like a laugh in an approximate way. One could say that a laugh in general is a sign of amusement. One could go on to categorize laughs into various types (titters, giggles, guffaws, etc.) and attribute different meanings to these categories. But this is not to say that one can describe all types of laugh or fully translate their meaning into words. The same is true of the paralanguage of writing: consider the meaning of a scrawl, as opposed to copper-plate script, and the number of intermediate possibilities.

In these respects, human paralanguage maintains the graded signalling used by animals. The bark of a dog creates meaning in much the same way as a human smile, by varying intensity. The difference is that some human paralanguage also carries linguistic meaning. If you hear my voice, the sound waves carry the information you need in order to perceive the syntagmatic relations of the signs of my message, and set about decoding and interpreting them; but you will also know, from the volume, pitch and intonation of my voice, something about my emotional state and social identity – whether I am angry, or bored, or excited, and that I am an adult middle-class English male. For this reason human communication is sometimes characterized as utilizing a 'double channel' (Ellis and Beattie 1986: 16–77). Every utterance carries both linguistic and paralinguistic meaning. This is not to say, however, that any given instance of paralinguistic behaviour is natural or instinctive or universal. In this respect the analogy with animal communication is misleading, for while the communicative behaviour of an animal is, generally speaking, common to all members of that species, human paralinguistic communication varies considerably. Contrastive cultural analysis reveals many cases of the same paralinguistic action having widely different meanings in different cultures. A particular kind of touch, proximity, eye contact, laughter or voice volume may mean nothing, or something quite different, when transferred from one culture to another. (See Morris (1977) and Morris et al. (1979). For a discussion of attempts to find universal elements in paralanguage, see George Lakoff (1987: 38)). This causes considerable problems for advertisers organizing international campaigns, who must realize that it is often more than the words of an ad that need translation. The term **copy adaptation** has been coined to emphasize this difference from translation (*Marketing* 17 January 1991: 28).

The signification of paralanguage is generally quite as arbitrary as that of language. Yet, although it is erroneous to think of paralanguage as natural and culture-free, aspects of it are beyond conscious control. A laugh or a smile may be used deliberately (not necessarily hypocritically) to send a particular message; at other times they may emerge spontaneously against the will of the communicator, as when people 'cannot help' laughing or smiling. Many paralinguistic features communicate relatively permanent features of a particular individual, including sex, social class and age. Language – with the exception of some instances of swearing and prayer (Ellis and Beattie 1986: 263) – is much more under conscious control. One of the most distinctive features of human communication is lying (Lyons 1977: 83).

It is possible to argue, as many linguists do, that paralanguage is of no concern to linguistics, because language is best understood when it is rigorously isolated from such distracting phenomena. This is an odd view, for language never occurs without paralanguage. The two constantly interact, and communicative competence involves using both together – but it is a view which has mesmerized later-twentieth-century linguistics. Chomsky (1965: 3–4), though differing from Saussure by describing language as a psychological rather than a social phenomenon, is in agreement on this point. Long before the rise of Chomskian theory, the Russian thinker Bakhtin (1895–1975), in a critique of Saussure, suggested that the dogmatic divorce between the study of language and paralanguage derives in part, despite linguistics' professed belief in the primacy of speech, from an overemphasis on written discourse and in particular on literature (Volosinov [1929] 1988: 52–62).[7] Though writing has its own paralinguistic features, they are commonly less potent than the paralanguage of spoken interaction. In literature, such features are, with rare exceptions, considered to be of no significance at all. (Imagine the unorthodoxy of saying that the effect of a novel was altered by its binding or the size of its print.) Yet literature is in this – and in other respects – an unusual discourse. Certainly, an analysis of advertising will not get far with a linguistics which excludes paralanguage on principle, for advertising, like many other types of discourse, carries a heavy proportion of its meaning paralinguistically.

4.1.3 Peircean semiotics

The semiotic theory of the American philosopher Charles Peirce (1839–1914) provides categories which supplement those of Saussure. Defining a sign very broadly as

> Something which stands to somebody for something else, in some respect or capacity.
>
> (Peirce [1931–58])

Peirce suggested further types of sign in addition to those of a purely arbitrary conventional nature. Two of these, which are particularly useful in analyses of advertising, are the **index** (plural **indices**) and the **icon**.

An index is a sign which points to something else by virtue of a causal relationship. This category can include such natural co-occurrences as smoke and fire, dark clouds and impending rain, a human footprint and the presence of a human being, but it can also encompass more consciously controlled meanings. The imprint of a signet ring is an index of the ring itself, and of its wearer (though its signification of the wearer's approval is arbitrary). A wedding ring, as well as being a symbol (in the sense defined in 4.1.1),[8] is also an index of marriage. An ad, in a current magazine or tv programme, is an index of the existence and availability of a product. The notion of the index is particularly useful in the description of paralanguage. A slurred voice is an index of drunkenness, for example; expensive clothing is an index of wealth. Yet the interpretation of indices is not a process of decoding. It depends on knowledge of the world, and will vary from one language-user to another. Sweaty palms may have quite different indexical meaning to a doctor than to a person with no skill in diagnosing illness. (It is the idiosyncrasy and sensitivity of indexical interpretation, incidentally, which is the charm of Sherlock Holmes.)

An icon is a sign which means by virtue of resemblance to the signified. Maps and photographs are good examples. Yet this type of sign is almost always more complex than at first appears. Most icons resemble their signified only in some respects. A blue and white photograph of Elvis Presley having his famous GI haircut (used in an ad for Stubbs watches) is in a degree an icon of the person Elvis Presley (or our concept of him); but this does not entail that he was four inches tall, two dimensional, motionless or blue. The meaning of photographs, moreover, despite the widely held view that they show life 'as it is', is also created by arbitrary semiotic paradigmatic choice and syntagmatic ordering (Barthes [1964] 1977). (Who is Elvis seen with? Who was he chosen instead of?) Many signs are believed to be iconic because the perception of a connection between signified and signifier is so habitual that it begins to seem natural. (Does the ⚹ on a lavatory door really look more like a man than a woman?) For a sign to be truly iconic, it would have to be transparent to someone who had never seen it before – and it seems unlikely that this is as much the case as sometimes supposed. We see the resemblance when we already know the meaning. This is especially true with onomatopoeic words which supposedly imitate the sound of their referent. The Russian words *puknut'* and *pyornut'* for example are regarded as onomatopoeic by Russian speakers, but it is not possible for someone who does not speak Russian to work out their meaning from the sound alone.[9] It is not a question of a sign or combination of signs being wholly iconic, indexical or arbitrary. Many combine all three.

4.1.4 Shortcomings of semiotics

A weakness of the semiotic approach is its exclusive devotion to similarities, and then an air of finality once these similarities are observed, which blinds it to what is unique. Although it undoubtedly contributes to the analysis of an ad to see what it has in common with the myths of earlier cultures, or with other discourse types of its own period and place, or with other ads, there are also important elements which are unique in advertising, or in a given ad, as there are in any discourse type or instance of it. Under the influence of semiotics, academic thought has devoted its attention to those features of a phenomenon which allow one instance to be seen as equivalent to another; and in its analyses it has concentrated on those features to the detriment of others. Forty years ago, the method was a revolutionary one, and justly captured the intellectual imagination, not only for the added complexity it could bring to analysis but also for its political and philosophical implications. Its vision of cultures and cultural artefacts, no matter how superficially different, as fundamentally similar was a powerful weapon against racism and cultural chauvinism, and held out hope of the discovery of abstract structures universal in human culture.

Yet the semiotic approach also runs a danger of simplification and partial analysis. Its insights are useful but incomplete. It both derives from and exerts influence upon linguistics and semantics. From Saussure it derives the idea of meaning as being an equivalence between a surface signifier and something else. In semantics a word is seen as equivalent to its **denotation** (components) or **reference** (what it describes in the world). Utterances are reduced to **propositions** (declarative statements of the relationships between entities) and discourse to the logical connections between these propositions. These statements and their relations are then seen as the 'underlying' meaning. In Chomskian linguistics there is a similar concentration on the 'underlying' deep grammatical structure of a sentence, which generates the sentence we actually see or hear. Such concentration on underlying structures (whether semantic or linguistic) neglects the fact that there may also be surface forms which are important in themselves. There is moreover a contradiction in such an approach. Talk of 'deep' and 'surface' meaning is metaphorical and also pejorative. What is on the surface – 'superficial' – is trivial, false and empty-headed; what is 'deep' is serious, genuine and thoughtful. Ironically, in both semantics and linguistics, the claim that deep structures are the most important is insinuated through this purely surface metaphor. If we transform the words 'deep' and 'surface' to some underlying representation, this value judgement within them disappears!

One area of surface form often simplified or neglected by semantics and linguistics is paralanguage.

4.2 EXPLOITING THE DOUBLE CHANNEL

Writing, of its nature, makes less use of paralanguage than speech. The physical substance of some written texts exists only to realize linguistic form. This tendency is accentuated by the high esteem accorded to the written word, and the belief that its function is to relay information objectively and impersonally. The function of paralanguage is more often to express attitudes and emotions, to regulate and establish social relations, to mediate between words and a particular situation. Paralanguage is also more concerned with facilitating the process of communication, rather than with its product: the meanings which literate people believe are somehow stored in a written text, quite independently of situation and speaker. A literate culture typically believes in, and elevates, the importance of 'objective scientific facts', regarded as persisting independently of speakers and situations. As such, many written texts aspire to eliminate all traces of either the situation in which they were composed, the process of composition, or the person who originated them. The nature of writing makes this possible, for it displaces language from the time and place of its composition, enabling the sender to work upon it as an object. You, the reader, do not see me, the writer, as you read this book, or know anything about the circumstances in which I am writing. You do not know what changes I have made in this sentence, when I added it to the manuscript, or whether I paused to have a cup of coffee between these dots . . . and these. . . . And by the conventions of our culture you do not care. You read this book for the information or ideas it carries, not to communicate with me as an individual physical presence. Writing makes this language no longer dependent on me and my situation in any way. You can read this book in any order, when and how you want: and I will not even know. I may even be dead. As far as the paralanguage of this writing goes – the shapes of the letters and so on – it is considered so immaterial that I, typing these words on to the screen of my word-processor, do not even know how they will appear to you. Nor is that considered to be my business, but that of the publisher, whose choice of typeface will be influenced more by the desire for clarity which aids linguistic interpretation than by any other considerations.

This perceived unimportance of paralanguage varies with discourse type, even in writing. It is also very much a feature of contemporary scientific culture. In illuminated medieval manuscripts, and in traditional oriental calligraphy, the shape of letters has an intrinsic importance beyond the linguistic signs they realise. Even in our cultures, though academic books aspire to ethereal impersonality, there are also anxious love letters where everything is considered important: the paper and its perfume, the fact that it is handwritten instead of typed, and 'sealed with a kiss' – or as the Lypsyl ad says 'LYPSYLed with a kiss' (Figure 25).

Figure 25 Lypsyl lipsalve slogo: 'LYPSYLed with a kiss'

4.3 PARALANGUAGE IN LITERATURE AND ADS

In the exploitation of written paralanguage, literature and advertising differ considerably.

Etymologically the word 'literature' is very closely associated with words referring to written language. It derives from the Latin word *littera*, meaning a letter of the alphabet, a root which it shares with the words 'literate' and 'literal' (Williams 1983: 183–8). In a phrase like 'the biology literature', it is still used simply to mean 'written material', and despite all difficulties of definition, whatever else a literary text may or may not be, it is always written (though it may also be spoken too). It is true that in its most usual contemporary sense – the sense which is so hard to define, but which refers, let us say for the sake of argument, to highly esteemed verbal art – it *appears* to include both written and spoken material: novels and short stories which are primarily written texts, but also poems and plays. These last two, however, and especially poetry, have been increasingly treated as written rather than spoken. The importance attributed to exact wording is possible only when poems are written down. It is hard to imagine a poem or play being accorded literary status in the twentieth century on the basis of performance only, though the reverse – the high acclaim of an unperformed written text – is quite feasible. Certainly, in academic study, the merits of a poem or a play are judged to be the merits of the written text; these may include a perceived potential for oral performance, though not the merits of any particular rendering. Such a bias, however, like the notion of 'literature' itself, is a relatively modern phenomenon. Many works now regarded as literary classics, such as *The Iliad* or *Beowulf*, are transcriptions of oral performances. The force of the modern partiality for writing is revealed not only by this tendency to assimilate the spoken verbal art to writing, but also by the anachronistic projection of modern values into the past in the oxymoron 'oral literature', which attempts to treat the verbal art of an oral culture as though it were fixed and written text. In our culture any oral creation which is valued is immediately written down: highly valued pop songs and film scripts quickly appear as books.

Yet despite this tendency immediately to shift valued speech towards writing it remains true that poetry and drama, especially away from the clutches of academics, preserve features peculiar to speech, and only realizable in speech.

One feature which literature of all kinds preserves in common with spoken discourse is its affective role, its strong association with emotion rather than with fact. Literary discourse is commonly perceived as the expression of some extraordinary individual personality, whose ideas, experiences, memories and emotions are somehow transmitted to us through the text. (Such a view clearly shares the conduit view of language – though with reference to feelings rather than to information.) The displacement of writing leads literate societies towards a depersonalization of the text, a divorce from individuals and situations, and a belief in objective scientific fact. Literature, when perceived as the expression of an individual, is at odds with this. Yet its association with the voice of an individual persists strongly, despite the efforts of various schools of literary theory to displace it. Russian Formalism and the New Criticism insist on the autonomy of the text and the irrelevance of the writer's biography or the circumstances of production. Psychoanalytic and Marxist criticism, despite their differences, have in common a tendency to believe that writing reveals the struggle of forces (in the mind or in society respectively) of which the author was unaware, and to which he or she may have been explicitly opposed. Reader-response theory has tried to shift the focus of attention away from the writer and the writing and towards the reader and the reading.

Just how unsuccessful such critical movements have been in affecting the popular view of literature is witnessed by the fact that everywhere – in bookshops, schools, universities and casual conversations – literature continues to be classified by author. ('Have you got any Pirandello?'; 'We're doing Balzac this term'; 'I am reading another Kundera'.) Nor has interest in the lives of authors diminished. In some respects, this obsession with literature as the expression of a unique personality, and the conception of the self which is necessary to it, is a relatively modern phenomenon, dating from the Romantic emphasis on an artist's extraordinary personality and powers (Foucault [1969] 1979). In another sense this intensely personal emphasis of literary communication is rooted in the pre-literate past. It preserves the individual nature of oral communication which can never be divorced from a particular speaker. This is perhaps part of the appeal of literature, for the transition from oral to **chirographic** (i.e. written) communication is a feature of **ontogenetic** as well as **phylogenetic** development:[10] we all lived in an oral, personal, affective world in infancy. This kind of communication remains powerful and pleasurable throughout life, while the depersonalized voice of objective facts remains somewhat alien. Advertising identifies itself with the former, while its opponents, by trying to associate it with incorrect facts, identify it with the latter.

Like literature, advertising inhabits a borderland between writing and speech, though in a different way. Although the language of tv ads is predominantly speech, while that of magazine and poster ads is writing, this difference exists only in reception, not in production. The words in contemporary ads are always carefully scripted and subjected to so much scrutiny and rewriting that in this respect they stand comparison with the drafting of laws or poetry. This has not always been so. Some early tv ads in the 1950s and 1960s contained ad lib and improvised passages (Geis 1982: 130–62). By the 1980s such improvisation had become extraordinary, and a subject for remark (as when the actresses Sara Crowe and Ann Bryson satirized their roles as 'bimbo' secretaries in a popular Philadelphia Cream Cheese ad by adding an ironically vacuous 'lov-er-lee': 'We just tagged that one line on to the end of the take and they loved it' – *TV Times* 2 November 1990.) The scripts of spoken or sung ads, unlike those of poems and plays, however, are neither available to their audience nor required by them. In this respect ads are closer to oral communication than to literature.

Recognition of the author, however, is less widespread. Outside the confines of the advertising world itself, ads are not commonly linked to an individual creative personality. Though exceptionally innovative talents, like those of Adam Lury and Dave Trott, are known to other advertisers, their names are virtually unheard of elsewhere,[11] and the general public certainly does not identify ads by author. This may be partly because an ad is not an individual creation, but involves many people. Joint authorship in literature, by contrast, is so unusual that exceptions (like Beaumont and Fletcher) stand out. Another reason may be that creators of ads often feel too constrained by their brief to describe the ad as truly their own. Ads, then, unlike either speech or literature, do not draw attention to their sender. They do, however, by associating writing with pictures, anchor their communication firmly to a specific non-linguistic situation, simulating the paralanguage of face-to-face interaction. Consider, for example, how essential facial expression and gesture are to the tv ads analysed in Chapter 3. The situation of the picture is not the situation of the ad's creation, however, but fictional.

4.3.1 The double channel in literature: use of graphology

Ads and literature thus have a much closer relation to orality than many other kinds of written text, but the nature of this closeness in the two discourses is rather different. They also differ in the degree to which they exploit the potential for paralinguistic meaning in sounds and letters.

Literature makes so little use of the paralinguistic potential of writing that exceptions are both striking and well known. George Herbert arranged the lines of his poem 'Easter Wings' to look like wings (when viewed on their side) and the lines of his poem 'The Altar' to look like an altar. Lewis Carroll wrote 'The Mouse's Tale' in *Alice's Adventures in Wonderland* in the shape of a tail (Figure 26). The twentieth century has produced many examples of such attempts to evoke both the arbitrary semiotic meaning of words and their potential to form pictures. Guillaume Apollinaire, for example, wrote 'Calligrammes' in which words are arranged to form pictures of falling rain, the Eiffel Tower, a train or a starry sky. The signification of these poems is both iconic, because the words look like their subjects, and conventional, because the words create linguistic meaning through an arbitrary code.

Another well-known literary use of written paralanguage is found in *Tristram Shandy* in which Laurence Sterne uses blank and black pages, squiggles, pointing hands and paragraphs of dashes. These are neither iconic nor conventional signs, and convey nothing very precise, though they are indices of narrative stance. In harmony with this is the book's unconventional simulation of face-to-face interaction. The author addresses the reader as though he or she were present before him:

> How could Madam be so inattentive in reading the last chapter? I told you in it that my Mother was a papist. – Papist! You told me no such thing, Sir. Madam I beg leave to repeat it over again.
>
> (Sterne [1759–67] 1986: 82)

'Fury said to a
mouse, That he
met in the
house,
" Let us
both go to
law : *I* will
prosecute
you. – Come,
I'll take no
denial ; We
must have a
trial : For
really this
morning I've
nothing
to do."
Said the
mouse to the
cur, " Such
a trial,
dear Sir,
With
no jury
or judge,
would be
wasting
our
breath."
" I'll be
judge, I'll
be jury,"
Said
cunning
old Fury :
" I'll
try the
whole
cause,
and
condemn
you
to
death."

Figure 26 The mouse's tale from *Alice's Adventures in Wonderland*

and as though the reader's immediate situation, including its time, were the same as the plot:

> It is about an hour and a half's tolerable good reading since my Uncle Toby rung the bell . . . and nobody can say, with reason, that I have not allowed Obadiah time enough, poetically speaking, and considering the emergency too, both to come and go
>
> (Sterne [1759–67] 1986: 222)

The immediate and personal nature of the paralinguistic and the visual, also a feature of face-to-face communication, fits well with such apparently interactive and dialogic discourse, though both are at odds with the distant, non-reciprocal nature of communication through print, and it is from the tension between the two sub-modes of writing and speech that the book gains its energy.

Yet it is indicative of the attitude of a chirographic culture to the paralinguistic that poetry or prose which exploits the paralanguage of writing is usually relegated to the status of whimsy, or regarded as childish. In cultures closer to orality, arrangements of words in patterns are often of intense ritual significance, or convey more serious meanings. In an analysis of Psalm 137, Halle (1989) shows how the Hebrew words create a picture of the temple in Jerusalem. As this psalm describes the agonies of exile, slavery and defeat, beginning 'By the rivers of Babylon, there we sat down, yea, we wept . . .' and ending

> Happy shall he be that rewardeth thee as thou has served us.
> Happy shall he be that taketh and dasheth thy little ones against the rocks.

it could hardly be described as light or children's verse.

Yet in literary exploitations of the double channel, making printed words behave both symbolically and iconically, there is a striking reluctance to vary the shapes of letters themselves. The placement of letters on the page may form pictures, but the actual shape of individual letters is unimportant.

4.4 THE DOUBLE CHANNEL IN ADVERTISING: USE OF GRAPHOLOGY

In a hierarchical, bottom-up model of language and discourse (see section 1.4), advertising is distinguished by its extraordinary innovative profusion in the lower levels. The number of ways in which advertising exploits the paralanguage of writing is staggeringly large. No catalogue could be complete, for original uses of lettering are constantly appearing. (A spectacles ad uses blurred print; a cat tip-toes along the top of three-dimensional letters spelling 'Kattomeat': see Exercise 3.4d.) This section gives examples of technique, and also looks at some individual ads.

Some might argue that this lower-level inventiveness is balanced by a certain rigidity and unimaginativeness up above. The notion of higher and lower levels in discourse, however, is a metaphor, and like most metaphors it is loaded. What is 'higher' is also considered to be 'better', just as what is lower is considered to be 'worse' (as in the phrases 'high ideals' and 'low standards'). It is worth considering whether the hierarchy could not be reversed.

4.4.1 Iconicity with words

This is the technique used in the ad for Maxwell House coffee in Exercise 3.4a, and in many others as well. The tv version showed a suburban family drinking coffee in the garden of a semi-detached house. This house – a Maxwell House – is secure, friendly and homely. The photograph merges into a stylized drawing, in which the angle of the roof is represented by two lines, one saying 'Is yours a Max', the other '-well House'. The imitation of the roof by the letters is iconic. The name 'Maxwell House' now seems to be both the name of the coffee and to refer to the house in the picture. The coffee thus gains some of the attributes of that house. It too is 'secure', 'reliable', 'homely' and 'restful'. It is also linked to the visual image of the roof. As a roof protects and warms and is part of a house, it signifies the qualities of warmth and protection symbolically (as defined in 4.1.1) and also signifies 'house' metonymically. Thus 'Maxwell House' comes to mean protection and warmth too.

Another example of iconicity can be found in the ad for the perfume Elizabeth Taylor's Passion shown in Figure 27. Here, the slight displacement of the second line leftwards makes the outline of the block of words hexagonal, like the bottle. (A distinctive bottle shape is important in perfume branding, and invariably features in perfume ads.) The shape of the copy thus signifies the bottle iconically, because it imitates its shape. There is (as always) a further complication: the bottle and the words are also shaped like a heart.[12] The heart is a symbol of passion (arguably partly metonymic, because a thumping heart accompanies passion, but now largely conventional). 'Passion' is also the name of the perfume, so it refers back to the bottle. There is thus a circularity of signification leading from 'passion' in its usual sense, via two icons and one symbol, to 'Passion' as a name which leads us back to 'passion' in its usual sense again. There are other iconic echoes too. In the photograph the sparkle of the eyes resembles the sparkle of the diamonds.[13]

4.4.2 Iconicity by letter shape

Some logos and ads exploit or slightly alter conventional letter shapes, to create an iconic representation of the product or of something associated with it. The initial A of Alitalia is written in the shape of an aeroplane tail;

Figure 27 Elizabeth Taylor's Passion perfume ad

the G of Guinness is sometimes a picture of an Irish harp; the elongated upstrokes of the dunhill logo when it appears on cigarette packets look like the long cigarettes inside.[14]

4.4.3. Connected icons and symbols

In the advertisement for the Sun Alliance insurance firm in Figure 28, a couple (heterosexual as are all advertising couples!) are seen tumbling helplessly in a whirlpool drawn with the words: 'Clause two which relates to section two. Clause four which relates to section one'.

IF HOME INSURANCE
GOES OVER YOUR HEAD

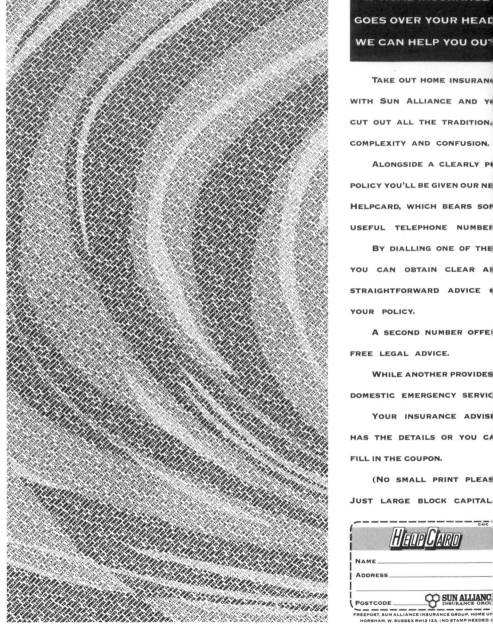

Figure 28 Sun Alliance insurance ad: whirlpool of words

WE CAN HELP YOU OUT.
TAKE OUT HOME INSURANCE
WITH SUN ALLIANCE AND YOU
CUT OUT ALL THE TRADITIONAL
COMPLEXITY AND CONFUSION

The words in the drawing are in small print. They are also used iconically to signify a whirlpool, which is a symbol (or metaphor) of 'complexity and confusion'. In the copy alongside, the phrase 'goes over your head' creates a pun, signifying 'is incomprehensible to you', while also maintaining its literal meaning, paralleled in the image of people drowning in a whirlpool. In addition the copy is itself in large block capitals thus iconically signifying the behaviour demanded. The connections are complex and various (Figure 29).

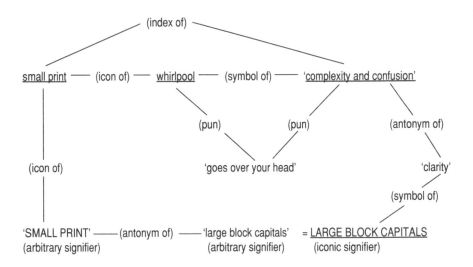

Figure 29 Signification in the whirlpool of words

4.4.4 Connected icons and arbitrary signs

The copy of the Lypsyl ad referred to (in section 4.2) employs both arbitrary linguistic signs ('sealed with a') and a further arbitrary sign (X = kiss), but also iconicity as the cross-strokes of the X are pictures of tubes of Lypsyl.

A well-known example of such a mixture is found in stickers saying such things as 'I ♡ PARIS' in which the iconic signifies a heart which is the symbol of love. An ad for Black Heart rum extends this.

Figure 30 Black Heart Rum ad: 'I love Black Heart'

4.4.5 Writing which provokes iconic behaviour

A double-page magazine ad for Philips colour tv displays its copy over a tv picture of a professional tennis match, as follows:

you	haven't
seen	tennis
on	television
until	you've
seen	it
on	a
philips 41″	screen

thus causing its reader to move his or her eyes from side to side, as though at a tennis match. The same device is used in Roger McGough's poem '40 – 0'.

4.4.6 Indexical graphology

The AA insurance ad in Exercise 3.4b signified a child indexically by using a child's handwriting. As the punctuation and spelling are by contrast not childlike, the child's presence is almost entirely graphological.

Indexical scripts and typefaces are frequent in junk mail. Addresses are printed to look handwritten, thus signifying an individual rather than an official addresser.

4.4.7 Writing imitating another writing system, creating an index of another culture

In an ad for the perfume 'Xi'a Xi'ang', the name is written in the Latin alphabet, but the stylized strokes of the letters are reminiscent of the calligraphy used for Chinese characters. Thus, although the words use the

Figure 31 X'ia Xi'ang perfume logo

Latin alphabet, their form is indexical of the Far East, even to someone who does not know Chinese. (In Chinese the words mean 'Distant thoughts' or 'Daydream'. On the bottle, they are accompanied by the Chinese characters of which 'Xi'a Xi'ang' is the Pinyin transcription – but these facts will not be known by most purchasers.)

A similar technique is used in many products associated with Russia. A Cyrillic letter is used, though it is read as the Latin letter whose shape it most resembles. Near my home, there is a restaurant called Rasputin's whose name is written

ЯASPUTINS.

The Cyrillic equivalent of the Latin R is not Я, but P; in Russian the letter ___ is read as 'Ya'. The letter is thus not only an arbitrary sign forming part of the word as read in English, but also an index of the Russian language, and therefore of Russia, because, even when its arbitrary connection with the sound 'Ya' is unknown, it is known to be a Cyrillic letter. This technique should not be confused with that used in ads which do actually use a different writing system, such as an ad for *The Economist* which appears in shorthand.

A very particular use of different writing systems can be found in Japanese ads (see Figure 6). As Japanese uses three different writing systems – the indigenous *hirogana* and *katakana* syllabaries, and *kanji* ideograms borrowed from Chinese – texts can shift backwards and forwards between one writing system and another. Predictably, Japanese ads have not been slow to exploit this property of their written language. Characters are combined in unexpected ways to attract attention, in old-fashioned ways to suggest that a product is traditional, or mixed with the Latin alphabet to suggest that the product is modern and international (Kanehisa 1985).

4.4.8 Mood evocation through typeface

Many successful brand names are inextricably connected with the typeface in which they are written (see Exercises 3.1 and 3.2). So strong can this association be that some ads can refer to their product, not by naming it, but by using this typeface. The British newspaper *The Independent*, for example, ran an ad which said only

It is. Are you?

Reference to the product was achieved not only because the word 'independent' completes the elliptical first sentence

It is (independent).

but also because the typeface used was the same as that of the publication's title. A Guinness ad whose copy was only 'Pure Genius' relied on the same association, as did a Benson & Hedges cigarette ad showing an unmarked cigarette packet next to a safety razor covered in shaving cream, in which, like shaved stubble, could be seen the jumbled letters of the product's name.

In all these instances, a typeface is used to signify the product, in addition to, or sometimes instead of, the word or words which signify it arbitrarily in the code. It is difficult to categorize this kind of signification using the semiotic terms employed so far. In part the connection is indexical: we associate a particular kind of print with a particular product. But there is also an element of mood evocation, of 'brand personality', which is hard to define. The advertising magazine *Campaign* (21 December 1990) carried a light-hearted article in which a handwriting analyst commented on well-known logos, suggesting interpretations such as 'warm, sensitive' for Coca-Cola and 'respect for tradition' for Ford. The status of such judgements is dubious, and the nature of the meanings of typefaces unclear; but that choices matter seems indisputable. The signification is both indeterminate and powerful. Advertising therefore adores it.

4.5 GRAPHOLOGY IN ADVERTISING: TWO EXAMPLES

In section 4.4, I have tried to generalize about the use of graphology. Yet, as with other types of signification, there is always a potential for truly original exploitation of the code. I shall finish this section with analyses of two unusual ads.

4.5.1 Example one: Tsar

This ad creates patterns of letters and letter combinations which become clear when the wording of the ad (both the copy and the name of the manufacturers) is set out as shown in Figure 32b.[15]

The majority of patterns are purely graphological. Exceptions are the repetition of 'P' which is also pronounced /p/ in all three cases, and the echo between 'eef' and 'iv' which is only phonological. 'Ts' is a mirror image of 'st' in writing but not in sound; 'ar' is pronounced differently in

Figure 32a Tsar eau-de-toilette ad

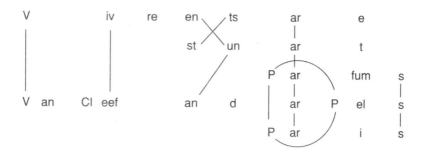

Figure 32b Repetitions in Tsar ad

'Paris' and 'parfums'; none of the three final 's' letters is pronounced at all. The theme of repetition and reflection is echoed in the picture of a man contemplating a statue, which is itself 'a work of art'.

4.5.2 Example two: Dubo Dubon Dubonnet

In a version of this ad from 1932 (Figure 33), the hollow letters of the product name are increasingly shaded, thus iconically representing the filling of a container with liquid; the body of the man beside them is increasingly shaded in the same way, as though he too were filling up. As

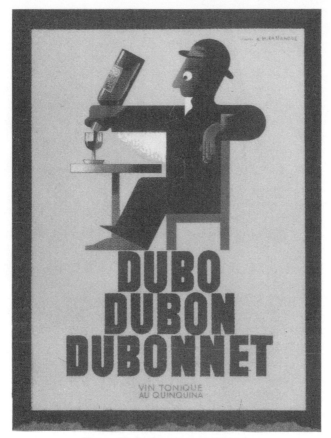

Figure 33 Dubonnet aperitif ad

the filling also turns the man red, and a flushed complexion can be an index of drunkenness, it also signifies increasing intoxication. The darkening tone is also a metaphor of inebriation. (Only the last drawing is shown in Figure 33.)

4.6 WRITING AND SPEECH

Whether finally destined for tv or a magazine, the words of an ad are almost always written down at some stage in its creation. By freeing language from time and projecting it into space, writing enables more concise and less redundant expression, and creates time to choose words carefully for maximum effect. Yet it also entails a divorce of text from a particular situation, person and voice, depriving it of the emotive richness of paralanguage, which may be so useful to the advertiser. Writing also focuses the receiver's attention upon the words themselves, and on what is perceived to be the objective meaning or content of what is said; it enables the receiver to go back and contemplate the text more carefully – perhaps finding inconsistencies and untruths – making it less likely that he or she will be swept along by the tide of what is being said without time for reflection. In short, though writing may be to an advertiser's advantage in composition, it is not always so in reception, as it may both deprive the message of some of its power and also enable criticism and contestation. This ambivalent relation of ads to writing is perhaps the cause of the intense exploitation of written paralanguage, as illustrated in the last sections. Writing is used both to create text and simultaneously to distract attention from it by using letter shapes and patterns to create parallel iconic and indexical meanings quite separate from the linguistic ones. This reveals, perhaps, a certain lack of confidence in the text itself.

The losses of written text can in part be compensated by reading aloud, and by pictures. The contemporary world is full of such discourse, which seeks the advantages of both channels. In a chirographic culture, where the fundamental advantage of writing over speech is the opportunity it brings for the displacement of a message from its point of origin, and its distribution to a wider audience in time and space, the loss of speaker and situation are felt to be the lesser of two evils. The technology of mass communication partly redresses this necessary loss. Radio, telephone and tape recorder enable the displacement of language, while preserving the sound of an individual voice. In television and film, the reading aloud of written texts allows the sender some of the advantages of writing, while also reinstating or creating an image of both a speaker and a situation. Yet the speaker on tv is not always the sender, and what is happening is not truly on-line like face-to-face interaction. Broadcasting, moreover, from the receiver's point of view, despite its achievement of displacement and wide dissemination, lacks other attributes of writing; it does not enable the receiver to process a message at any pace and in any order, to glance backwards and forwards, to juxtapose linearly separate segments, and to obtain an overall impression of structure. Broadcasting, in short, gives the sender an edge over the receiver. Television lacks the advantages of reading, though they are to some degree made possible by video (for a discussion see Cubitt 1991). Television also delivers words more slowly than they can be read. (The average speaking rate, depending on discourse type, is estimated at around 240 syllables or 170 word per minute – Tauroza and Allison 1990: 97.)

Literary discourse in novels, by remaining content with writing, in general eschews the paralanguage made possible by recording and pictures. Yet it is not true that it cannot, and does not, exploit paralanguage at all. It can describe, through the conventional signification of written words, such paralinguistic behaviour as tones of voice, facial expressions and gestures, though their audialization or visualization, if it takes place at all, will vary considerably from reader to reader.

Again she turned her face to him and her clear, bright eyes, bright likeshallow water, filled with light, frightened, yet involuntarily lighting and shaking with response. 'Oh isn't it! I wasn't able to come last week.' He noted the common accent.

(D.H. Lawrence, *The Rainbow*: 228)

How you and I see and hear this are unlikely to be the same.

So literary discourse in novels does not exploit the capacity of mass communication or live performance to reinstate both speaker and situation to its texts. (When we treat plays and poems as written texts – as most educational institutions do – then this is true of these literary genres too.) Though novels may appear to set great store by the 'voice' of an author, narrator or character, or upon fictional situations, their abstinence from pictures and sound ensures that the receiver's representation of these voices and settings will be far more heterogeneous, far more dependent upon the reader, than that imparted by the pictures or the recorded voice. (I do not claim by this that everyone's perception of a recording or picture is the same, but only that they are closer than perceptions of verbally described sounds and pictures. It is in the nature of pictures and recording to constrain interpretation.)

As already discussed in Chapter 3, pictures and sound create both their own meanings and meanings resulting from their interplay with each other and with text. It is not only that sound recording makes it possible to use music. Sound also enables language to maintain, regain or have added to it the paralanguage of an individual or choral voice. (Choral singing – so common in ads – carries with it a message of solidarity, of social harmony, and of friendship.) Voice quality serves as an index of such passing emotional states as happiness, sensuality, optimism. The advantage of such associations for the advertiser is that they are both powerful and elusive. Though everyone may experience the optimism of a voice, it is difficult either to prove or measure the existence of this graded quality.

There is likely to be far more agreement about the more permanent characteristics of the speaker conveyed by the voice. These include age, class, sex and individual identity, all of which are carefully selected in ads, and are strong clues to the ideology which advertisers attribute to their target audiences. The voices of celebrities (or mimics of celebrities) bestow upon a product all the values signified by that individual: the strength of the athlete, the glamour of the star or the authority of the politician. (Here, again, the fact that celebrities whose voices are imitated without their permission are unlikely to prove deception illustrates the simultaneous power and elusiveness of paralinguistic signification.) Perhaps the most telling evidence of sexism in advertising is not to be found in 'what happens', but in the ubiquity of the male in the final voice-over, even in ads portraying or aimed at women, or which pay lip-service to the 'modern liberated woman'. (An example is an ad for Birds Eye Menu-Master, shown as a convenience food allowing the woman time for a career, aerobics and amateur dramatics, but described to her by a man.) Although women's voices are used for tampons; foreign accents for exotic food, alcoholic drinks or perfume; regional or working-class accents for humorous effect in the advertising of cheaper necessities; the most authoritative summarizing voices are almost always those of indigenous educated middle-class males, especially in safety campaigns and ads for expensive durables and financial services.

4.7 PROSODY

The fact that writing is in part a representation of speech which, even when not actually read aloud, may form a 'sound image' in the mind gives rise to another paralinguistic phenomenon, which is prevalent in both advertising and literary discourse. This is **prosody**, the paralanguage of the patterning of sound most commonly associated with verse and poetry, but also present in prose and in spoken discourse, especially conversation or polemic (Tannen 1989). It includes such phenomena as rhyme, rhythm, assonance, consonance and alliteration, and can be found both in speech and in writing perceived as speech. It is discussed in Chapter 6.

EXERCISES

1 How do the following signify:

a Maroc (sticker on fruit)
b On the side of a bus: 'Bus advertising works (You've read this)'
c The Lypsyl slogo in Figure 25
d In the USA, CNN News run ads listing hotels which run CNN news.
e 'Polo: the mint with the h le'
f The P&O ad (see Figure 34)

2 What are the effects of handwriting in the following (Figure 35)
    (a) Help the Aged   (b) Gianni Versace profumi

3 Look back at the ads for Tsar and Dubonnet (Figures 32 and 33). To what extent do you find their exploitation of graphology
    • original
    • artistic
    • effective in selling the product?
    How do these criteria relate to each other?

4 Watch, and if possible record, an advertising break and a news bulletin. Analyse and compare the uses of paralanguage in each.

a

b

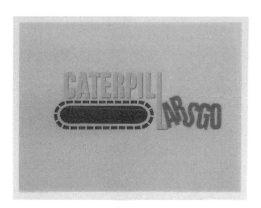

c

d

e

f

Figure 34 P&O Scottish Ferries ad

If undelivered please return to:
P.O. Box 464 London EC1B 1BD

Recycled paper

You have this gift... Could you give it to others?

LC

Help the Aged

Figure 35a Help the Aged charity envelope

IN MAN'S FRAGRANCE
lies his CulTure.
love and PASSioN,
The TheATre of life,
The seNse of oNe's origiNs ANd fAmily.
The sigNs of MAN. ThaT
liNger iN The Memory.

GiANNi VErsAce
ProfUMi

Figure 35b Gianni Versace perfume ad

FURTHER READING

The theories of Saussure are easily accessible and readable in the *Course in General Linguistics*. Wade Baskin's translation (Fontana [1915] 1974) is particularly good, and the most relevant parts are the Introduction III–VI; Part 1 I–III; Part 2 I–V)

Peirce's own writings are both more voluminous and more obscure (though see Peirce in the Bibliography). A good introduction to his ideas, together with an analysis of semiotics in general, can be found in Chapter 4 of Lyons (1977) *Semantics*.

An excellent introduction to the relation of language and paralanguage is the first four chapters of Ellis and Beattie (1986) *The Psychology of Language and Communication*.

Part II
Text

5 Words and phrases

People don't want a mortgage,
they want a home.
(Leeds Building Society)

5.0 MEANING AND DISCOURSE TYPE

Part I has examined the many ways in which advertising exploits both what is around the language of ads (situation, accompanying discourses, music and pictures) and what is, as it were, 'inside' that language, created by imaginative use of graphic and phonic paralanguage. These exploitations change the linguistic message, making it more personal and more immediate, more dependent upon particular people and situations, more emotive, and less determinate. Working against this kind of communication is a literate culture's belief and ideal that a written text – and thus by extension language itself – can, and should, free communication of such qualities, creating meanings which are unambiguous and determinate, no longer dependent on individuals or situation, and shared and objective rather than personal and subjective. This perceived potential of text to embody impersonal facts is commonly striven for in scientific prose, news reporting and legal documents, where reference to both sender and situation are removed by such linguistic strategies as the use of the passive ('It was placed' rather than 'I put it'), impersonal constructions ('There are growing fears that' rather than 'We are worried that . . .') and nominalizations ('non-payment of the tax will result in prosecution' rather than 'if you don't pay, we shall fine you'). Ironically, in view of their pretensions to objectivity, these habits imply a belief more in keeping with magic than with science: that a particular form of words somehow alters what happened, deleting the real agent as well as the grammatical one.

This striving for objective fact, intertwined with a faith in objective language, has been widely challenged in recent years, most notably by the philosophical movements of hermeneutics and deconstruction, although paradoxically (as the leaders of these movements are well aware) the discourse of the challenge is also very often similar to that of its target.

This, however, only reinforces the deconstructionist point that there is no neutral discourse.

Yet even if there is a potential in language – and in particular in writing – to eliminate the personal and emotional, and to be more precise, it is not the case that text, when insulated from its substance and situation, carries only these shared, precise and unambiguous meanings. While the lawyer and the scientist may strive – albeit without hope of total success – to rid words of a subjectivity which they deem undesirable, other writers may seek to maximize it. These opposite tendencies have often been used to distinguish two major categories of discourse. A third tendency is to use words conatively, prescribing the behaviour of others. This yields a classification of discourse into three broad types. This widely accepted tripartite division of discourse has its roots in Plato's rhetorical 'trichotomy'.

	Discourse	Trichotomy	Function	Use
1	Scientific	Cognitive	Descriptive	Informative
2	Poetic	Affective	Appraisive	Valuative
3	Religious	Conative	Prescriptive	Incitive

(adapted from Holbrook 1987)

Different suppositions about the intentions of a writer and the discourse type will yield quite different value judgements about the same text. Expressions which might be perceived as lies, or as too personal and vague in a scientific treatise, yield positive reactions when presented as a work of fiction or as a poem. Compare, for example, the effect of

As Gregor Samsa awoke one morning from uneasy dreams he found himself transformed in his bed into a gigantic insect[1]

as the opening of a novel with its effect as the opening of a biography; or of

I have been one acquainted with the night.[2]

as the opening of a poem or of a conversation. The lesson of such comparisons is that the 'truth' of a sentence cannot be assessed in isolation from its discoursal context, as logicians have rashly supposed. There are many types of utterance, including metaphorical ones, to which the issue of truth or falsehood is of no relevance. They can, as E.H. Gombrich wrote of pictures

No more be true or false than a statement can be blue or green.

(Gombrich 1977: 68)

A major problem in the evaluation of advertising arises from the difficulty of assigning it neatly to any one of the three macro categories, leading to dispute over its moral and aesthetic status. It is unusual in being balanced between all of these categories, and may thus necessitate a change in this ancient classification. In the eyes of both manufacturer and consumers, its major function is conative (if most frequently in soft-sell ads by implication), yet it is often judged by the standards of the descriptive for misrepresenting or distracting from the facts. Yet its use of language and other modes is often closer to the poetic, tending towards the personal, the specific, the ambiguous and the indeterminate.

5.1 DETERMINATE AND INDETERMINATE MEANINGS[3]

Chapter 1 discussed descriptions of meaning which break words down into components, and then use these components to establish sense relations between words (section 1.2.1). Like scientific discourse, such descriptions of the denotation of words dwell upon, and elevate, the degree to which meanings are both fixed and shared by all speakers. They derive from Saussurean semiology: the denotation of a word is an analysis of its signified; its sense is its relation to other signs. Nor has this semiotic approach been undermined by prototype theory or notions of family resemblance (see section 1.2.1), for they too seek to find what is held in common by speakers and to relate words to each other through these common meanings. It is often assumed, usually without much question, that semantic representations of meaning also have psychological reality: that they are not, in other words, just conveniences for linguists, but are used by expert speakers in the processing of language and the understanding of what words refer to. In recent decades the notion of **pragmatic meaning** – what a word or utterance means and does in a particular context – has also gained ground, and in some areas of research has almost eclipsed the importance attributed to semantic meaning.

The current general view of meaning thus comprises semantic meaning, with pragmatic meaning appended to it as a kind of extra. Pragmatic meaning is not usually conceived as an alternative to semantic meaning, but as dependent upon it, deriving from the interaction of semantic meaning with context: so the importance attached to pragmatic meaning does nothing to end the primacy of semantic meaning. Yet a word has many aspects for its user other than its denotation, which supposedly persists across different contexts, and its pragmatic function, which supposedly varies systematically across contexts. These aspects of a word are so many and so vast that knowledge of them will vary considerably from user to user. A word has an etymology, a diachronic history, connotations, **collocations**,[4] translation equivalents, personal associations, metonymic and metaphorical uses (both standard and original), echoes of **homonyms** exploited in puns,[5] associations with certain discourse types, with images, with encyclopedic knowledge, and meanings which derive from the patterns it forms when taken with the words around it (see Chapter 6). Both semantics and pragmatics derive from theoretical descriptions of language and language in use. Both assume that meaning is arrived at by the application of rules: componential analysis, sense relations, logic from semantics; conversational principles (see section 7.2) and conditions necessary to particular speech acts from pragmatics. But neither fully describes what meaning is to participants in discourse. They come from theoretical description of language and of language in use. As such, they reflect partly the accidents of the development of twentieth-century linguistics, and partly an understandable desire to have some reasonably solid ground to stand on, in an otherwise treacherous landscape. If your job is to describe language, it is quite sensible to tackle meaning through semantics and pragmatics, because they do provide reasonably clear-cut procedures for formulating meaning. These kinds of meaning are important to participants in certain discourses – of legislation, commerce, science – where people attach particular importance to the social or practical consequences of exact wording, or feel responsible for outcomes which they judge important, and where they seek to maximize, through precision, the degree to which meaning is shared. Such discourses are often confrontational, and the relationships they embody are competitive, making people actually seek to misunderstand, to catch each other out! This is not to say, however, that this is always or entirely how participants in discourse make their own meanings or perceive those of other people, especially in secure situations. It is quite possible that, while an observer of behaviour may describe what is happening by rules, the doer, the person behaving, may be using experience, rules of thumb, and guesswork (Dreyfus 1987). This is an argument advanced by Searle (ironically a leading formulator of rules for pragmatics: Searle 1975a; 1975b). In a television debate, he argued fervently against the premises of Artificial Intelligence which seek to explain behaviour in terms of rules and procedures which can be modelled on computer.[6] He pointed out that there are complex mathematical formulae for calculating the trajectory of a ball bounced off a wall relative to the position of a person and a dog running alongside that wall. His own dog, he tells us, is an expert at catching such a ball in its mouth – but it is unlikely that it does this by using the formulae, either consciously or subconsciously. As Searle said, very excitedly: 'THE DOG JUST KNOWS!' In many situations the relationship of words to participants is rather like the relationship of Searle's dog to the ball. Both language and bouncing balls may move too fast for calculation, and are better handled by experienced guesswork.

   It is the less determinate, less rule-bound types of meaning which are most frequently exploited in advertising, and on which analysis of advertising must therefore concentrate. For advertising, unlike linguistics, does not seek to steady the ground beneath our feet, but to make it sway. Nor does it share much in common with the logical public debate of law and science; it rather adopts the features of personal interaction. Coming at its addressee when he or she is at home, relaxing, in front of the television, behind locked doors, it talks to him or her as 'you', in the most colloquial language, about the most personal subjects (food, toilets, condoms, under-wear) in settings which assume access to the most private – if most common – fantasies, fears and aspirations. Nor is the communication between advertiser and consumer always discussed; the experience often remains private, even if it may take place in company. In analysing this situation, to exalt logical and literal meanings of advertising copy, as many analysts have done, is to miss the point. A linguistics for advertising – and many other discourses – must be one which can consider the indeterminate and emotive. This second part of the book attempts to consider some of these types of meaning: first in individual words, and then in longer linguistic units.

5.2 INDETERMINATE MEANINGS IN ADS: CONNOTATIONS

Advertisers have a predilection for strategies which distract from or add to the literal meaning (denotation, reference or logical content) of language. This may be effected at the graphic level, as we have seen in Chapter 4, or through deviant spellings: Theakston's Old Peculier Ale; Beanz Meanz Heinz. It may be done within words by exploiting a resemblance between a product name and one or more syllables of another word, enabling a fusion between the two, in which the product becomes a **morpheme** (a meaningful part) of the longer word: 'Cosmeau. Neauvember 1990' on the spine of a *Cosmopolitan* magazine advertising Eau Perrier (Figure 36), or this more protracted ad for the Linn Motor Group:

Linndividual   Linngineering   Linntelligent   Linnvironmental
Linntensive care   AdrenaLinn   Linnvestment   Linn Motor Group

At word level it is effected in many ways, most obviously by puns.

5.2.1 Perfume and cars

Paramount among the techniques for extending denotational meanings is the exploitation of **connotation** – the vague association which a word may have for a whole speech community or for groups or individuals within it. Connotations are both variable and imprecise. The connotations of 'dog' might include such different qualities as loyalty, dirtiness, inferiority, sexual promiscuity, friendliness; of 'stallion' such qualities as sexual potency, freedom, nobility. I shall examine connotations in ads by looking at the presentation of two very different products: perfume and cars. Both are advertised extensively on tv and in magazines; cars are also often advertised – appropriately – on roadside hoardings. As products they are in some ways polar opposites, in others very similar. Cars are perceived as an expensive necessity, while perfume is a relatively cheap luxury.[7] Yet, more than other products, they are both marketed and perceived as expressions of the self and of sexuality: a woman is her perfume, a man is his car.[8]

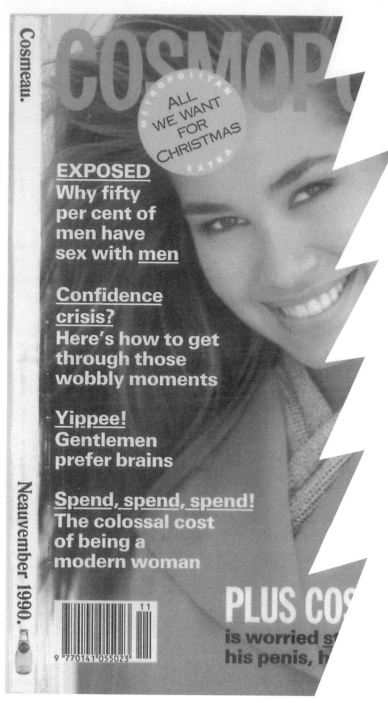

Figure 36 Eau Perrier ad: *Cosmopolitan* magazine spine

Traditionally, perfume advertising has been aimed at women. Prejudice against homosexuality led male perfumes to be described euphemistically, and with a false functionalism, as 'after-shave' and 'anti-perspirant'. Although the general bias still persists, the traditional target markets of both products have been opened up slightly to the other sex. There are now numerous ads for men's perfume, and a number of car ads ostensibly aimed at women, or purporting to acknowledge the woman's interest in a couple's purchase of a car. To some extent this reflects changing social attitudes to the roles of men and women; but, while the target markets may be merging, the roles ascribed to users are not, thus preserving the narrower range of roles offered by society to women. While perfume ads appeal to both men and women almost exclusively as lovers, there is a difference in the presentation of the two sexes in car ads. Men are not only lovers but also husbands, fathers, loners, careerists, technical experts, general status-seekers and responsible guardians of the planet's ecology (!); women are almost always only wives, lovers or careerists. A further complication to this association of product with one sex is that perfume – by virtue of its price, size, luxury and sensuality – is very frequently a gift of one partner to another, and as such is likely to be purchased by someone of the opposite sex from its consumer (though 'unromantic' partners may say what they want beforehand, or take their gift back afterwards[9]). Like other products concerned with sexual relationships, perfume ads wrongly assume an exclusively heterosexual market, although some recent ads may have been deliberately ambivalent about the sexual orientation they portray.

The differences between the products lead to different techniques. Perfume ads are 'ticklers' with very short copy (typically around ten words, though sometimes no more than the brand name itself). Car ads, on the other hand, though also 'ticklers', mix in reasons and are thus typically long-copy ads. (This distinction is complicated by the fact that some 'reasons' in car ads are so abstruse that they become ticklers: the Fiat Tipo, for example, has an 'aerodynamic drag factor of 3.1'.) In keeping with their status as necessities purchased by the user rather than as gifts, campaigns for cars are typically slow-drip, while perfume, a luxurious gift, is intensely sudden-burst, especially before Christmas. The two products thus provide contrasts as ad types along many of the parameters described in section 1.3. Those features which they share, on the other hand, may point to general features of advertising.

5.2.2 Perfume names and ads

As a product, perfume not only contrasts with 'big-buy' durables like cars, but also is very different from many other luxuries. It is not one of the growing number of items which owe their existence to advertising – 'panty shields' (worn *between* periods!), 'shake-and-vac' (a powder sprinkled on the carpet and then hoovered up!!). Its history is ancient, its cultural importance universal. Gell (1977), for example, describes its importance in the hunting, magic and dream augury of the Umeda of Papua New Guinea – a society as different from urban industrial capitalist society as it is possible to imagine.[10] Yet, though it predates advertising, it also suits it as an archetypical luxury. Unless it has exactly the smell of something widely known, it is also, of its nature, indescribable in words. Descriptions of a smell are indirect: **synaesthetic**, referring to one sense in terms of another ('sharp', 'sour', 'gentle', 'dark'), metonymic ('high society'), metaphorical ('poisonous'). A perfume may be described in terms of its effect ('seductive', 'overpowering'), the kind of person who might use it ('manly'), the place where one might find it ('oriental'), or by reference to its availability ('cheap', 'rare'). All such descriptions may serve as indices of a particular smell, but depend very much upon that individual knowledge and association. It is impossible to describe the smell – which is apparently what matters – with any precision. (Arguably, this applies to all descriptions but, in degree, perfume is an extreme case.) A smell has no denotation, no component which distinguishes it from another! Paradoxically, this resistance to description increases rather than decreases the verbal freedom of the advertiser. For this reason perfume, more than any other product, has attracted the attention of analysts (e.g. Bonney and Wilson 1983; Vorlat 1985; Cook 1990b). A new perfume can be called virtually anything. The naming of cars, by contrast, is more circumscribed. The name 'jaguar' could not easily be given to a small, slow, two-door, two-cylinder hatchback. The peculiar relation of perfume to language allows the naming and description of perfumes to illuminate a process which is more limited and disguised in the naming and description of products whose features are more amenable to precise description. The Jaguar car, for example, shares certain (but not all) denotational components with the animal. Though it may not suckle live-born young, it is streamlined and accelerates faster than others of its kind. This degree of equivalence between signifieds justifies the metaphor. But the name also invokes the connotations of 'jaguar', which might include – always allowing for imprecision and personal variation – such associations as rarity, beauty, superiority, aggression, violence, sexuality, devouring of smaller creatures, and so on. (Unfortunately for the advertiser a successful naming contains its own destruction, for a well-established trade name like Jaguar soon comes to signify the product directly, rather than via another signified. In Britain, 'Ajax' is primarily the name of a cleaning powder, not a Greek warrior.) In the naming of a perfume, as the topic has no components to be denoted, there can be no components shared between topic and vehicle[11] – though there may be components shared between the effect of the perfume and the effect of the vehicle ('Magie noire') or a relationship of metonymy between user and perfume ('Paula Yates'). The only way of denoting the perfume itself is by a unique name ('Armani', 'JHL') combined with direct experience of it, though even here the name carries connotations of its country of origin or other products of the same manufacturer. All other descriptions create qualities for the perfume by fusing it with something else, and with the (variable) connotations of that something else. To call a perfume 'Jaguar' would not be to *point out* that it is fast and streamlined (as in the case of the car) but to *create* an association with such qualities.

It is sometimes claimed that advertising proliferates where there is little difference between one product and another (Hoshino 1988; Williamson 1978: 25). One bar of soap washes your hands very much like the next. Yet even where there are differences between products they are often quite obvious, and can be easily stated, without elaborate or figurative explanation. This car costs x; its maximum speed is x; it uses x litres per mile; it has a luggage capacity of x cubic feet, etc. Though mention of such facts is occasionally adopted as a gimmick – attracting attention by its break from advertising tradition (see Chapter 10) – the contemporary ad does not dwell upon such qualities – as did, say, the eighteenth-century ad in Figure 1 – but links the product to some other entity, effect or person (all or any of which I shall refer to as **sphere**), creating a **fusion** which will imbue the characterless product with desirable qualities. Fusion is a major aim of contemporary advertising. It is for this reason that puns, metaphors, symbolism and endorsements[12] are the stocks in trade of contemporary advertising, rather than direct appeals such as

'Lovely bananas, 50 pence a pound!'

In the naming and description of luxuries like perfumes (cigarettes, alcohol, etc.) this process is stripped of the disguise of any literal or logical equivalence to the other sphere, which is evoked in the naming of such entities as cars. In the case of perfume, the only relevant 'fact' is whether it is liked by 'you', or by people 'you' want to like it. As Thompson (1990) puts it:

> The rational consumer chooses at the point of purchase by comparing smells. So the rational core of a perfume ad can only really consist of a sort of nudge: 'Remember, when you *are* comparing perfumes, you might want to give X a try'. The situation would be very different if you were about to purchase a computer.

> (Thompson 1990: 211)

Consider the perfume name 'Opium'. Semantically the word refers to a narcotic obtained from the juice of a poppy, and this primary meaning is a well-known one (unlike 'Ajax'). The word 'opium' is a co-hyponym of 'morphine', which refers to a narcotic refined from opium, and to 'heroin', which is refined from morphine. There is thus little semantic difference between the terms, other than their strength and addictiveness, and a difference of effect (which, like the smell of a perfume, is beyond description). That it is the connotation and not the denotation of 'opium' which is evoked as a metaphor of the perfume is strongly suggested by the unsuitability of either 'morphine' or 'heroin' as perfume names: for whereas the connotations of 'opium' may include the nineteenth century, the Orient, dreams, Romantic poetry, and bohemian illegality, 'morphine' is more likely to be associated with painful diseases, hospitals and accidents, while 'heroin' has connotations of organized crime, premature death, HIV infection, unwilling prostitution and urban poverty.

The name 'opium' thus relies on connotation. Yet it is not necessarily the case, as many analysts assume without evidence, that denotational meaning must precede connotational meaning in language processing. Bonney and Wilson (1983), for example, discussing an ad for Fidji perfume, which shows the naked shoulders of a woman with a snake entwined round her neck like a necklace, write:

> But the picture is to be read not simply as a woman holding a bottle of perfume with a serpent round her neck. The point of the serpent is to signify temptation, which it does by virtue of it place in the story of the Fall in 'Genesis'. Thus it is the connotation of that element, not its denotation, which is of prime importance. However the denotation is not irrelevant. Indeed, it is a condition of the connotation. For if the coloured shape round the woman's neck were not read first as a serpent, it could not also be read as signifying temptation.
>
> (Bonney and Wilson [1983] 1990: 192)

Yet it is possible that the image is perceived firstly as a signifier of 'temptation' (which may be attractive) and only optionally as a snake (which may well be repulsive). (In a similar way, the processing of a dead metaphor – 'he hit the roof' – may not involve its literal meaning.) Thus 'Opium' may be interpreted only connotationally. If it is interpreted in both ways, its connotations hover between the repugnant and the attractively illegal: a border area which exerts a compelling fascination. Many other names select such daring choices, often elevating attitudes – especially sexual attitudes – in a way which seems to defy both traditional patriarchal morality, and the new morality of an anti-patriarchal feminism. The name 'Tramp', for example, is, in a patriarchal system, a term of sexist abuse for a woman who 'sleeps around', and as such would not be welcomed by a woman who accepts traditional values. Yet the word, and the attitude to women it encapsulates, would be rejected by feminists. Nevertheless, the name is presumably assumed to appeal to women.

In the name 'Poison' there is an intermediate stage of equivalence between 'poison' and 'perfume'. Both share the supernym 'liquid'. 'Poison' is a liquid which kills. 'Poison' perfume is a liquid (literally) which kills (metaphorically), and both are used by a *femme fatale*. Perhaps the most effective names are those which arouse many different connotations simultaneously, allowing the product to appeal to incompatible desires within one person, or to different types of people. In an informal survey of forty young adults, very different connotations were suggested by them for the perfume name 'White Linen'. Associations included 'purity', 'a freshly made bed (ready for sex)', 'a holiday in a good hotel', 'cleanliness', 'first communion' and 'a rite of passage from girlhood to womanhood'. (A current ad for White Linen restricts such connotations by showing a modestly dressed woman pacing pensively on a sunny Mediterranean balcony.)

The effect of names is often modified by their preservation, untranslated, for a foreign market. Many French and Italian perfumes are marketed with their original names to English-speaking consumers. Where the meaning is widely known (L'aimant, Exotique, Eau Sauvage) they may preserve their original connotations, simply attracting the extra connotations of the culture of which they are an index. Where the word is unlikely to be known, the situation is different. In a French-speaking market 'Ma Griffe', for example, effects a three-way union of elements which may be represented as follows:

FRENCH *Denotation*:	*Meaning 1* my designer label	*Meaning 2* my claw mark	*Meaning 3* the perfume
Possible connotations:	elitism, wealth, snobbishness; I am an object for sale	selfishness, sadomasochist sexuality	(gained from 1 and 2)

In English, where the meaning of this word is unlikely to be known to most purchasers, a quite different fusion is effected, which may be represented as follows:

ENGLISH *Denotation*:	*Meaning 1* (unknown)	*Meaning 2* the perfume
Indexical of:	Frenchness	
Connotations:	romance, sophistication, etc.	romance, etc. (gained from 1)

Even where naming is motivated by some sharing of components, it is the connotations which follow from the comparison which matter. This broad difference exists in literary metaphor too. In Ezra Pound's poem 'In a Station of the Metro'

The apparition of these faces in the crowd;
Petals on a wet, black bough.

the comparison is justified by a degree of equivalence – both metro and bough are cylindrical and dark, both passengers and petals are paler and smaller than this background. Yet it is the variable and indeterminate connotations of the 'petals' and 'bough' (of fragility, transience, etc.)

which give the equivalence its power (for some people). In other meta-phors, sometimes included under the term **catachresis** (Durand 1987), the nature of an abstract topic can be understood only by attracting to itself the qualities of a vehicle, which provides what T.S. Eliot termed an 'objective correlative' for the ineffable (Myers and Simms 1989: 211). Such meta-phors are common – perhaps essential – to the description of the abstract and spiritual (freedom, peace, the love of god, poetic genius) and also the most physical (smells, pain, sexual pleasure). Indeed, the abstract entity or the sensation may only be able to exist conceptually through the metaphor (G. Lakoff and Johnson 1980: 110). In perfume ads the vehicle creates features for both the physical and abstract nature of the perfume:

Valentino. Not just a perfume. A rite of passage.

Where a product is both unnamed and indescribable the options for the advertiser are immense. The wide connotative power of the names of new perfumes is a testimony to the seizure of this opportunity. (In literature the naming of characters offers similar potential, though options are limited by temporal and historical setting.) Not all products offer such freedoms. They may inherit a mundane name from a less publicity-conscious age or be constrained by obvious facts. In either case the nature of the imposition may be neutral, positive (by happy chance) or in the worst cases negative (Milka Lila Pause chocolate, Shmuckers mustard, Pre-Gestive Tea). This is complicated by the positive connotations which a firm or brand name attracts to itself as years pass (Heinz, Kelloggs, Ford – or PG Tips, as Pre-Gestive Tea was renamed in 1955). One way for the advertiser to escape a negative connotation is to confront it with humour:

Milka Lila Pause – hate the name, love the chocolate.

Shmuckers – with a name like that, it's gotta be good.

5.3 CAR NAMES AND ADS

Cars, more than perfumes, typically belong to this category of products which inherit a neutral name. They may make use of metonymy (a 'Fiesta' car goes to a fiesta; a 'Skylark' is to be found in the open country) but such names combine with trade names,[13] the alliterative 'Ford Fiesta' or the rhythmic 'BUick SKYlark' (two trochees), and these names are often followed by a figure indicating cylinder number or engine capacity. This restricted potential of cars to effect fusion with another sphere through names, combined with the tendency of car ads to use longer copy, means that the fusion more often takes place, not at word level, but at the textual or discoursal level. Yet it still happens. Despite a sprinkling of technical data in the long copy of car ads, 'you' are rarely sold a car alone. Just as much as with perfumes, though more verbosely, 'you' are also sold yourself in an attractive persona, role or environment. Thus in an ad for the BMW5 each part of the car is equated to a feature of a fit and healthy human body: the seats are its flexible spine, the warning devices its alert ears, the dials its eyes. An ad for the Volvo 740 Turbo leaves 'you' embracing a lightly clad woman on an empty beach after a happy day's surfing.[14] A Toyota moves with the elegance of a thoroughbred racehorse. A Saab driver is as alert as a fighter pilot and supported by the same computer technology. Et cetera et cetera. There are perhaps as many examples as there are makes and marques of cars.

5.3.1 Long-copy car ads: an example

In illustration of how fusion is created in text, and of how words and phrases take on extra dimensions of meaning from context, as discourse, we shall consider in detail a magazine car ad for the Subaru estate 1.8 and Justy 1.2 (Figure 37). The text is as follows:

The Subaru of his and hers

The Subaru of his and hers. Or how to keep your marriage on the road. Faithfully through the rough and the smooth. Through stormy weather and the big freeze. Gripping stuff, Subaru four-wheel drive. The world and his wife's favourite in fact. With 1½ million four-wheel drives to prove it. Mind you, it only takes two to make a perfect marriage. The Justy for one. The world's first 1.2 4WD supermini. A poetic little mover. 3 valves per cylinder. 5-speed box. 3 or 5 doors. From only £6,198 what's more. The other partner? A Subaru estate, of course. Marries all the practical virtues to sheer desirability. With seven models to choose from. Starting at just £8,599. Which means you can both be in Subaru four-wheel drive for less than £15,000. A small price to pay for lasting harmony, don't you think?

Of the twenty-two **orthographic sentences** (groups of words bounded by a capital and a full stop) only one contains a main verb ('marries'). The text is presented alongside a picture, in which the two cars are shown parked outside a house beside the sea with roses growing around the doorway. Two Labrador dogs are beside the upper car. The dogs and the cars face in opposite directions. What is not clear from the black-and-white reproduction is that the picture is in two colours only: the cars and the roses are red, everything else is blue. The picture presents a number of pairs, pairs of pairs, and pairs within pairs: picture/text; blue/red; pets/cars; dog/bitch; house/car; car/car; land/sea; front wheels/back wheels (4WD).

The text imposed on the picture, 'The Subaru of his and hers', which is also the first line of the copy, contains a verbal pairing: 'his'/'hers'. It is also linguistically odd. A more usual way of expressing the same meaning, in narrow semantic terms, might be: 'His Subaru and her Subaru' or 'A man's

Figure 37 Subaru car ad: 'The Subaru of his and hers'

and a woman's Subaru'. The oddness attracts attention, it may even be intended to evoke Japanese English, but, more importantly, it fuses meanings and discourse types. Its grammatical structure – a definite noun phrase post-modified by a prepositional phrase with 'of'

(The NP (of NP))

is typical of story titles: *The Rape of the Lock, The Master of Ballantrae, The Lord of the Rings, The Tale of Jemima Puddleduck.* The next unit further encourages this impression, for 'or' after such a construction often introduces a subtitle, and a non-finite noun clause with the structure

	VP	NP	A/PP
[how	(to x)	(your x)	(x)]

is typical of subtitles of advisory or cautionary tales with a humorous bent ('How to make friends' or 'How to get ahead in business'). Interpreted as the title of a story, the product name, by virtue of its position in the opening unit, fuses with words which might occupy the same slot:

	tale	
the	story	of his and hers.
	Subaru	

With only the slightest alteration (the replacement 'the' with a demonstrative 'this' or 'that') the phrase becomes one typical of casual conversation.

(DEMONSTRATIVE	NOUN	(of (POSSESSIVE PRONOUN)))
(These	scissors	(of (mine)))
(That	dog	(of (yours)))
(That	friend	(of (his)))

I am omitting the words 'and hers' because, though they *can* be included in the grammatical analysis

(The Subaru (of (<his and hers>)))

discoursally they do not belong. They are like an afterthought:

The Subaru of his and – oh, I almost forgot and it's not so important anyway – of hers.

If the speaker or story-teller had had this phrase in mind from the beginning he (not she) would have said

The Subaru of theirs.

As it stands, the construction not only presents 'of hers' as an afterthought, but also iconically represents in its grammatical form a separation between 'him' and 'her'. The addressees are not 'they' but 'he – and she': a man and a wife who go their separate ways. This same odd separated pronominal is used to similar effect by James Joyce at the end of *The Dead* when describing a couple who are alienated from each other:

> He watched her while she slept, as though he and she had never lived together as man and wife.
>
> (Joyce, *The Dead*: 219)

Semantically, the signified of 'his and hers' is the same as that of 'theirs', but the effect is quite different (Cook 1986). Yet another surface distinction which is lost in analyses appealing to 'depth'!

This initial relegation of the woman to a secondary place by means of grammar rather than meaning may explain a rather unusual but unanimous interpretation of this text, by people asked to recall it after one reading.[15] The ad creates the impression that it is addressed to the man of the couple rather than the woman, and secondly that it is the larger of the two cars which is for the man. Yet neither of these ideas is expressed directly – they are only insinuated. Certainly, they are partly activated by cultural schemata which the ad does nothing to contradict, but they are also immediately reinforced by the secondary position of 'and hers'.

From its outset, the copy evokes the discourse types of story and casual conversation. The ad's 'own' style is difficult to identify; it exists parasitically by attaching itself to these hosts. The verbless orthographic sentences use both the elliptical utterances of conversation and the verbless phrases and clauses of titles and headlines. Story-telling, already suggested by the title, is again evoked by the phrase 'gripping stuff' (punningly referring both to the story and the car's four-wheel drive), though as a comment *on* the story rather than part *of* it it also belongs to casual conversation. From this phrase onward story-telling gives way to a conversational style which persists to the very end, evoked by fillers typical of conversational discourse ('in fact', 'mind you', 'of course'), interrogatives which imply the presence of an interlocutor ('The other partner?', 'Don't you think?') and ellipses which appear to complete and support utterances of that interlocutor:

> Which means you can both be . . .

> Marries all the practical virtues to sheer desirability.

These last sentences both presuppose a grammatical head recoverable from a previous sentence – respectively a noun phrase which the relative clause can post-modify, and a noun phrase to act as subject for the verb. Although these can be found, they lend the whole text an air of being one half of a conversation, the answers to questions supplied by 'you'. Alternatively one may read the whole as a dialogue between two speakers with breaks in text corresponding to a change of voice, or as two voices both addressed to 'you'. In all these readings, the form of the text – whether as story or as conversation – is interactive. It is not disembodied information, but a personal communication. The discourse types imply this presence: a story needs an audience as well as a teller, a conversation involves at least two people. Who are these two participants? Two men talking about cars in the absence of women? The probability of this impression cannot be ignored simply because it cannot be proved by semantic or logical analysis. Elusiveness and resistance to proof are the strength of such insinuation. It is equivalent at discourse level to the connotation of a word: personal, variable and more powerful than literal meanings.

The skilful avoidance of explicit reference to the male point of view under cover of addressing two partners is rather spoiled at the end of the copy, where the coupon to cut out says:

Please send *me* details of the Subaru range

not 'Please send *us* . . .'. Could there have been a lack of communication between skilful copy-writer and clumsy coupon designer? We know, I think, which partner 'me' refers to.

Within the general frame of these two dialogic discourse types (story and conversation), the sphere with which the product fuses is marriage. The cars are *like* a husband and wife, *for* a husband and wife, and create marital harmony. Like the picture, the text is full of verbal pairs, noun phrases co-ordinated by a conjunction: 'his and hers', 'the rough and the smooth', 'stormy weather and the big freeze', 'The world and his wife'. Semantically, there are many words which refer to dualities: 'marriage', 'two', 'partner', 'marries', 'both', 'harmony', 'other'. In addition there are many words and phrases which collocate equally with cars, with marriage, or one or other of the sexes. The metaphorical clause

how to keep your marriage on the road

takes a dead and clichéd metaphor in which marriage is compared to driving, and revivifies it by reversing it – it is driving which is compared to a marriage rather than vice versa. Once this fusion is established, every subsequent description can apply to either the marriage, or one of the partners, or one of the cars: 'Faithfully through the rough and the smooth', 'stormy weather and the big freeze', 'it only takes two to make a perfect marriage', 'lasting harmony'. The phrase 'a poetic little mover' can be both a male-to-male description of an attractive woman or of a car; while 'marries all the practical virtues to sheer desirability' sounds like a traditional description of the perfect husband. (These are perhaps the clearest indications in the text as to which car is for which partner.)

The ad, aimed at the man of a middle-aged couple, is presented as a solution to marital tension. The disjunction of the opening 'his and hers' becomes the 'lasting marital harmony' of the end. As with the single-word or short-phrase names of perfumes, it is not the literal denotational meaning which matters – that the car has four-wheel drive, grips the road, or is reliable – but, rather, the indeterminate and unprovable implications. This is not only the case with those shorter phrases, such as the 'rough and the smooth' or 'gripping stuff', which are ready-made chunks and can be treated as though they are single lexical items; it is also true of longer units, like 'marries all the practical virtues to sheer desirability'. Unlike word connotation, which a word may activate on its own, these extra dimensions of meaning are dependent on the pictorial and discoursal context.

In this ad, the marriage metaphor (itself a marriage) is multi-dimensional, for there are many interlocking figurative and literal marriages in both picture and text: between man and woman, car and car, two people and the two cars, car and road, practical virtues and sheer desirability, big car and man, little car and woman, purchase and marital harmony, funds and expenditure, front-wheel drive and back-wheel drive (a pair of pairs), as well as the additional pairs I have already listed for the picture. What these pairings effect is an image of a harmony in which everything in the human, natural and social world fits complacently together (as in the Wrigley's ad in 3.3.2). Sexual stereotypes are reinforced without being explicitly stated, and nothing, not even the sea and the land, is allowed to exist outside this binary universe. The abstract qualities of the relationship between the sexes are expressed by concrete metaphorical vehicles. If we split each pair and arrange them so that each component relates not only syntagmatically to its partner but also paradigmatically to the other pairs, then the world of this ad becomes much clearer:

Male	Female
driver	car
rough	smooth
Estate	Justy
£8,599	£6,198
1.8	1.2
road	home
world	wife
cars	pets
red	blue
practical	poetic
dog	bitch
car	house

In semiotic terms, the ad not only uses existing denotations and sense relations, but also creates new ones, in which each term relates to each other term in its own column, attracting qualities from the other terms to itself, and antithetically to each term in the other column.

5.3.2 A literary comparison

Lest one suppose that it is only in the trivial discourse of ads that such a seamless mythology of the masculine and feminine could exist, it may be instructive to compare the binary oppositions established in this ad with those in a literary text on a similar theme: the speeches at the opening of the third act of *Romeo and Juliet*. Here Romeo, after a single night with Juliet, is anxious to depart for fear of discovery by her family. Initial discord has yielded briefly to harmony, though one which is soon to be broken. The text is as follows:

JULIET: Wilt thou be gone? It is not yet near day:
It was the nightingale, and not the lark,
That pierc'd the fearful hollow of thine ear;
Nightly she sings on yon pomegranate tree;
Believe me, love, it was the nightingale.

ROMEO: It was the lark, the herald of the morn,
No nightingale: look, love, what envious streaks
Do lace the severing clouds in yonder east;
Night's candles are burnt out, and jocund day
Stands tiptoe on the misty mountain tops:
I must be gone and live or stay and die

(Romeo and Juliet III: v:1–11)

Though comparison of so respected a passage with one so lightly dismissed may seem far-fetched, artificial or pretentious, it has more in its favour than might at first appear, and rejection of the comparison may need arguing quite as much as acceptance. Both the Subaru ad and the parting speeches create an image of masculinity and femininity through a series of binary opposition. Those in the Subaru ad have been listed above; those in the speeches are as follows:

Female	*Male*
Juliet	Romeo
question	answer
stays	goes
night	day
garden	mountain tops
nightingale	lark
death	life
sleeping	waking
hollow	candles

In the ad, as we have seen, there are parallels between pairs both within the picture, between picture and text and within the text. In the speeches, when considered as written text, such interconnections are inevitably linguistic only (although on stage or film, there may be visual and visual-textual parallels too). Thus many utterances of Romeo's either repeat the grammatical structures of Juliet's while substituting new lexis which re-verses or changes the meaning –

	S/NP	P/VP	C/NP
Juliet:	(it)	(was)	(the nightingale)
Romeo:	(it)	(was)	(the lark)

			C/NP
Juliet:	and	(not)	(the lark)
Romeo:		(no	nightingale)

	P/IMPERATIVE VP	Od/NP	VOC NP
Juliet:	(Believe)	(me)	(love)
Romeo:	(Look),		(love)

	P/VP	Od/NP	PP	o/NP
Juliet:	(pierced)	(the fearful hollow	(of	(thine ear)))
Romeo:	(do lace)	(the severing clouds	(in	(yonder east)))

– or maintain the semantic content while transforming the syntactic structure, as in Romeo's declarative echo of Juliet's interrogative:

Juliet: Wilt thou be gone?

Romeo: I must be gone.

The last line sums up this tension between parallel structure and divergent meaning in

(go)	and	(live)
(stay)	and	(die)

This counterpoint of repetition and alteration represents the conflicting motivations of the two speakers: repetition reflecting convergence and the desire to stay; changes reflecting divergence and the need to go. Perhaps the most obvious pairing – and one so obvious that it is easily overlooked – is that of the two speeches themselves. They are almost equal in length, although Romeo's, with significant asymmetry, has an extra, summary line. They have a number of lexical items in common (five content words and numerous pronouns and functors) and also an unusual rhythm, in which the ten-syllable line is divided, by reason of grammatical boundaries, either into four and six syllables, or seven and three, thus potentially lending to these words, when spoken, a certain breathless and passionate irregularity.

To some extent such comparisons of literature and ads are mere provocations – though with a serious point. It is true of course that these speeches are only an extract from a much longer text within which they establish many more echoes and parallels than those I have ascribed to them here. Their sentimental and romantic view of love is but one voice within the play, balanced with others and undermined by them (the wisdom of the Nurse and the cynicism of Mercutio). It is also true that this moment of harmony is broken by subsequent disaster, and, viewed retrospectively, has a quite different meaning. Rarely are the harmonious myths of the advertising world ever set up to be shattered (though see Chapter 10). Yet so strong is the reverence for Shakespeare and other literary 'giants' that speeches such as these are often artificially isolated both from their co-text and from performance, and approached as if, even in isolation, they were works of art of intrinsic and autonomous merit. In one view the comparability of these lines with an ad may be viewed as a condemnation of this isolating, extract-worshipping approach.

Whatever one's final judgement of the relevant merits of these speeches and the Subaru ad, they are similar in their formal complexity and compression, and in their ideology. Both are formally highly complex; both express very traditional patriarchal images of sexual roles. In this light, though the superior acclaim accorded to Shakespeare may indeed be justified, it may also need arguing.

EXERCISES

1 An ad for Cindy Tights shows only the lower half of a long-legged young woman, seen from behind, walking down a street in a short skirt slightly lifted by the wind, over the copy

Cindy Tights Are Right Up Your Street

How is the connotation of the words affected by the picture?

2 Consider the following names of literary characters. What connotations do they have and how do they influence expectations? How have names been chosen or formed? What limitations are there on naming?

Jay Gatsby	Daisy Buchanan	Mrs Rouncewell
Mr Allworthy	Constance Chatterley	Mr Knightley
Mr Murdstone	Maurice Zapp	Sergeant Troy

What could be done to maintain the connotations of names in translation? (The name Raskolnikov in *Crime and Punishment*, for example, derives from the Russian for 'dissent', but this is lost in English.)

3 What are the connotations of the following perfume names? Can they be sorted into groups? Which are for men and which for women?

Boss	Pagan	Paris	Intimate	Liaisons
Open	Valentino	Sport	Classic Gold	Rive Gauche
Rebel	Bogart	Coco	Lace	Samsara
Decadence	Nightmusk	Joy	Obsession	Byzance
1000	Tuscany	Fidji	Eau Sauvage	L'Air du Temps
Eternity	Loulou	Brut	Anais Anais	Members Only

What would *you* call a new perfume?

4 Make a list of car names and consider their connotations.

5 Consider the ad for Volkswagen Seat (Figure 38).

> WHAT'S MINE IS MINE
> 'Wow,' he said, 'a System-Porsche engine. That's high-performance.'
> 'I think I was supposed to be impressed or something. Frankly, all I ask from my car is that it'll get me from A to B.'
> Reliably, of course. And safely.
> Rather like the car in question – a Seat Ibiza. It did look stylish.
> And it drove like a dream – light, precise steering that made it incredibly easy both to turn and park.
> While he was raving about the meticulous German engineering and quality control, I was rather more impressed with interior design: controls closer to hand, instruments easier to read.
>
> WHAT'S HIS IS OURS
> Happily we both agreed that the price (from £5,099) and running costs (ridiculously low) were absolutely ideal.
> (Although we bickered a bit about whether to go for three or five doors.)
> I won, on condition that the boy-racer got to drive it home.
> He thought I was joking when I told him: 'Just this once.'

What discourse type is fused with this ad?
List any words and phrases which led to this conclusion.
Who is speaking to whom and where?
What attitudes to the roles and relationships of the sexes are implied, and how?

FURTHER READING

The ideas in this chapter were influenced by Bakhtin's theory of the indeterminacy of meaning in Volosinov [1929] (1988) *Marxism and the Philosophy of Language*, and also by G. Lakoff and Johnson (1980) *Metaphors We Live By*. My own ideas on indeterminate meaning are further developed in 'Indeterminacy, translation and the expert speaker' (Cook 1991).

An excellent and more technical introduction to theories of meaning (including connotation) can be found in Leech (1981) (2nd edn) *Semantics* Chapters 1–7. Prototype theory (also discussed in Chapter 1) is expounded in Rosch's (1977) 'Human categorization', and its implications developed and discussed extensively in G. Lakoff (1987) *Women, Fire and Dangerous Things*.

Figure 38 Volkswagen Seat car ad: 'What's mine is mine'

6 Prosody, parallelism, poetry

6.0 PROSODY IN DISCOURSE

Prosody, the patterning of sound, lends a text an extra dimension which reinforces, contradicts or adds to its linguistic meanings, or interpretations of them. Like music and paralanguage, its communicative effect is impossible to define or relate to precise referents; the subjective and disputable attempts of literary critics to do this only emphasize its impossibility. Universal, and highly valued in all societies, prosodic patterns can be described, but the reasons for their powerful attraction remain mysterious. From an ontogenetic perspective, it has been suggested that rhythm and repetition recall the regular sound of the mother's heartbeat in the womb or mimic the vital processes of the body (Langer 1967: 324; Stetson 1951) or, from a phylogenetic perspective, the dances of ritual magic (Olson 1950), that they have an enhancing effect on neuronal circuits in the brain (Newman 1986), or that, by drawing attention to chance connections between linguistic structures, they beneficially break down rigid schemata which may impede creative thought (Cook forthcoming). Undoubtedly, they have a powerful emotional and mnemonic effect, yet descriptions of this power are commoner than explanations, and explanations all remain highly speculative.

All discourse uses prosody to some extent, though with differing degrees of prominence. In discourse where prosody is less prominent, both words and syntactic structures are selected more by semantic and pragmatic than by prosodic criteria. To put it more plainly: in such discourses, we choose our words for their meaning, or to have a desired effect, rather than for sound. If patterns of sound occur, they generally do so accidentally. Highly prosodic discourse, on the other hand, chooses words to create sound patterns, as well as for their meanings and functions. On occasion phonetic and phonological criteria may dominate, and a word or other linguistic unit be chosen primarily for its rhyme, rhythm or syllabic structure, and in spite of its meaning.

The dichotomy between non-prosodic and prosodic discourse is, like most dichotomies, a descriptive convenience only. Actual discourse occurs on a continuum between these two theoretical poles. Though poetry is exceptional in the degree to which it exploits prosody, and bureaucratic prose in the degree to which it does not, most discourse types make more use of it than is generally supposed (Tannen 1989). The two motives behind linguistic choice are not mutually exclusive. A given word or grammatical construction may be doubly determined, by sound and by meaning – and doubly apposite – for though it may be the quest for prosodic patterning which brings a particular wording to mind it may still have a semantic and pragmatic appropriateness, despite its origin.

6.1 PROSODY IN ADS

In advertising, prosodic patterning is extensive. I shall approach it under five headings: poems, borrowed poems, jingles, borrowed songs and prosodic ads. I do not share the view that prosodic patterning is a feature of interpretation, brought into existence by ways of reading and varying considerably between different users. I regard it rather, despite some group variation, as a feature of the code, perceived in very much the same way in a given text by competent speakers of English, and indeed partly indicative of that competence. Though the appreciation of some prosodic techniques may be enhanced by education in poetic appreciation, to claim that the perception of verse rhythm in general is limited to some groups of speakers seems quite contrary to experience. Not everyone may know a means of formal description, but the perception and enjoyment of prosody is an early and universal aspect of competence in any language.

6.1.1 'Poems'

PLEASURE IN EVERYTHING

The day begins
            warm tones of light
surround me
            an island of delight
washing the night
            from sleepy limbs
to greet the day
            re-born.

In languages using alphabetic writing, a feature of written poetry is that its lines end before the margin, motivated by some other criterion than a simple lack of space. Writing which does not do this, yet presents itself as 'poetry' (Oscar Wilde's 'Prose Poems', Rimbaud's 'Les Illuminations'), is perceived as, and was presumably intended to be, odd. Line-breaks and gaps between stanzas enable us to identify writing visually as likely to be poetry, even when it is out of focus or written in another language. This visual unit of the line has a conventional connection to a unit of sound, a

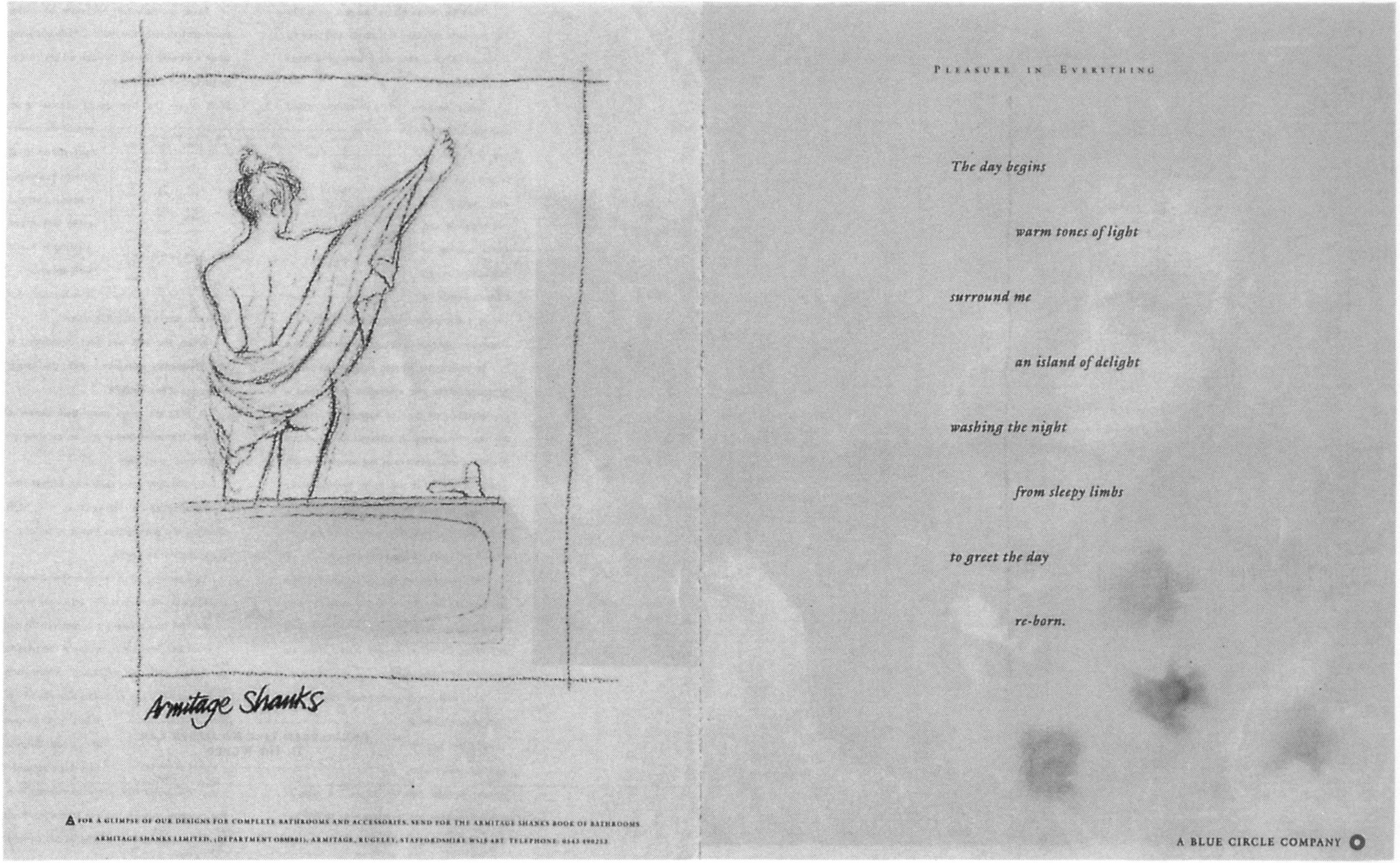

Figure 39 Armitage Shanks bathrooms ad

spoken 'line' composed of one or more metrical units (**feet**). The fact that sophisticated poetry may depart from this convention, breaking metric units through enjambment, pausing where there is no line-break,[1] or writing in lines which do not correspond to any metrical unit, does not invalidate this characterization. Such innovation can be defined only by reference to the norm it abandons.

Yet, although both written and spoken lineation are common in poetry, they are not commonly perceived as either sufficient or essential to it. The appellation 'poetry' has become a value judgement. To present writing in lines in the main body of a book is a bid for this accolade, and signifies (conventionally) that one wishes the text to be read as poetry. Though there are critics and literary theorists who espouse the extreme view that 'poetry' refers to a manner of reading, and that any prose passage written out in lines becomes poetry, it is still the case that writing in shortened lines, away from contrived deceptions, signals that a text should be read as poetry. The layout makes a claim that the reader will find a particular kind of interest and value, and that the sound patterns contribute to this.

There are discourses and parts of discourses, however, where writing in lines does not signal that a text should be read as a poem. Title pages, notices, labels, tickets and menus, for example, employ lineation without making any such claim, and it would be quite inappropriate to accuse them of pretensions to poetry! What I have said above applies to text placed in the main body of books or magazines. In this respect, advertising is anomalous. It is very common for short copy to be presented in broken lines, or – on tv – to be spoken rhythmically. Yet this practice need not necessarily attract the reading strategies evoked by poetry, even when it is accompanied by sound patterning, metre or rhyme. The more prominent the picture, and the greater its connection to the copy, the less likely that copy is to be perceived as an attempt at poetry. This is revealed in the contrast between the ad in Figure 27 (Elizabeth Taylor's Passion) and in Figure 39 (Armitage Shanks). Here the latter, by its clear separation from the picture (a line drawing of a naked woman towelling herself in the bath on the opposite page) seems to demand a more independent status, and therefore consideration as a 'poem', while the former, by placing the words on the picture, and relying on the picture for their interpretation ('*the* woman', '*the* fragrance'), encourages a more integrated perception of words and pictures which (despite exceptions like Blake's 'Songs of Innocence and Experience') is unusual in poetry.

Mercifully, attempts to produce 'poems' in ads are rare. This particular example is outstandingly banal and clumsy. The rhythm and rhyme scheme are irregular to no purpose; there are no other phonological patterns of note; and the sentiment and imagery are trite. But it is a bad ad as well as a bad poem.

6.1.2 'Borrowed' and commissioned poems

Some ads pick up another discourse and turn it to their own devices. This is more carrion than parasitic. When it cannot write its own poems, advertising appropriates others. An interesting and unusual relationship between ads and poetry is illustrated by 'The Night Mail', a poem commissioned from W.H. Auden for an ad for the Royal Mail. In a later version of the ad, the poem (not all by Auden) goes as follows:

> This is the night mail crossing the border,
> Bringing the cheque and the postal order,
> Letters for the rich, letters for the poor,
> The shop at the corner, and the girl next door.
> Pulling up Beattock a steady climb,
> The gradient's against her, but she is on time.
> Passing the shunter intent on its toil,
> Moving the coke, and the coal, and the oil,
> Girders for bridges, plastic for fridges,
> Bricks for the site, are required for tonight.
> Grimy and grey is the engine's reflection,
> Down to the docks for the metal collection.
> The passenger train is full of commuters,
> Bound for the office to work in computers:
> The teacher, the doctor, the actor in farce,
> The typist, the banker, the judge in first class,
> Reading *The Times* with a crossword to do
> Returning at night on the 6.42.

6.1.3 Jingles

Though it also employs prosodic patterning, the jingle is very different from the 'poem' of Figure 39. It is heard rather than read; it has no pretensions to be poetry; and it is sung to music which alters and dictates the rhythms of the written word. Yet it often makes more interesting and effective use of sound patterning in language.

The jingle of two consecutive Wrigley's Spearmint Gum ads, 'Poster' and 'Neon' (the predecessors of 'Last stick' described in section 3.3.2) is as follows:

> Wrigley's spearmint, it's the one.
> Cool fresh taste, share it with someone.
> So minty cool, through and through, it
> Tastes so great, you'll just love to chew it.

In one of the two tv ads using this jingle ('Poster'), the sung rhythm is a clear four-beat line, as represented below

1		2		3		4
WRI	gley's	SPEAR	mint	IT'S	the	ONE
COOL	fresh	TASTE	share it	WITH	some	ONE
So MINT	y	COOL		THROUGH	and	THROUGH it
TASTES	so	GREAT	you'll	JUST LOVE	to	CHEW it

As with most songs, the music dictates the rhythm, and stresses may fall on syllables which would be unstressed in speech (for example 'WITH'). Unstressed syllables between the major beats are pushed up together when they are numerous, or drawn out when they are few. Thus, in the sung rhythm represented above, the words slow down and gather force in the third line with a marked pause between 'COOL' and 'THROUGH'. The resulting climax is reinforced by a tension between the units of rhyme and the units of grammar. Grammatically 'through and through' belongs to cool, while 'it' belongs to 'tastes'. (The analysis here assumes that there is an ellipsis of 'being' from an opening clause: 'Being so minty cool through and through'.)

[[Ø (so minty cool) (through and through)] (it) (tastes) (so great [(you) ('ll) (just) (love) [(to chew) (it)]]]]

While this grammatical structure encourages a pause between 'through' and 'it', the rhyming of 'through it' and 'chew it' forces the two words together. As each line in the music is followed by a pause, the subject of the sentence 'it' is left doubly suspended, held back from its predicator by both rhythm and rhyme. The fourth line thus effects a sudden and swift loosening of tension, creating an effect of 'arrest' and 'release' (Sinclair 1966). In this case the hold is not only grammatical, but also musical and phonological, for the music and rhyme delay the completion of the grammatical unit, which, when it comes, is accentuated by the resumption of the rhythm, leading to the acceleration of the double beat on 'JUST LOVE'. The effect is also pictorial – and this again illustrates the dangers of analysing the words of ads without their images – for the scene changes smartly at line endings. Both versions use a succession of incidents involving young men and women sharing sticks of gum (and perhaps by implication each other). Relationships are ambiguous, as a member of one couple smiles at, kisses, or offers gum to a member of another couple, or a single young woman is seen with a group of young men, bestowing a kiss on the one who gives her a stick of gum. In both ads using this jingle, the transition from line 3 to line 4 is matched by a camera shift, so that the last 'releasing' line accompanies an image of the final young woman flirtatiously folding and inserting a stick of gum slowly into her mouth. The result is a unity in which music, images, prosody, grammar and acting come together to produce a powerful and successful ad.

The effect of a jingle is achieved through a combination of words, images and music, rather than, as in written poetry, through the interplay of the lineation, implied pronunciation and linguistic structure. The jingle is a genre in its own right, rather than one which attempts to emulate another, like ad poems. For this reason perhaps it lacks the pretentiousness of such attempts at poetry as the Armitage Shanks ad.

6.1.4 Borrowed songs

The borrowing of songs is far more common than the borrowing of poems. Following the success of the 501 ads of 1985 onwards, there has been a spate of ads using the pop songs of earlier decades. Economically, the relationship is symbiotic, for the song is often re-released, and sells successfully once again. Choices are occasionally based on meaning, creating a pun ('Let Me Wrap You in My Warm and Tender Love' for a wool ad), or, more frequently, on mood.

6.1.5 The prosodic ad

We have examined two opposite cases. One is the unpretentious jingle, relying heavily on music and pictures, whose words are heard but not seen, but which can nevertheless make skilful use of the sound patterning of words. The other is the ad whose words attempt to stand on their own unaided by music or image, inviting comparison with poetry by linear layout. Between these two poles is a third category I shall refer to as **prosodic ads**. These are magazine or poster ads which superimpose short copy on to an image, arranging it, like poetry, in lines which suggest some correspondence between these graphological units and spoken units when the ad is read aloud, or pronounced as internal 'sound-images'. Such ads cannot, by definition, exploit the speech, music and moving images of the tv ad. They are bound to a still photograph and the written word; yet they do not attempt to divorce the two.

An example of this category is the ad for *SHE* magazine in Figure 40.

SHE
is a woman and a lover
SHE
is a worker and a mother
SHE
is the magazine for women who juggle their lives
SHE
is changing . . .

The accompanying picture shows a young woman in four situations: on her own, in evening dress with a man, at work with a Filofax and holding a baby. Each 'SHE' is written in letters eight times the size of those in the other words. When read aloud – or to oneself – the words fall into a regular rhythmic pattern emphasized by the line changes.

Figure 40 SHE magazine ad

```
    /      ˘     ˘          /      ˘      ˘      ˘         /     ˘
  SHE
         is     a     WO   man   and    a        LO    ver
  SHE
         is     a     WOR  ker   and    a        MO    ther
  SHE
         is    the    MA   ga    zine   for      WO    men
who JU
              ggle their   LIVES
  SHE   is                 CHANGing . . .
```

Lines 1, 3 and 6 are a single powerful stressed syllable (echoed in the layout by the large lettering and being on a separate line). The alternating lines 2, 4 and 5 are two identical metrical units: two unstressed, one stressed, and a further unstressed syllable (˘˘/˘). In traditional prosody, the conclusion of a line with an unstressed syllable is known as a **feminine ending**. (A **masculine ending** is one whose last syllable is stressed.) Words in parallel position in this metrical scheme are brought into contrast with each other, and this parallelism is further emphasized by a number of phonological repetitions. 'Woman' and 'worker' both occur in the same metrical slot and both begin with /w/; 'lover' and 'mother' also occur in parallel metrical slots and have the same vowels: /ʌ/ /ə/. All four words are disyllabic with an initial stress. The harmony of this prosodic parallelism iconically represents the meaning of the ad, for what is claimed in these lines is that a woman can reconcile these traditionally incompatible roles: femininity and a career, maternity and romance. This apparent feminism is, however, undermined by the order of both the words and the rhythm. The strong ('masculine'?) metrical unit occurs first ('SHE'), but each line finishes with a less emphatic and more delicate ('feminine'?) unit. This retreat is paralleled in the order: first 'woman' then 'lover'; first 'worker' then 'mother'. Despite the claim to a balance between roles, it is the traditional ones which are finally settled upon, both rhythmically and semantically. In the ideology of this ad, a woman should start life as a woman and a worker, but finish as a lover and a mother.

A further example of this category is the ad for Elizabeth Taylor's Passion (discussed in section 4.4.1). Its prosody is as remarkable as its graphological shape, for when spoken it forms four **amphibrachs** (a metrical unit consisting of one stressed syllable with an unstressed syllable on either side) as follows:

```
                 ˘        /          ˘
               be    TOUCHED   by
               the     FRA     grance
               that   TOUCH    es
               the     WO      man
```

This rhythm moreover mimes that of the product name, which is also amphibrachic

e	LIZ	a
beth	TAY	lor

Nor is this patterning unconnected to the meaning, for the repetition of the rhythm of the name in the rhythm of the copy echoes the theme of reflection and contemplation of the self in this (and many other) perfume ads. The succession of amphibrachs creates a further icon of reflection, for they are the same backwards and forwards, and a succession of four means that the second half of the copy is a mirror image of the first

$$\quad \text{♩}_\smile \qquad \text{♩}_\smile \quad - \quad \text{♩}_\smile \qquad \text{♩}_\smile \, .$$

A similar prosodic symmetry, together with a pictorial evocation of self-contemplation, is attempted, rather less successfully, in the Tsar ad (see Figure 32)

/	‿	/	/	‿	/
VIVRE	en	TSAR	EST	un	ART

The identification of such prosody, and its interaction with graphology, music, images, grammar and meaning, raises the issue of the degree to which such devices are used consciously and intentionally by the advertiser. A common reaction to such analyses is to say that they 'read too much into it', or that 'the advertiser could not possibly have meant this'. Yet there is no reason why such formal patterning should be any more conscious or intentional in poetry than in advertising. There need be no claim in the analysis of formal patterns that these were either fully recognized or intended by the creator. In discussion of poetry, the reader-response critic Stanley Fish (1980) argues that such patterns as alliteration are not features of the text, but features of the reading: they come into existence only through such analyses. This argument leaves two important issues out of account. One is the degree to which such patterns can be perceived at some tacit or unconscious level; the other is the degree to which all member of a speech community read in a similar and predictable manner. Whatever differences may exist between members of an English-speaking community in ideology and experience, there is considerable homogeneity in word stress (despite well-documented differences). Most English speakers would stress the texts analysed above in the same way (saying LOver and not loVER for example). The rhythm suggested by a written text is thus far more predictable, and far less individually variable, than such aspects of language as connotation or pragmatic function. Prosody has an objective quality; it is a feature of text as well as of reading.

6.2 ROMAN JAKOBSON'S POETICS

At a conference in Indiana in 1958, the linguist Roman Jakobson (1896–1982) summed up a view of literature which – whether accepted or rejected – has exerted a profound influence upon the relationship between poetics and linguistics ever since.[2] Using a model of communication similar to that in section 1.0, but with text at its centre, he proposed that language has a number of macro-functions, each with a 'set' towards one element of communication as follows[3]

Element	*Function*	
addresser	emotive	(expressing feelings and states)
addressee	conative	(influencing behaviour of addressee)
world	referential	(imparting information)
channel	phatic	(checking or establishing contact)
code	metalingual	(negotiating or checking the language)
form	poetic	(foregrounding linguistic structures)

It is the poetic function which is of particular importance for the linguistic study of literature, and is also relevant to the study of ads. When this function is dominant, each linguistic unit is effective not only for its meaning (its semantic reference to the world, and its difference from other units which could have been chosen in its place) but also for the patterns it makes – or breaks – in its formal relationships (of grammar and sound) to other units. Thus the arbitrariness of the sign is partially suspended; each signifier is important not only for its relation to its signified, but also for its relation to other signifiers. This may depend on quite specific and superficial features: whether two signifiers rhyme, for example, or whether two sentence structures are the same.

If meaning is equivalence, then this concentration on linguistic form for its own sake, rather than only to stand for something else, creates a new kind of 'meaning'.

> The poetic function projects the principle of equivalence from the axis of selection into the axis of combination.
>
> (Jakobson 1960)

In this view the 'meaning' of a poetic message is not wholly embraced by paraphrases and translations which are regarded as semantically equivalent. It is inseparable from the message's unique graphological, phonological, grammatical and lexical structure. 'Meaning' is not to be found somewhere else at all – which is the usual idea of theories of meaning – but in, and only in, the message itself.

6.2.1 Parallelism

Let us look at an extract from a literary text with particularly salient parallel linguistic structures: a stanza of Oscar Wilde's *The Ballad of Reading Gaol*

Yet each man kills the thing he loves
By all let this be heard
Some do it with a bitter look
Some with a flattering word
The coward does it with a kiss
The brave man with a sword

To a degree the 'meaning' is shared by a paraphrase such as

I'd like everyone to know that in a manner of speaking everybody destroys the object of their affection, either openly with violence, or in an underhand way with flattery and hypocrisy.

Although a paraphrase may set up new formal relationships of its own (which may also be deemed poetic), no paraphrase maintains the unique relationships of the signs within the original: the graphological layout in lines as a stanza; the iambic rhythm of the alternating eight- and six-syllable lines ($\int\int\int\int \int\int\int$); the rhyming of 'heard', 'word' and their eye-rhyme with 'sword'; the alliteration of 'coward' and 'kiss'; the grammatical parallels of the lines

S/NP	P/VP	Od/NP	A/PP	o/NP
(Some)	(do)	(it)	(with	(a bitter look))
(Some)	Ø	Ø	(with	(a flattering word))
(The coward)	(does)	(it)	(with	(a kiss))
(The brave man)	Ø	Ø	(with	(a sword))

All these formal parallels emphasize semantic parallels and antitheses. The equivalent phonological and grammatical positions of

bitter look
flattering word
a kiss
a sword

emphasize their shared semantic role: that they are all instruments of destruction.

6.2.2 Deviation, foregrounding, compression, representation

In Jakobson's view such parallels are the hallmark of the poetic message. They entail four further characteristics: deviation from normal usage, foregrounding, compression of meaning, and representation. (I shall return critically to the notions of deviation and normality at a later point, but accept them as unproblematic for the moment.) If we take non-prosodic text as the norm, then the syntactic reorderings and unusual paradigmatic choices needed to create the rhythms and rhymes of verse are also likely to create deviant grammatical structures and lexical combinations. In non-prosodic English speech, though the beat falls regularly, the number of unstressed syllables between stresses is irregular; in most English verse, however, they are patterned.[4] Thus from the perspective of non-prosodic text, verse itself is deviant.

Parallelism and deviation cause the **foregrounding** of linguistic units, 'throwing them into relief' against either the background of the norms of the language of the whole or those established internally by the parallelisms within the text. The idea of foregrounding was first suggested by a group of literary theorists known as the Russian formalists (in the 1910s and 1920s) and further developed by the Prague School of Linguistics (1920s and 1930s). In both movements, Jakobson was a leading figure. The Russian formalists claimed that the distinctive feature of literature is its ability to **defamiliarize**, to make the reader see afresh experience which has become automatized. In the view of the Prague School, the function of foregrounding is to effect such defamiliarization. Deviant forms create compressed meanings, for they evoke both the form from which they deviate – present, as it were, as a ghost – and themselves. A Hopkins sonnet, for example, begins with the line:

I wake and feel the fell of night not day

The odd and ambiguous choice of 'fell' evokes more 'usual' variations on the phrase structure

(NP   (PP   (NP)))
the x   of   night

such as 'the black of night' or 'the dead of night', thus attracting their meanings to itself. But 'fell' also means 'a blow', 'an animal pelt', 'a moor' and 'cruel'. Phonologically, it parallels the verb 'feel'. The Hopkins line is deviant in two senses: it departs from set patterns, and it tolerates ambiguity.

The following poem by Malcolm Williams illustrates a different kind of deviation. Here the departures from expectation are syntagmatic rather than paradigmatic.

> Pipe Song
>
> Plant, Spirit,
>   In me your power.
> I suck burning
>   From the bowl of a pipe,
> And blow clouds of smoke

> From my mouth,
> And see with the eye of
> Leaf buds, grass shoots.
> I enter your world.
> Enter mine.

In any poem, each line is both an autonomous unit, and also part of a longer grammatical unit which may continue into the next line. Each line is thus complete and incomplete simultaneously, and this often creates conflicting interpretations. In the opening line of this poem, 'Plant' and 'Spirit' can each be read as noun or verb, depending on how one reads on into the next line. There are four possible readings, equivalent to

1	Voc NP	Imperative VP	PP		
	(Oh Plant)	(spirit)	(in me) . . .		
2	Imperative VP	Voc NP	PP		
	(Plant)	(Oh spirit)	(in me) . . .		
3	Voc NP	Voc NP	PP	VP	NP
	(Oh Plant)	(Oh Spirit)	(in me)	(is)	(your power)

with 'is' ellipted.

4	Voc NP	Imperative VP	Imperative VP	A/PP	Od/NP
	(Oh you)	(<Plant	and spirit>)	(in me)	(your power)

with 'Oh you' and 'and' ellipted. In the third line, 'I suck burning' can be interpreted as

S/NP	P/VP	Od/NP
(I)	(suck)	(burning)

or as

S/NP	P/VP	C/NP
(I)	(suck)	(burning)

In other words as 'I suck something which is burning' or 'I suck and I am burning'.

S/NP	P/VP	Od or C/NP
(I)	(blow)	(clouds of smoke)

can be interpreted as in

S/NP	P/VP	Od/NP
(I)	(blow)	(bubbles)

in which case the blower stays still and the clouds move, or as in

S/NP	P/VP	C/AjP
(the wind)	(blows)	(cold)

in which case the speaker has become or feels himself or herself to have become part of these clouds.[5] The words 'buds' and 'shoots' may be read as either nouns (when taken with the line before) or verbs (when the line is read in isolation).

These formal ambiguities multiply and compress the possible textual meanings of the poem. They are all encoded (see section 4.1.1) and may affect any literate speaker of English – even if he or she cannot describe them grammatically. Interpretations, varying from one speaker to another, will multiply these meanings considerably. For this reason any paraphrase must be both longer than the original and incomplete. Textual deviation may also add to meaning through **representation**, in which form imitates its reference or refers to itself (Widdowson 1984b; 1992). If we assume 'Pipe Song' to be about the smoking of marijuana (rather than just tobacco), the ambivalence of the word classes and functions contributes to the communication of this. Clumsily paraphrasing, the speaker is also in a state of flux and loss of identity. Subject and object, process and entity, doer and done to, all fuse. The poem does what it means. Representation is a kind of iconicity. In a simple form it is often found in graffiti:

I can't spel

I used to be able to finish things but now I . . .

The form of the signs resembles their conventional meaning.

Formalist and stylistic criticism often assumes without much debate that compression of meaning through parallelism, deviation, foregrounding and representation is a virtue in itself. Yet there is no necessary correlation between devices creating a density of meaning and positive evaluation. This is the major, if often unaddressed, problem for stylistics. In poetry, quite as much as in music, value and formal complexity have no necessary connection. While the exegesis of formal complexity seems to explain the power of a poem, and thus satisfies the critic who cannot tolerate the unexplained, there are many poems whose power does not yield in this way. Advertising further disrupts this approach, in that it often has the same formal complexity as lyric poetry, but its evaluation by the critical establishment is quite different.

6.3 PARALLELISM IN ADS: AN EXAMPLE

Parallelism may be not only graphological, phonological (i.e. prosodic) and grammatical, but also semantic and discoursal. These different levels of parallelism may coexist in a single text. In the opening line of the ad for Sunny Delight orange juice (Figure 41), for example, there is graphological parallelism between the phrases 'Good Mother' and 'Great Mom' because both use the same word-initial capitals (a repetition which could be perceived even by someone who knew neither English nor the Latin alpha-

Figure 41 Sunny Delight orange juice ad

'I FOUND A WAY TO BE A GOOD MOTHER AND STILL BE A GREAT MOM.'
Every time you buy Sunny Delight, you win two ways. You're still a good mother because you're giving your kids something healthy. Plus, they'll think you're great because they're getting something delicious. Kids love the refreshing taste of orange, tangerine and lime. You'll love the vitamins they get in every glass.

bet). There is also phonological parallelism because, when spoken, both phrases repeat sounds in the same sequence: \g\ \m\ \g\ \m\. There is lexical parallelism: 'great' is a synonym of 'good' and 'mother' of 'mom'. (Denotationally equivalent, the phrases 'Good Mother' and 'Great Mom' can be distinguished only by connotation, or discoursally, in terms of who would use them to whom in what situation.)

Both in this opening line and in the remaining copy, there are grammatical parallels. The copy has five parallel constructions. (In the following analysis only elements in parallel are labelled grammatically.)

```
1.   S/NP    P/VP    Od/NP   RCl    P/VP          C/NP
     (I)    (found)  (a way  [      (to    be)    (a Good Mother)])
and   Ø       Ø      (Ø  Ø  [(still) (Ø    be)    (a Great Mom)])
```

```
2.              S/NP    P/VP
Every time      (you)   (buy)    (Sunny Delight)
                (you)   (win)    (two ways)
```

```
3.              S/NP    P/VP
                (You)   ('re )   (still) (a good mother)
because         (you)   ('re giving )    (your kids) (something healthy)
```

```
4.              S/NP    P/VP
Plus,           [(they) ('ll think)      [(you) ('re) (great)]]
because         [(they) ('re getting)    (something delicious)]
```

```
5.   S/NP       P/VP            Od/NP
     [(Kids) (   love)          (the refreshing taste (of (<orange,
                                tangerine and lime>))]
     [(You)  ('ll love)         (the vitamins [(they) (get) (in
                                (every glass)])]
```

These grammatical equivalences are reinforced by lexical repetitions, for the second of each pair of structures repeats, in the same grammatical slots, some of the words of the first: 'be' in 1, 'you' in 2, 'you' in 3', 'they' in 4, 'love' in 5. The effect, as in *The Ballad of Reading Gaol*, is to create equivalence of meaning between those units which are lexically different, but occur in the same grammatical positions:

to be a Good Mother	=	to be a Great Mom
buy Sunny Delight	=	win two ways
being a good mother	=	giving your kids something healthy
they think you're great	=	they're getting something delicious
the refreshing taste of orange, tangerine and lime	=	the vitamins they get in every glass

There are also two discoursal parallels. The first is between the mother in the picture and 'you' the reader. She is for this reason black in a magazine whose readership is black (*Ebony*), and she looks directly out of the page. A second discoursal parallel is between two ways of perceiving a relationship: with regard to people outside, or with regard to people inside it. (A similar dual perspective on a relationship occurs in the Wrigley's 'Last stick' ad in section 3.3.2.) In the first perspective, being a mother is a position in society; in the second, it is a relationship with one's child(ren).

6.4 THE PRODUCT AS A FUSION OF PUBLIC AND PRIVATE

The product as a mediator between public and private is common in ads targeted at women, for it promises reconciliation between the apparently rival claims of femininity and feminism. The *She* ad in section 6.1.5 and the Seat ad in Exercise 5.5 are further examples. Their parallelism at many levels represents this message of reconciliation, for its linguistic harmony suggests the social harmony it claims to offer.

The fusion of public and private can also be expressed more directly. An outrageously illogical – and for that reason amusing and memorable – example occurs in an ad for Charnos lingerie (Figure 42).

A sophisticated young woman is seen in a café in France, a moment after confidently sending back her order – the waiter can be seen departing in the background. The copy reads:

> What gave her the nerve to send back her espresso? Was it her underwear?

and underneath

> Be bold in Fever. A sultry range of lingerie. Try it on. With Charnos.

Inset in the corner is a photograph of the same woman reclining with a self-contemplative air in a black lace bra and pants.

In this ad, what is traditionally important in the sexual sphere suddenly becomes important in that of the public service encounter, though it remains unseen and irrelevant.

The fusion of these two spheres in representations of women is prevalent in many other contemporary discourses besides advertising: in the stage acts of Madonna, for example, or, as MacCannell (1987) observes, in the name of the popular tv sexologist, Doctor Ruth:

> a name which perfectly embodies a contradiction of scientific formality and informal familiarity, a name ideally suited to a female eunuch, which is the only possible cultural figure that could be empowered with the capacity for unrestrained sexual discourse.
>
> (MacCannell 1987: 259)

As a general phenomenon this tension between public and private motivates the intense interest in the private lives of public figures. Each member of the British Royal Family, for example, is known for his or her position in the family and in the state. In all these cases the formal syntagmatic and paradigmatic relations are important. In the lingerie ad the punning 'try it on' enables the copy to refer to both spheres at once. Visually, Madonna departs from the syntax of clothing by appearing in a wedding veil and mini-skirt,[6] and 'Doctor Ruth' breaks a rule that the title 'Doctor', as a modifier, must modify a surname rather than a first name. All these are amusing departures from expectation. Princess Diana on the

What gave her the nerve to send back the espresso? *Was it her underwear?*

Charnos
LINGERIE

Be bold in *Fever*. A sultry range of lingerie. Try it on. With Charnos.

Figure 42 Charnos lingerie ad

other hand demonstrates conformity to both syntactic and paradigmatic rules, appearing in jeans or tiara in the appropriate surroundings, but never wearing both together.

6.5 DEVIATION IN ADS

Deviation assumes a norm – in language as anywhere else – and consensus about linguistic norms is as problematic as consensus about norms of behaviour. Is the standard against which deviation is measured that of some institutional but arbitrary authority? Or is it just the majority view? Neither possibility is straightforward. The acceptance of an arbitrary authority is susceptible to changes in political power, and assumes that there will be no conflicts between rival authorities. The argument that normal usage is that of the majority of speakers, however, soon becomes circular, for speakers of a language are defined as people who use the language in the 'normal' way. Language data, moreover, reveal divergences between what speakers do and what they say they do, suggesting that intuitions are not always the best indicators of what actually happens.[7]

There are also the dimensions of historical change, group and individual variations, and differences between discourse types. 'Normality' exists in the context of specific participants, a time, a place and a purpose. What is normal in one context may seem quite deviant in another. Yet, despite the absence of any rigorous definition of norm and deviation, or any indisputable method for identifying instances of them, it remains true that there is substantial agreement among speakers of a language about instances of both.[8] If there were not, communication would not take place. This misfit between theory and practice is no cause for alarm. It throws more doubt upon the validity of a descriptive method which insists on rigorous proof than it does upon the validity of the terms 'deviant' and 'normal', and it provides further evidence that what is most powerful and effective in language is also what is most indeterminate, variable and indefinable. The idea of linguistic deviation is still valid – despite the fact that all judgements are relative and open to challenge.

Deviation in advertising, as in any other discourse, may involve deviation from an external norm – however elusive – or from a pattern established within the text: **external deviation** and **internal deviation** respectively.[9] An instance of internal deviation in a text may conform to an external norm, and conversely an instance of external deviation may conform to an internal norm. In a text where every sentence is verbless the sentence with a verb stands out; in a similar way, there is nothing odd about one misspelt word in a text which is all misspelt. A third category of deviation is that which is relative to the conventions of a particular discourse type.

Yet all kinds of departure from the norm, if over-used, soon become coated with 'the glass armour of the familiar' (Shklovsky [1940] 1974: 68).

This phenomenon is especially pertinent to advertising, a genre where such external deviations as graphological innovation, misspelling, puns, ungrammaticality, sustained ambiguity and so on have become so expected that in a sense the most truly deviant ad is that which has no external deviation at all.

External deviation is frequent in ads at every linguistic level. Thus we find new words or phrases formed by **compounding** ('oatgoodness', 'fairy liquid'); **affixation** ('provodkative', 'cookability'); **clipping and blending** ('liquidarnosc', 'telecom', 'mucron'). At the grammatical level we find **functional conversion** in which a word of one class behaves as though it were in another ('A Kwik-Fit Fitter'; 'B&Q it'), and many syntactic constructions 'which cannot be generated by an English grammar but are nevertheless interpretable' (Widdowson 1972).

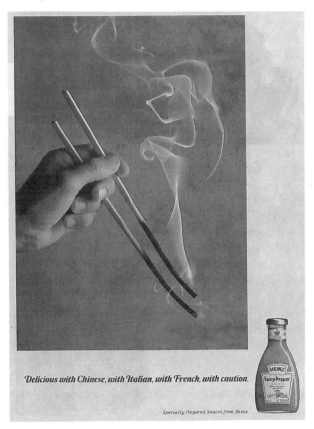

Delicious with Chinese, with Italian, with French, with caution.

Specially Prepared Sauces from Heinz

Figure 43 Heinz Spicy Pepper Sauce ad

Internal deviation also abounds. An ad for Heinz Spicy Pepper Sauce (see Figure 43) shows a hand holding two charred and smoking chopsticks over the copy

Delicious with Chinese, with Italian, with French, with caution.

Here the last word is foregrounded because the established pattern (with (x Ø)) (where x is an adjective denoting a nationality and modifying an ellipted head noun 'food') is broken by 'caution'. This example is also an instance of the figure of speech **syllepsis**

> in which one word is used in two senses within the same utterance and the effect is of putting together two co-ordinated constructions with ellipsis. It is frequently used with comic or satiric effect, eg 'She went home in tears and a sedan chair'.
>
> (Wales 1989: 445)

6.5.1 Foregrounding in ads: an example

The words of the P&O ad (already presented in Exercise 4.1.e, Figure 34) are

Lorries go
Drills go
Lambs go
Caterpillars go
Cargo
P&O

On tv, each of the first four lines is accompanied by an appropriate noise. This ad sets up a number of grammatical and semantic parallels which are broken in the last two lines, thus foregrounding the name of the ferry company P&O. The first four lines all have the grammatical structure

NP + VP

the VP being the same verb ('go') in all cases. 'Go' is a pun meaning both 'make a noise' and 'travel/are transported'. The first meaning is suggested by the sounds which accompany each shot. It is a meaning restricted to discourse of, or for, small children – 'Cows go moo', etc. The second comes into being retrospectively when the receiver realizes that this is an ad for a ferry company – and this double meaning will then operate on subsequent viewings. The nouns all refer to entities which make noises, and which also might be transported by a Scottish ferry service. They also fall into two broad semantic categories: the inanimate and mechanical ('lorries', 'drills') or animate ('lambs'). 'Caterpillar' (itself a dead metaphor when applied to a vehicle) can be either. This ad is parasitic on the discourse types of child's game or rhyme, in which the reactivation of the literal meaning of 'caterpillar' is quite appropriate. In this context, the fifth line 'cargo' lends itself to an initial and disturbing interpretation as a deviant (or child's) version of a sentence on the same pattern as the first four:

Cars go

A further step away from the pattern is

P&O

which, though it rhymes and has the same rhythm as 'Lorries go', cannot be interpreted as NP + VP. The name of the firm is thus not only foregrounded by its difference from, but also made equivalent to, the movement of lorries, cars, animals and machines.

6.6 JAKOBSON'S POETICS IN PERSPECTIVE

It has become fashionable to disown, criticize and even ridicule the Jakobsonian approach, and in particular the suggestion that parallelism and deviation are in any way peculiar to or characteristic of literary texts. Werth (1976) found parallelisms in a newspaper article on pest control, while Tannen (1989) observes that they are a recurring feature of conversation, political oratory and storytelling. They are also common in graffiti, songs and jokes (Cook 1989b). Conversely, there are many texts regarded as literary classics which manifest neither deviance nor patterning. Such criticism of Jakobson accepts the general idea of deviant and patterned language, while not accepting the claim that it is unique to literary discourse. A more radical attack denies that there are linguistic norms so independent of differences between speakers or situations that they can be treated as features of text. In this view, such features as alliteration may not *be in* the text but *read into* it, only becoming important if importance is attributed to them (Fish 1980). There is also the dimension of historical change. What can be said, in Jakobsonian terms, of the literariness of seventeenth-century verse, when it is encountered – as it often is – away from the context of the non-literary language of its period? Culler (1975: 113–30) argues that even in contemporary texts the perception of patterns and deviations may not be part of the linguistic competence of a native speaker, but a 'literary competence' dependent on education. As deviation often depends upon knowledge of different discourse types, it will vary with the reader's experience. Science fiction, for example, often plays off the 'plain' language of the scientific account against fantastic facts, in much the same way as some toothpaste ads invoke the language of empirical science.

Though all of these criticisms have their strengths, it is a tribute to the stature of Jakobson's approach that thirty years later it still continues to attract both flattering imitations and violent rejections, and to be at the centre of critical attention (Carter 1989: 1; Attridge 1989). Many criticisms, moreover, find their mark only by significant simplification of the original argument.[10]

The language of advertising – with its frequent foregrounding of parallelism and deviation – is a key exhibit in the case against Jakobson, and its status as evidence has grown considerably since Jakobson's statement of 1958, made at a time when tv advertising was still in its infancy.[11] The issue is complicated by the tendency of ads to set up parallels, compressions and deviations, not only textually but also – increasingly – by cross-reference between text and pictures, situation, music and substance (see Chapters 2 and 3), although this use of non-linguistic features can be viewed as an extension rather than an abandonment of such techniques (Durand 1987; Forceville 1990).

The problems which advertising poses for the Jakobsonian approach are formidable, but not catastrophic. His methods may be combined with, rather than substituted for, the study of context. There is more to literary discourse than textual complexity, but that does not mean that textual complexity does not also play a part. If the poetic function is present in other discourse types, this does not mean that it is not relevant in litera-ture. Advertising may share some aspects of this feature with literature but lack others and have still others peculiar to itself. Nor do exceptions undermine a general characterization of the prototypical literary text.

One way around the definitional impasse would be to drop the claim that literature is characterized by formal features. Another would be to admit certain ads – or even advertising in its entirety – to the status of literature. But this is playing with definitions in a way which departs radically and unusually from normal usage (Cook 1988). Whatever may be understood by the term 'literature', ads are not included in it, and though they may tickle they do not attract the same acclaim. But they do not necessarily undermine all attempt to characterize literature in terms of its language. Ads are a parasite discourse which has attached itself to literary discourse (among other types) as a host. The indefinable function of literature, its adaptability and range, and the number of literature graduates and aspiring writers in creative departments of advertising agencies, all make this inevitable. But the reasons for the continuing exclusion of advertising from literature lie more in the reader than in the text. However poetic advertis-ing language may be, many people prefer to deny its 'poetic licence', emphasize its conative function, and continue to criticize it as though it were purely referential: presenting facts whose truth, unlike those of poetry, can be checked.

EXERCISES

1 Part of the poem in section 6.1.2 is by Auden, another part is written for the ad. Is it possible to tell which part is which? If so, how? Would your judgement of the original poem be different if Auden had not written it for the ad?

2 Identify and evaluate the parallelism, deviation, compression and rep-resentation in the following:

   a Beanz Meanz Heinz.

   b X'ia X'iang
       To travel forward to the past

To allow what is forbidden
To obtain that which is elusive

c   The see-sawing sea (Dylan Thomas)

d   The woods are lovely, dark and deep,
But I have promises to keep,
And miles to go before I sleep,
And miles to go before I sleep. (Robert Frost)

e   You may not cross the Volga's might
Nor hear the boatman's lusty cry,
But you can still experience
The true spirit of Russia.
Stolichnaya vodka.

f   (opposite a red image of a woman and perfume bottle)
Born to reveal
the woman you've become.
Not just a perfume
a rite of passage.
Valentino

3   Do you think the following is
   • part of an ad.
   • a poem by William Carlos Williams.
   • neither.

Why?

I have eaten
the plums
that were in
the icebox
and which
you were probably
saving
for breakfast

Forgive me
they were delicious
so sweet
so cold

FURTHER READING

The original formulation of Jakobson's theory can be found in his (1960) 'Concluding statement: linguistics and poetics'.

Two useful introductions to linguistic approaches to poetry are Leech (1969) *A Linguistic Guide to English Poetry* and Widdowson (1975) *Stylistics and the Teaching of Literature*.

An excellent discussion and demonstration of the dependence of poetic text on specific surface choices, together with practical exercises and suggestions for the teaching of poetry, can be found in Widdowson (1992) *Practical Stylistics*. Arguments against the stylistics approach can be found in Fish (1980) *Is There a Text in This Class*. The two sides, and the whole issue of the application of linguistics to literary analysis, are very well discussed in Chapters 2, 3 and 7 of Jefferson and Robey (1986) *Modern Literary Theory: A Comparative Introduction*. A stimulating book on parallelism of all kinds in non-literary discourse, especially conversation and political rhetoric, is Tannen's (1979) *Talking Voices*.

7 Connected text

7.0 CONNECTIVITY IN DISCOURSE

Some linguists confine their studies to the formulation of rules for the selection and combination of units below the sentence. They regard the sentence as the upper limit of linguistic enquiry on the assumption that rules governing the combination of sentences – if they exist at all – must make appeal to areas other than the linguistic: the shared situational, cultural and world knowledge of the participants. When this is taken into account, the perception of connections between sentences varies from participant to participant – what appears connected to one speaker may not appear so to another – so *both* language and participants must be described. The resultant proliferation of variables has led some linguists to the hasty conclusion that there are no rules above the sentence, while others have attempted to extend to discourse the kind of rules which apply within sentences, but are quite alien to the open, context-dependent and indeterminate nature of discourse. The idea that discourse may be governed by factors which vary between people and places is quite alien to 'scientific' linguistics. Ironically, the 'harder' natural sciences and mathematics, from which it derived its approach, have more easily accepted relativity.

The most productive view is one which steers between the extremes of abandoning discourse as a realm of impenetrable anarchy, and one which tries to colonize it with sentence grammar. The 'rules v no rules' debate is unhelpful. In discourse analysis, the notion of 'rules', in the sense of dictates and restrictions on choices and combinations which constitute a language, is best replaced by that of 'regularities': probable choices and combinations which can be related to specified participants and discourse types, but are always prone to innovation and extension. The distinction between rules and regularities, however, is a fuzzy one. It is not that there are regularities above sentence level and rules below it; rather, that this point in the linguistic hierarchy marks a radical change in the degree of flexibility. Like discourse, grammar is also subject to contextual variation and change over time – though less evidently than discourse.

Phonological and syntactic parallelism is one kind of connection between sentences which can be described in purely formal terms, without appeal to semantic reference or pragmatic context. For this reason it is often overlooked in descriptions of **cohesion** (formal connections between sentences in a text) which appeal to semantics. The fact that the connection through parallelism is one of surface form rather than of logic or underlying meaning, dependent on coincidences between signifiers rather than between signifieds, does not endear it to the 'scientific' approach (for which 'cat' and 'bat' are alike because they are mammals rather than because they rhyme, and certainly have nothing to do with 'hat'). Parallelism retains a child's inability to separate signifier from signified (Vygotsky [1934] 1962: 223) or the approach to language of a pre-literate pre-scientific culture, where it is often used (and presumably needed) as a mnemonic.[1] In pre- or recently literate cultures the signifier is held in greater esteem (the name of a god, the words of a spell) than in a literate culture, where, with the exception of taboos on certain words in particular spheres (such as sex, excretion and death), the signifier is often regarded as mere packaging for a 'fact', which can be disposed of once opened. Consequently, though parallelism continues to exert its power in poetry and song, it is often disdained in a scientific culture, and associated with 'lower' discourse types. Even in literary discourse, it is regarded as insufficient to warrant acclaim for itself – hence the distinction between 'verse' and 'poetry'.

Though tolerated in fiction and poetry, parallelism is often regarded as deceptive in the treatment of 'facts', where it is perceived as a substitute for logic and reference to the world. In the popular view of a science-dominated culture, political rhetoric and advertising (two common non-literary sources of parallelism) are blamed for replacing facts with rhetoric (in the pejorative sense). Poetry has no facts to hide, and is forgiven. Yet the discourse of advertising and politics often has scant referential function. It is largely emotive, conative and phatic, using language to establish identity and differentiate that identity from others. The discourse of some sports competitors and their supporters is also of this kind, and the enthusiasm for it indicates a need. It may be reduced to a single message endlessly elaborated:

HERE I COME.

This is a phrase which Halliday (1975: 37) uses to characterize what he calls the Personal Function in the language of a child, but it is equally pertinent to some adult discourse too.

It is, as Goffman observes, equivalent to **display** in the animal kingdom:

the capacity and inclination of individuals to portray a version of themselves and their relationships at strategic moments – a working agreement to present each other with, and facilitate the other's presentation of, gestural pictures of the claimed reality of their relationship and the claimed character of human nature.

(Goffman [1976] 1979:7)

Like spells and prayers, display elevates a signifier – the name of a product, a team or a political party – above what it signifies. Though similar to the phatic function of language, it is nevertheless distinct from it; for, while phatic communication establishes and maintains relationships, the main purpose of display is to establish and maintain identity. Our harsh judgements of display might soften if we regarded it as akin to the ritual boasting of warriors – a genre which survives in the modern world in the pre-fight hype of boxing. If we despise such talk, we do so because we share the assumptions of our age and the elevation of fact and logic over other forms of truth. Incantation, bragging, name-calling, and the repeated patterns they engender, may have functions which we do not fully understand. The persistence of poetry and the burgeoning use of parallelism in ads – quite out of proportion to its conative or referential function – both testify to this possibility. Yet we should also notice that in the contemporary world participation in display is often passive and vicarious. We express our identity by accepting somebody else's product, political programme, sporting prowess or art, rather than by making our own.

7.1 COHESIVE DEVICES

Linguistic description of cohesion between sentences emphasizes semantic links. Units at any level between morpheme and clause may refer to the same entity, relation or process, or have some logical or sequential connection, indicated by such devices as

- the repetition of lexical items
- lexical items or phrases with some sense relation, e.g. hyponymy, synonymy, antonymy, etc. (see section 1.2.1)
- referring expressions (especially pronouns) understood by reference to a unit in another sentence
- ellipsis, in which an omitted unit is recoverable from a previous sentence
- conjunctions, (words and phrases which indicate a logical, temporal, causal or exemplifying relationship).

All of these cohesive devices are present in the words of a tv ad for Pretty Polly tights (set out here with each sentence on a new line for ease of reference).

1 In the 1930s one man touched the lives of millions of women.
2 He wasn't a film star or a singer but a scientist.
3 He invented nylon.
4 Yet two years later, beset with doubt, he took his own life.
5 Wallace Carothers dedicated his life to women.
6 Nylon by Wallace Carothers.
7 Nylons by Pretty Polly.

- **Repetition** the lexical item 'women' is repeated in 1 and 5, 'life' in 4 and 5, 'Wallace Carothers' in 5 and 6.
- **Sense relations** 'man' in 1, and 'film star', 'singer', 'scientist' in 2, are all related semantically by a single component of meaning: 'human'.
- **Referring expressions** The noun phrase 'one man' in 1 has the same reference as the chain of referring expressions ('he . . . he . . . he') in 2, 3 and 4. These pronouns refer back (**anaphorically**) to 'one man', and forward (**cataphorically**) to 'Wallace Carothers', and are continued by 'his' in 5.
- **Ellipsis** There are two instances: 'but ØHE ØWAS a scientist' in 2, and 'two years later ØTHAN ØTHE ØTIME ØHE ØINVENTED ØNYLON' in 3.
- **Conjunctions** 'but' and 'yet' are both conjunctions.

All these phenomena, which can be described without reference to non-linguistic context, give this text cohesion, and help to link the sentences within it together. Yet they do not account entirely for the perception of these sentences as coherent discourse, with meaning and purpose. This can be illustrated, by maintaining the cohesion, but making some other changes.

> In the 1870s one man touched the lives of sixty women. He wasn't a greengrocer or an astronaut but a stationer. He invented the paper clip. Yet two years later, tormented by mosquitoes, he took his own life. Harold Digby dedicated his life to women. The paper clip by Harold Digby. Paper clips by . . .

This passage does not make sense. Only lunatics and linguists invent such texts. But it does reveal a number of factors which establish coherence. So strong is our desire to *make sense* that, if it were encountered outside a book such as this one, the reaction would be to try to do so. When such attempts fail, and a text remains incoherent, even though the failure may be that of the receiver, its sender, as a last resort, is likely to be described as 'mad'.

Firstly, the ad assumes a great deal of cultural knowledge in the receiver. We know that stockings and tights are made of nylon, and that their use is widespread. We know that famous and successful male film stars and singers have female fans; that scientists can be successful too, but are considered less glamorous. We also know that scientists invent things; that the inventor of a successful product, because of patent laws, could become very wealthy; that wealth is desirable. Following from all this, it is surprising and unexplained (hence 'yet') that such a man should commit suicide. This factual gap, which maintains the interest of the text, may also activate a stereotype: the pauper inventor who foolishly sells a patent; the wealthy and successful person who is nevertheless miserable. The quantity of knowledge needed for interpretation is vast, and its boundaries indeterminate. This summary only skims its surface. Each assumption makes further assumptions, and depends on further shared knowledge for interpretation, thus revealing a paradox in the notion of communication as transferral of knowledge: communication can only take place where there is knowledge in common in the first place. It is impossible to say everything.

The text also establishes connections through surface form. 'Star', 'singer' and 'scientist' alliterate. There are lexical and grammatical parallels

S/NP	P/VP	Od/NP	
(one man)	(touched)	(the lives (of (millions (of (women))))	
(he)	(took)	(his own life)	
			A/PP
(he)	(dedicated)	(his life)	(to women)

suggesting, illogically, that these actions are in some way equivalent. 'Touched' – meaning both to move and to come into physical contact – is a pun. The second sense suggests the contact between nylon and skin. In the last two sentences, which adopt the verbless grammar of a title, parallelism is the ascendent means of connection, for the equivalent position of 'Wallace Carothers' and 'Pretty Polly' suggests that the latter has all the scientific genius, sensitivity, altruism and tragic glamour of the former.

7.2 PRAGMATIC PRINCIPLES AND COHERENCE

Coherence is the overall quality of unity and meaning perceived in discourse. Although aided by cohesion, and almost always accompanied by it, it is not created by it (as the incoherent version of the Pretty Polly ad illustrates) but depends upon other pragmatic factors. Before proceeding with a discussion of cohesion, let us consider some of these pragmatic factors, and how they influence the type and density of cohesive ties.

One of the standard explanations of how addressers organize text and how addressees perceive it as coherent – how in other words a text becomes discourse – is an appeal to theories of **conversational principles**. According to Grice ([1967] 1975) discourse is interpreted as though the speaker were following four maxims of a **co-operative principle**: to be true, clear, relevant, and as brief or as long as necessary. At times these demands pull in opposite directions, and one may oust another. They may also be flouted to produce a particular effect (irony, for example, flouts the truth maxim). Lakoff (1973) suggests a further **politeness principle**. Speakers follow three further maxims: to avoid imposing, to make their hearer feel good, to give him or her options.

The balance between the two principles changes with the purpose of the communication and the relationship between the participants. In interaction whose function is primarily phatic – to establish or maintain social relationships – the politeness principle may be uppermost. The desire to make someone feel good may win out over truth or brevity. (Consider how you would answer a host's question about a tasteless dish prepared in your honour.) The reverse holds where the communicative purpose is collaboration to effect some change in the social or physical environment. (Consider the same question when two chefs are making a joint entry to a competition, and trying to decide which dish to submit.)

Participant relationships also affect the balance between the two principles. (How well do you know your host? How touchy is the other competitor?) Where the relation is already established and secure, there may be less need for politeness strategies. This accounts for a similarity in behaviour in relationships of marked power difference on the one hand (say, police officer and suspect) and of equality and intimacy on the other (say, close friends or partners) (Wolfson 1988). Both generate bald statements and commands, physical proximity without apology, the broaching of intimate subject matter, interruption and abrupt topic switch.

Though the co-operative and politeness principles may be a cultural universal, there is considerable cultural variation in their manifestations, or the balance between their demands. Tannen (1984), for example, suggests that some cultures favour a 'high involvement' politeness, making the hearer feel good by taking interest in personal affairs, while others favour a strategy of non-imposition, making the former seem intrusive and the latter unfriendly when the two come into contact. Brown and Levinson (1978; 1987) suggest that while every culture recognizes territory on to which the polite person should not trespass without reason or redressive action, the nature of that territory may vary considerably from culture to culture. In different cultures, different emphasis is given to different types of territory: time, property, friendships, body functions, expertise, etc. These differences are a further source of cultural misunderstanding.

While the two conversational principles may well be culturally universal, they are not equally applicable to all discourse types. They belong very much to spoken phatic discourse in which relationships are neither of unequal power nor of great intimacy. Such civil relationships are of a kind so common in modern urban industrial democracies that Wolfson (1988) has termed them the 'bulge'. Yet, while such relationships may be numerous, they do not account for all interactions, nor for those which the participants themselves deem most important. A brief consultation with a doctor or a short exchange with a partner may well outweigh hours of civil intercourse in service encounters or the workplace. For discourse analysis, the easiest data to collect are from the bulge or from public interactions of differentiated power, such as legal proceedings, but a comprehensive approach to discourse, which is qualitative as well as quantitative, needs to consider intimate discourse too.

Neither advertising nor literature can be easily accounted for in terms of conversational principles. The relationship of addresser to addressee, and the purpose of the discourse are far removed from the phatic communication of the bulge. What is the truth, relevance, clarity, brevity or politeness of a novel or poem? The standards against which these questions can be answered are internal rather than external (Iago was lying, but within a fiction) and judgements by external measures can seem quite beside the point. Literature is both true and untrue, relevant and irrelevant, often economic in expression but also, by utilitarian yardsticks, superfluous. The relationship of addresser to addressee is simultaneously one of extreme distance – the author not even knowing his or her readers – yet one of extreme intimacy. Like the voice of a friend, the literary voice addresses us, not for some practical or social purpose, but sometimes to understand itself, or for the pleasure of talking. Both the subject matter and the language of literature are often those reserved for intimate relationships, and many people experience a sense of companionship and intimacy with their favourite authors.

Advertising shares – or attempts to share – many of these qualities. Admittedly, it usually has a clearer purpose than literature – to sell – and the information which it gives in pursuit of this aim may be judged by the standards of the co-operative principle as true, clear, brief or relevant. Yet factual claims and direct persuasion take up less and less space in contemporary ads. Attention is focused away from them to a world where questions of truth, relevance and politeness seem as beside the point as they do in literature. As advertising has matured, formidable restrictions have grown up alongside it, imposed by publishers, broadcasters, the law or advertisers' own organizations. If factual claims are untrue, the advertiser is held responsible. Ads are withdrawn, goods are returned; and, because literal untruth is also bad advertising, it is now shunned by advertisers quite as much as their moralistic critics. Of course, advertisers continue to use deceptive strategies for disguising or avoiding unattractive facts, for presenting descriptions in such a way that the inattentive may miss the bad aspects or imagine good aspects of a product. But these strategies are well known, over-analysed, and distract attention away from more powerful strategies. In many ads (perfume, chewing gum) there is no truth value to assess (Thompson 1990). In ads where there are 'facts' (about cars, insurance, orange juice) they are often far from the focus of attention. In the curtain track ad in Figure 44, for example, there is no reason to doubt that the product allows curtains to close smoothly – all its competitors probably do the same – but what is one to say about the truth or relevance of the story of the woman and her lover?

7.3 ECONOMIC EXTRAVAGANCE: COHESION IN ADS

Cohesive devices all serve the co-operative principle and vary with the emphasis on its four maxims. Repetition makes connections in text clear, though it may be at the expense of brevity; lexical cohesion may add new information economically while also aiding clarity; referring expressions

Superstyle Twin Track/Designers Guild Lichen-Buff

New Superstyle ready corded curtain track, unbeatable in a tight corner.

Whether you're in a tight corner or just playing it straight, fit Harrison Drape's new Superstyle ready corded track and you'll discover it has some unexpectedly handy features.

The unique beaded cord is remarkably strong and won't snag or jam even round tight corners.

With Superstyle's Masterglider the problem of getting corded curtains to meet perfectly in the middle is solved effortlessly, in seconds.

And with Superstyle Twin Track, a valance rail allows you to add a little extra style even in those awkward situations.

So, with Harrison Drape's Superstyle you can get in and out of the most tricky situations, with unashamed ease and style.

Harrison Drape

A McKECHNIE COMPANY

Figure 44 Harrison Drape Superstyle curtain track ad

are brief, though they may sacrifice clarity; conjunctions make connections clear, though they also increase length. Broadly speaking, where there is mistrust and/or an accompanying desire to minimize ambiguity, the truth maxim will be elevated over the clarity maxim. (Instruction manuals and legal documents favour repetition over referring expressions, in the belief that the latter, being more ambiguous, are conducive to misunderstandings and the construction of loopholes.) Where there is trust, where connections can be inferred or clarification obtained, brevity may be ascendant. Narrative thus often lacks the repetition, explicit connectives and density of conjunctions of legal and technical prose. Casual conversation is full of ellipsis – although this is balanced by conversation's own peculiar prolixity: apparently meaningless phrases designed to gain or hold turns, signal turn type or topic change, or simply gain the time necessary for the production and processing of speech (Levinson 1983: 284–370).

Where there is repetition or lexical cohesion which cannot be accounted for by the co-operative principle, it is often motivated by the politeness principle. An excess of language often indicates a sense of occasion, ceremony, respect or intimacy.

In referring to the product, or spheres it wishes to associate with it, advertising favours repetition over referring expressions. (Its idiosyncratic use of the latter is discussed in the next section.) In the curtain track ad, for example, in preference to 'we' and 'it', the name of the firm 'Harrison Drape' is repeated twice, the name of the product 'Superstyle' five times. One obvious function of repetition is to fix the name of the product in the mind, so that it will come to the lips of the purchaser lost for a name. But nominal repetition is also an index of rank, esteem, intimacy or self-confidence: consider the repetition of names in ceremonies, prayers, by lovers, or by arrogant individuals who just 'like the sound of their own name'.

Conjunctions are notoriously absurd in ads, and an easy target for analysts obsessed with demonstrating ads' illogicality. Commonly, conjunctions come, if at all, in the closing phrase, passing unnoticed (like Poe's purloined letter[2]) by their sheer blatancy and nerve:

So with Harrison Drape you can get in and out . . .

This use of 'so', however, exploits the ambiguity of the word; for, while, in written discourse, 'so' is often a synonym for 'therefore', in conversation – and the style of ads is conversational – it is only a filler, which holds or gains the turn for the speaker.

Many ads even start with a conjunction, elliptically referring to an inferred utterance such as 'Buy our product' or 'Use this'. An ad encouraging people to use seat belts said simply:

Because you know it makes sense.

Conjunctions, then, are used deftly, to omit that from which attention is best distracted, and maximize space for the overstatement of that for which attention is sought. The important and foregrounded fusion of product with user, situation or effect is more usually achieved through pun, connotation or metaphor, rather than through any logical or sequential connection in the world.

Lexical cohesion is used to allow fusion between the product name and other phrases, by treating them as though they were semantically related to it. It is a process which generates verbosity. Although ads pay for space and thus endure a discipline which can lead to economic and condensed expression, the lexical and phrasal chains in ads often appear extravagant and unnecessary:

Galaxy® Minstrels® chocolate
Silk with a polish. The rounded silk of smooth, creamy Galaxy® chocolate dressed in layer upon layer of chocolate shell. Coat after coat. Creating the softness of silk against the gentle crispness of chocolate shell. A delicate study in contradictions, Galaxy® Minstrels®.

Here there is nothing but the cohesive chain of noun phrases:[3] a seductively indulgent over-description whose excess iconically represents the luxury of eating the product, and successfully presents the nouns at the centre of the phrases ('silk', 'Galaxy®', 'coat') as equivalents, thus accruing the qualities of each other.

7.4 PRONOUNS IN ADS

A particular discourse type may have strong association with a particular type or density of cohesive ties. This does not mean they are definitive of that type, but only that they have an affinity with it.

One of the most distinctive features of advertising is its use of pronouns. In discourse in general, the third person pronouns may be either **endophoric**, referring to a noun phrase within the text – as 'he', for example, refers to Carothers in the Pretty Polly ad – or **exophoric,** referring to someone or something manifest to the participants from the situation or from their mutual knowledge ('Here he is', for example, on seeing someone who both sender and receiver are expecting). The first and second person pronouns are, other than in quoted speech, most usually exophoric (though they may be endophoric too, as in legal formulas such as 'I, Guy Cook, do hereby . . .'). Their exophoric reference is straightforward: 'I' means the addresser; 'you' the addressee.

Certain discourse types favour certain pronouns: diaries, for example, favour the first person; written narrative the first or third; prayers the second; scientific discourse the third – and so on. Ads use all three persons, but in peculiar ways. 'We' is the manufacturer; 'I' is often the adviser, the expert, the relator of experiences and motives leading to purchase of the product; 'he/she' is very often the person who did not use the product, distanced by this pronoun, and observed conspiratorially by 'you and I'; but most striking and most frequent, even in narrative, and most divergent from the uses of other discourse types, is the ubiquitous use of 'you'.

In face-to-face communication, 'you' assumes knowledge of the individual addressee. In printed and broadcast discourse, however, there are too many addressees to merit this personal and particular address. Before such use is condemned as superficial, it should be remembered that advertising shares this use of 'you' in displaced and disseminated communication with religious evangelism, official documents, political rhetoric, recipes, lyric poetry and songs. This similarity to the use of 'you' in other discourse types, however, may blind us to the particularity of 'you' in advertising.

The difference may be brought out by comparison with another discourse type. In songs, 'you' functions in a number of ways simultaneously. It is **multi-exophoric**, as it may refer to many people in the actual and fictional situation. Take, for example,

> Well in my heart you are my darling,
> At my gate you're welcome in,
> At my gate I'll meet you darling,
> If your love I could only win.
> (Traditional)

This is the plea of one lover to another. 'I' is the addresser, 'you' the addressee. But there are at least four ways of achieving specific reference for these pronouns. The receiver of the song is apparently overhearing one half of a dialogue. 'I' is the singer and 'you' is her lover.[4] Alternatively, and most frequently,[5] especially away from live performance, the receiver projects herself into the persona of the addresser and hears the song as though it is her own words to her own lover. Alternatively, the listener may project herself into the persona of the singer's lover and hear the singer addressing her. (Receivers are perhaps more prone to identify with singers of their own gender.) Lastly, but unusually, the pronouns of the song are interpreted as they would be in conversational face-to-face discourse: 'I' = the singer; 'you' = the addressee.

In another kind of song, still involving projection into the singer, the words are perceived as an externalization of an internal dialogue in which 'you' refers to the self:

> You load fifteen tons, what do you get?
> Another day older and deeper in debt.

The 'you' of ads, though also departing from conversational use, functions differently from either of these types of song. The tendency to project the self into the 'I' and address somebody else as 'you' is hampered by the frequent absence of 'I' and the clear address to the receiver. The 'you' of ads has a **double exophora** involving reference to someone in the picture (salient because pictures dominate words) and to the receiver's own self (salient because everyone is interested in themselves). The characters of ads sometimes look out of the picture (see Figure 41), making them both addressee and addresser. This double reference, originating in the text, encourages a completion of the triangle which effects a co-reference between the receiver and one of the people in the picture (Figure 45).

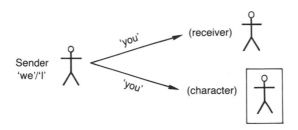

Figure 45 Double exophora of 'you'

This dual identity of 'you' is matched by the mysterious identity of 'I', which is not revealed. The visual presence of another person (the character) distracts from this absence, creating an illusion that the dialogue is between character and addressee.

In literary narrative, the reader may make a similar projection of the self into the pronouns 'he' or 'she' referring to one of the characters. The device of opening a narrative with a third person pronoun whose reference is unclear encourages such projection, for the character appears as *a* man or *a* woman rather than any specific person.

> He was working on the edge of the common.
> (D.H. Lawrence, *England, My England*)

> Now she sits alone and remembers.
> (Carlos Fuentes, *The Old Gringo*)

In lyric poetry third person pronouns can remain unspecified throughout ('She walks in beauty like the night') while the use of 'you' invites the same variety of interpretation as in pop songs. But these literary uses offer the reader both the option of involvement, projecting the self into characters, senders and receivers, and the option of detachment, interpreting any of the pronouns as referent to somebody else. Ads are more intrusive. Their 'you' is part of a high-involvement strategy which attempts to win us over by very direct address; they step uninvited into our world, expressing interest in our most intimate concerns.

7.4.1 The fusion of You and 'You': an example

The Harrison Drape Superstyle Curtain Track ad (Figure 44) is based upon an unusual and ingenious metaphor. The swift, smooth closure of well-tracked curtains resembles a deft, quick-witted and sophisticated act. By extension the owner of such curtains resembles the doer of such an act. In the picture the smart act, and drawing the curtains, are one and the same. The woman's dramatic tango-dancer pose, and her evident speed, suggest that she herself is like the curtains. (An elegant woman might also be draped in long dresses and swish by, though the woman here is in a short skirt).

These metaphors are sustained throughout the copy with words and phrases which can apply either to curtains (which exist both in the world of the picture and potentially in the world of the receiver) and to being caught with a lover (which probably – and no doubt regretfully for some prospective purchasers – exists only in the picture):

a tight corner
playing it straight
handy features
a little extra style
awkward situations
tricky situation
unashamed ease and style.

The only pronouns in this copy are 'you' and a single 'it' referring to the product. (The 'it' in the ready-made phrase 'playing it straight' refers to some vague concept such as 'life'.) 'You' refers to the addressee, the prospective purchaser, and also (by virtue of the double meanings listed above) to the woman in the photo: rich, quick-witted, hedonistic and enviably loved by two men. She also has the more easily imitated quality of having purchased Harrison Drape curtains. The text alone would refer to the reader's situation only. The picture creates an extra situation to which the text also refers. In some other discourses, 'you' refers simply to someone in the situation – but here there are two situations. 'You' refers exophorically both to the world of the picture, and to the situation of the receiver, and can thus refer to both the reader and the character at once. The conclusion (magical or superstitious) is that if two people are both referred to by one word ('you') they must both be the same person. This is not to say, however, that receivers are so gullible that they believe in the possibility of such a transformation, but that the ad allows them the pleasure of such a fantasy.

7.5 LEXIS, GRAMMAR AND COHESION IN INTERACTION: AN EXAMPLE

Part II has examined indeterminate and multiple meaning, parallelisms and cohesion. It is suitable to end this part of the book with an analysis which brings together these three areas of language, and the relation of

WALKING THE DOG-WITH A DASH OF PURE SMIRNOFF

SMIRNOFF
WHATEVER YOU DO WITH IT,
IT'S NEAT

Figure 46 Layout of Smirnoff vodka ad

language to pictures too, and illustrates the extraordinary complexity which brief advertising discourse can achieve.[6]

The ad we shall consider is for Smirnoff vodka. It is one of a series. Each ad begins with a different phrase.

WALKING THE DOG
MOWING THE LAWN
POOL SERVICE
BUILDING A SNOWMAN
CLEANING THE CARPET

but all continue with the words

WITH A DASH OF PURE SMIRNOFF
WHATEVER YOU DO WITH IT, IT'S NEAT (see Figure 46).

In each version, the photograph depicts an outlandish, futuristic image of the activity named in the opening phrase. 'Walking the dog' shows a fashionably dressed young man seated on a sheltered balcony, gazing out into torrential rain while his dog is exercised on an indoor electric walk machine; 'mowing the lawn' presents an aerial view of a woman with an outlandish hairstyle outstretched on a camp bed in the middle of a lawn that is being grazed by sheep; 'pool service' shows a couple relaxing on an inflated mattress in the middle of a swimming pool, while cocktails are sent to them on a radio-controlled model boat by a barman from the pool side; 'building a snowman' shows a couple relaxing in summer clothes inside, while outside snow falls to form the shape of a snowman as it settles on the branches of a tree which have been cut to create precisely that effect; 'cleaning the carpet' shows a man relaxing while a robot hoovers his carpet. Needless to say, in each variant the participants are drinking a cocktail containing Smirnoff vodka.

Underlying these apparently disparate images is a unifying theme. In each picture humans relax while a non-human agent (electricity, animals, radio waves, predicted natural forces, a computer) performs their work. This theme, creating fusion between the product and human technological ingenuity, is represented in the language of the opening phrases. All contain nominalizations of verbs:

	VP		NCl
somebody	(walks) the dog	*becomes*	[walking the dog]
	VP		NP
somebody	(serves) by the pool	*becomes*	(pool service)

This form eliminates or disguises the agent, thus echoing the pictures, where the human agent has also, in a different sense, been deleted.

The rhythm of the 'walking the dog' version is patterned. It can be read as six dactyls and one spondee (though there are alternative ways of stressing the second half).

WALKing the   DOG with a   DASH of pure SMIRnoff what
EVer you   DO with it   IT'S NEAT.

The multiplicity of meanings that can be generated by these sixteen words is vast.

To begin at the end: 'neat', has, in contemporary usage, at least three relevant meanings:

(a) undiluted (of liquids)
(b) smart, tidy (of physical entities, people, animals)
(c) elegant, sophisticated (of actions).

Confronted with this straightforward lexical ambiguity, the receiver may seek clarification from the 'it' (of 'it's'), of which 'neat' is the complement. The meaning of this 'it' should, in normal circumstances, define which meaning of 'neat' is operational. This 'it', however, is anaphoric, and presents a quadruple possibility of reference:

(i)   Smirnoff
(ii) the dog
(iii) whatever you do with the dog
(iv) whatever you do with the Smirnoff

of which (i) would suggest meaning (a) of 'neat', (ii) would suggest meaning (b), and (iii) and (iv) would suggest meaning (c). The situation is further complicated by the fact that the preceding 'it' (the first one) is also anaphoric, and presents a double possibility:

1 the dog
2 the Smirnoff

There are thus eight possible interpretations of 'Whatever you do with it, it's neat':

1 Whatever you do with the dog, the dog is neat.
2 Whatever you do with the dog, the Smirnoff is neat.
3 Whatever you do with the dog, that action is neat.
4 Whatever you do with the dog, what you do with the Smirnoff is neat.
5 Whatever you do with the Smirnoff, the dog is neat.
6 Whatever you do with the Smirnoff, the Smirnoff is neat.
7 Whatever you do with the Smirnoff, your action with the Smirnoff is neat.
8 Whatever you do with the Smirnoff, that action is neat.

If the ambiguity of the attribute 'neat' is included, and combined with these eight possibilities created by the anaphoric ambiguity of the two pronouns, no fewer than twenty-four possible interpretations will emerge – only some of which (such as 'the dog is undiluted') can be eliminated as nonsensical.

The receiver, having read the text once, is likely to re-read in a search for clarification[7] – which itself furthers the advertiser's aims. Instead of clarification, however, there is only mathematically multiplying possibility, in a bewildering land of stimulating linguistic uncertainty.

This uncertainty is further heightened by the first part of the text. The phrase 'with a dash of', in the context of discourse about alcoholic drinks, would normally have the meaning 'with a small quantity of another substance added for flavour':

1 (a drink)   with a dash of   (a liquid or substance)

where the names of the two must be different. This, however, contradicts the interpretation of 'neat' as 'undiluted', which seems, at first encounter, the most likely. If a drink has a small quantity of another substance added, then it cannot be 'undiluted'. So the combination of the two most likely meanings of the ambiguous terms 'dash' and 'neat' becomes conceptually impossible, and creates an oxymoron:

the diluted undiluted liquid

One possible answer to this problem is to select one of the other meanings of 'neat' or an alternative meaning of 'with a dash of' or both. We may choose to interpret 'with a dash of' in its nonphysical, more general sense (which is possibly derived from a metaphorical use of 'undiluted'), as in the phrase:

2 a holiday   with a dash of excitement
   (an event)   with a dash of (an abstract)

We may choose a different interpretation of 'dash', which also means 'a showy appearance or display', thus interpreting the phrase 'with a dash' positively as 'with panache' or 'with style', as in the sentence

3   he read the speech   with a dash
    (an action)   with a dash

'With a dash' seems to fuse the three possibilities:

(action)	with a dash of	(drink)
walking the dog	with a dash of	pure Smirnoff

This is disturbing, for it forces us to interpret either the Smirnoff as an action or abstract, or 'walking the dog' as a kind of drink. The result is a fusion between abstract and concrete, between action and substance. This is paralleled by the picture, in which a drink has indeed replaced an action.

All this affects the meaning of 'pure', caught up, as it were, in the crossfire between 'neat' and 'dash'. Qualifying the brand name of a spirit drink, it inevitably generates the meaning 'undiluted', a synonym of 'neat'. But, as the prime meaning of 'neat' has been interfered with, 'pure' inevitably goes with it. Like 'dash', 'pure' also has a non-physical and general meaning (deriving perhaps metaphorically from 'undiluted') roughly synonymous with 'simple' or 'unalloyed'. In this sense it often collocates with terms signifying emotions and concepts, as in 'pure delight', 'pure extravagance' or 'pure enjoyment'. The undermining of the prime meaning of 'neat' and the use of 'with a dash' to qualify an action rather than another drink is very likely to push the reader towards a partial inclusion of this meaning in the main one. The product becomes associated with emotions and concepts of an abstract, universal, positive and important nature, and is elevated into this realm. Through the creation of ambiguity, the violation and rewriting of usual combinations, Smirnoff vodka is pushed through the conceptual boundaries reflected in the language. It becomes not only an alcoholic drink, but an action and a concept as well.

Nor are these the only possible interpretations that might arise once the usual patterns of meaning have been disturbed and the receiver starts to seek, consciously or subconsciously, for new ones. 'With' can be interpreted either as 'in combination with' (as in 'with Uncle Bill') or as assigning an instrumental role to 'a drop of pure Smirnoff' (as in 'with an axe')

mowing the grass	with Uncle Bill
walking the dog	with a drop of pure Smirnoff

cutting up wood	with an axe
walking the dog	with a drop of pure Smirnoff

The second reading allocates the role of a tool (a technological innovation) to the drink, giving it the status of a feat of human ingenuity. A 'dash' could be interpreted as a punning reference to the text's punctuation, which connects the two noun phrases, rather unconventionally, with an orthographic dash. 'Neat' may be interpreted as (in addition to the three meanings listed above) 'well expressed, cleverly or smartly put or phrased',[8] thus making the first 'it' refer to the text itself. The second part of the slogan then becomes a self-congratulatory comment on the first:

whichever way you read this slogan, it (the slogan or your way of reading it) is clever.

Linguistically, then, the written text manifests a high concentration of 'deviation' and ambiguities. In the midst of the storm of linguistic and conceptual uncertainty created by this, it is worth noting that there is only one linguistic item whose reference is unequivocal: the brand name Smirnoff, which must become the starting point in any strategy of interpretation and to which readers – as they are of course intended to – may refer for clarification. The compression of language, the ability to yield many interpretations, the fusion of form and content allow the ad to make statements about its subject (Smirnoff vodka, technological innovation) which could not be expressed in any other way. The particular form of words mimes and reinforces the meaning, it represents it, indeed it *is* it. This is a kind of language associated with poetry, and it seems reasonable to me, in a general sense, to call this ad 'poetic'. Whether it is a valuable or appealing instance of poetic language is a matter of opinion.

EXERCISES

1 Look at the pictures for the Pretty Polly ad (Figure 47) and at the script for a later version of it. How is the meaning of the words affected by the pictures? Is it possible to talk about cohesion between text and picture?

VISION	SOUND
A photographer's studio, 1937. It is spacious and dramatically lit. The studio is propped with drapes and impressive, almost cumbersome, lights.	*MUSIC*: Ray Noble's 'The Very Thought of You'
The photographer is an elegantly dressed woman of about 30 years old. She is adjusting the camera, ready to take a shot of a man sitting in a chair. We do not really see him or his face.	IN THOSE EARLY DAYS, STILL LEARNING THE TRICKS OF THE TRADE, I TOOK A SHOT OF WALLACE CAROTHERS.

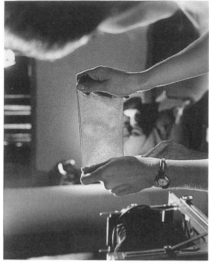

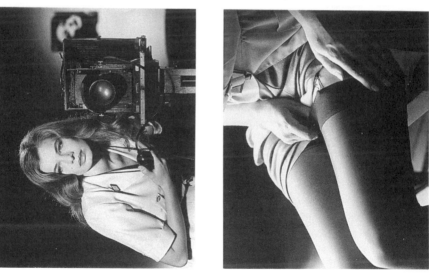

Figure 47 Pretty Polly nylons ad

She frowns, as if the setting is not quite right, after peering through the lens.	FOR A MAN WHO'D INVENTED NYLON, HE WAS SHY. . . FULL OF DOUBT.
Cut to her walking behind a screen. Smiling to herself, she takes off her stocking. Unravelling it, we see it's made of beautiful, sheer nylon.	I DON'T THINK HE EVER *REALLY* KNEW WHAT THOSE SOFT, SHEER NYLONS DID
Cut to her putting the stocking over the lens.	BUT I GUESS HE CHANGED A MILLION LIVES.
She takes the shot.	Click of camera.
End title: NYLONS NOW AVAILABLE FROM (PRETTY POLLY LOGO)	NYLONS NOW AVAILABLE FROM PRETTY POLLY

2 In this ad for the Saab 9000S identify links between sentences created by

- cohesive devices
- shared knowledge
- parallelisms.

It also leaves trees and forests standing.
Quietly nestled in the lush landscapes of Northamptonshire, lies the sleepy village of Silverstone. Every now and again however this wooded heaven is woken by the ear-splitting roar of its less tranquil neighbour. The famous Silverstone Circuit.

Yet for Saab, both provide the perfect surroundings for its latest green generation car. The new Saab 9000S 2.3. Out on the track the long-legged new 2.3 litre engine is able to flex its 150 bhp muscle. The car can demonstrate its controlled cornering, its swift, smooth and much safer overtaking, its higher torque. A powerful argument, the Saab 9000S 2.3.

But with power comes responsibility.

So the car leaves the circuit, and begins to weave its way more conservatively through the country lanes. This is where the ultimate green machine really begins to blossom.

A special 3-way catalytic converter removes a staggering 90% of harmful gases before they leave the exhaust pipe. That means no more unburned hydrocarbons, a dearth of deadly carbon monoxide, and far less nitrogen oxides – or nasty NOx as the environmentalists call it.

In other words, by driving a 'green' generation Saab, you'll actually be helping to stop the spread of acid rain across Europe. And the sooner that happens, the better.

3 Instead of merely repeating the name of the product, many ads refer to it in a number of different ways. What are the advantages of this for the advertiser? In an ad for rings, the following noun phrases were all used to refer to the product.

> The ring . . . this creation . . . a continuous band of 18 carat gold Forget-Me-Not flowers . . . the perfect eternity ring . . . a ring to treasure throughout a lifetime . . . a ring which binds your love . . . a ring to pass on to your loved ones . . . your ring . . . this fabulous piece of jewelry.

List the qualities claimed for the ring through this device.

4 Consider the use of referring expressions in the following. What is the cause of ambiguity? And what is its effect?

   a   (An ad for Mates condoms) 'My husband said Mates were for teenage sex. I said, when can we get some?'
   b   (An ad for Southern Comfort Bourbon, at the end of a film showing a young man and woman out on a romantic evening) 'Who are you mixing it with?'

FURTHER READING

The standard work on cohesion is Halliday and Hasan (1976) *Cohesion in English*; a shorter and slightly modified description is in Chapter 9 of Halliday (1985) *An Introduction to Functional Grammar*. Excellent and highly readable introductions to the theories of pragmatics referred to in this chapter are in Chapter 9 of Widdowson (1978) *Explorations in Applied Linguistics* and Chapter 8 of his (1984) *Explorations in Applied Linguistics 2*. 'Bulge theory', which deserves far more attention than it has received, is proposed in Wolfson (1988) 'The bulge: a theory of speech behaviour and social distance'.

Part III
People

8 Narrative voices

My face in thine eye, thine in mine appears
(John Donne)

8.0 INTRODUCTION

This section moves on from the materials and texts of ads to a consideration of the people who make them and the people who see them. The simple division into senders/addressers and addressees/receivers will now need elaboration, for there are many more distinctions to be made, to which these categories do not do justice.

It is important not to regard the three areas – materials, texts, people – as discrete, for each is better understood in conjunction with the others. People are the texts and materials they use; texts depend on materials and people; materials become significant when used by people to make texts. There is thus no clean break between this part of the book and the last one, but only a change of emphasis. In illustration of this, I shall begin, under the heading of 'people', with a re-examination of one element of cohesion
ellipsis – not this time in formal terms, but as an entry to the kind of participant relationships created by ads.

8.1 ELLIPSIS IN USE

As Chapter 7 has shown, ellipsis and other cohesive devices which serve the brevity principle allow the advertiser to achieve two commercially desirable effects: to save space where words cost money, and to avoid drawing attention to features of the message which do not serve the advertiser's interest.

An American ad for Cascade dishwasher detergent (Figure 48) exemplifies these reasons for economy. It shows three women sitting around a table, happily chatting, drinking white wine from spotless glasses. On the table is a vase of tulips, a white cloth, appetizers of fruit and cheese. The atmosphere is one of companionship, good humour, relaxation, cleanliness, luxury and harmony. The text reads:

Figure 48 Cascade dishwasher detergent ad

When Lisa made a surprise visit, you didn't have time to worry about spotted glasses. Fortunately, you didn't have to. Cascade. Because you don't have time for spots.

In the bottom right-hand corner, alongside the last two orthographic sentences, is a smaller picture, of a bottle and a packet of Cascade.

The second orthographic sentence contains ellipsis:

Fortunately you didn't have to   Ø   Ø   Ø   Ø
= Fortunately you didn't have to worry about spotted glasses.

with the ellipted elements corresponding to, and recoverable from, the preceding sentence. This is straightforward enough. Repetition of these elements would be quite superfluous; and, short of deliberate perversity, there is no room for misunderstanding what is omitted. The second instance of ellipsis, in the last two orthographic sentences, is complicated by unconventional punctuation. 'Cascade' (a single word) and 'Because you don't have time for spots' (a subordinate clause) are both presented as complete orthographic sentences. In the latter case, a main clause seems to have been ellipted in entirety:

[MAIN CLAUSE   [SUBORDINATE CLAUSE   ]]
[Ø Ø Ø . . .   [because you don't have time for spots]]

But the missing elements are by no means clear. One solution is to interpret the word 'Cascade' – despite its being marked off by a full stop – as part of that missing clause, and provide the other elements, creating perhaps

MAIN CLAUSE   SUBORDINATE CLAUSE
You ought to use Cascade
You ought to buy Cascade   because you don't have . . .
We recommend Cascade

In the age of the soft sell, such bald statements of purpose are avoided.

Though made much of by critics who believe in a gullible public, the two motives for ellipsis – to save space and omit direct appeal – are likely to be obvious in a general way to all participants, even when those participants cannot describe the phenomenon formally. Ads exist to sell, and every member of contemporary industrial society – other than very young children – knows this. Once an ad is identified, such conative components as 'buy our product' or 'we recommend that' are understood by default, and to condemn ads for omitting them is like criticizing a novel for not beginning with the words 'I have invented a fictional world which I should like you to share with me', or the writer of a tax demand for not saying 'It is my job to tell you that . . .'. We need to move beyond such criticisms, and consider the effect of such textual features as ellipsis on the relationship and identity of participants.

Besides economizing with words, ellipsis has other important effects, resulting from its association with particular discourse types, situations and relationships. Firstly, it frequently occurs in conversation and other face-to-face interaction, for the simple reason that failure to recover the missing elements can be remedied by a request.

A I think you ought to.
B Ought to what?
A Apply for the job.

Thus its frequent use creates a conversational tone. Secondly, it is associated with interaction in a situation which is mutually manifest to addresser and addressee.

A Scalpel!

It therefore suggests immediacy. Thirdly, it is indicative of shared knowledge and interests (as in both the above examples). Fourthly, it suggests a trusting relationship, in which people assume a desire to understand on the part of their interlocutor, and do not feel they need to spell out every detail legalistically. So its use can imply co-operation, informality, shared knowledge and intimacy.

The corollary of this is that, as these features diminish in communication, the more words we need to communicate. Participants need to make their discourse more explicit and complete. Lack of extensive ellipsis implies formality, social distance, or a lack of shared knowledge. This also applies to the use of explicit connectives (such as 'therefore' or 'for example').

Thus ads' use of ellipsis – a formal, textual phenomenon – has a discourse function, in that it creates an atmosphere of proximity and intimacy. It enables parasitism on the discourse type 'conversation': the prototype of interactive reciprocal communication in which formalities and differences of rank are often diminished or partially suspended (Cook 1989a: 51).

8.2 THE DIALOGUE OF ADS: GIVEN AND NEW INFORMATION

Another formal textual device with implications of reciprocity is the ordering and selection of information within clauses. This reflects the sender's assumptions about the knowledge and interests which he or she shares with the addressee, and also the focus of attention which the sender seeks to impose.

Even in written discourse this ordering and selection is motivated by an interpersonal concern: it pairs information which is assumed to be known to the addressee with information which is assumed to be new. Known information tends to come at the beginning of the clause, new information towards the end, where it receives greater attention. English possesses a number of grammatical options which allow the order of information to be shifted around, creating different **sentence perspectives**, such as:

> Grandma adored this old country recipe.
> What grandma adored was this old country recipe.
> It was this old country recipe which grandma adored.
> This old country recipe was what grandma adored.

As with parallelism, the difference between these sentences is a surface phenomenon, and disappears in any 'deep' grammatical or semantic analysis. They have the same 'meaning', in the sense that they refer to the same state of affairs. Yet what matters interactionally is their differences. In speech, this is complicated by the use of intonation to focus upon any element, and its interplay with grammatical focus.

> GRANDma adored this old country recipe.
> grandma aDORED this old country recipe.   etc. etc.

In speech, there is frequent ellipsis of known information. If I ask you what grandma adored, you might well just reply: 'This old country recipe.' In written and more formal discourse, on the other hand, known information is less frequently ellipted. This both allows greater ease of processing and makes the sender's perception of the nature of information quite clear. If all information were new, in a situation where clarification cannot be sought, the message might soon become incoherent and incomprehensible. If all information were already known on the other hand, it would simply be pointless and boring. But a balance of the two allows discourse to progress step by step, relating each new item to one which is already known. The new information of one clause becomes the known of the next, establishing an **information chain**.

The ad for Sun Alliance insurance (used as an example of innovative graphology in section 4.4.3) creates such an information chain. On the assumption that the ad is addressed to people who need home insurance, the opening of the first clause supplies no new information, while the second half supplies the name of a firm.

GIVEN ....NEW
Take out home insurance   with Sun Alliance.

In the second clause, it is clear the ad is addressing 'you', but not what will happen:

GIVEN ....NEW ....
and you   cut out all the traditional complexity and
                        confusion.

Assuming the knowledge that all insurance policies are documents, but not that they involve helpcards, the next clause divides as follows:

GIVEN ....NEW ....
Alongside a clearly put policy you'll be given our new helpcard.

(Note, however, how the claim about the clarity of the policy is placed as though it were taken for granted. This device of slipping a judgement into the given part of the clause is also commonly used in news.) As we can infer that the helpcard must carry some information, though its nature is unknown, the next clause divides into:

GIVEN ....NEW ....
which bears[1]   some useful telephone numbers.

As we now know there are telephone numbers on the card, and also, by general knowledge, that telephone numbers are to be dialled, then the next clause divides into:

GIVEN ....NEW ....
By dialling one of them   you can obtain clear and straightforward
                          advice on your policy.

As 'numbers' was plural, we know there is at least a second, though its function, again, is unknown.

GIVEN ....NEW ....
A second number   offers you free legal advice.

And we will not be surprised to hear of a third:

GIVEN ....NEW ....
While another provides   a domestic emergency service.

To organize discourse in this way the sender must predict both what the addressee does and does not know, and what he or she wants to know. Placed at the beginning of a clause, an item of known information becomes the **topic** of that clause.

Topics in discourse relate to each other hierarchically, so that we may talk about **main topics** of the discourse as a whole or **sub-topics** of a section or single clause. In this discourse the main topic is home insurance, and sub-topics include the helpcard and the telephone numbers on it. In a sense, the topic of a selling ad is always the product or service, though there is usually an apparent or surrogate topic too. (In a successful ad, this surrogate topic arouses interest, as people are eager to find out 'what this ad is for'. It may appear to be about people on a tropical beach, but turn out to be about chocolate bars!) In non-reciprocal written discourse the topic is imposed by the sender; in reciprocal discourse it may be more collaborative and influenced by the addressee.

Yet even in written non-reciprocal discourse the trace of a second voice is still present. Dialogue, which precedes monologue both phylogenetically and ontogenetically, may develop through a gradual deletion of this second voice. For this reason perhaps, from the dialogues of Plato through catechisms and sermons to university lectures and news broadcasts, there are many monologic non-reciprocal discourse types which present themselves in the form of two voices, or as face-to-face interaction. Yet the apparently independent second participant makes little contribution, and exists only as a foil.[2] The move towards the openly non-reciprocal discourse of extended writing[3] – from Platonic dialogue to philosophical treatise, from lecture to book – is a change of form rather than of participant power.

A way of dramatizing this trace of the second voice is to imagine non-reciprocal discourse as one half of a dialogue in which the sender pre-empts questions from the addressee (Widdowson 1978: 25–6). Each unspoken question prompts both the content and form of the next utterance. The dialogue imagined by the sender of the Sun Alliance ad may go something like this.

A Where should I take out home insurance?
B Take out home insurance with Sun Alliance.
A Why?

B You cut out all the traditional complexity and confusion.
A What would I be given?
B Alongside a clearly put policy you'll be given our new helpcard.
A What's on it?
B It bears some useful telephone numbers.
A What are the numbers for?
B By dialling one of them you can obtain clear and straightforward advice on your policy.
A What's the second number for?
B A second number offers you free legal advice.
A What's the third one for?
B Another provides a domestic emergency service.

In conversation, it is the first part of each clause which can most easily be omitted, and the following answers by B would be quite acceptable.

B With Sun Alliance.
B Cuts out all the traditional complexity and confusion.
B Our new helpcard.
B Some useful telephone numbers.
B Clear and straightforward advice on your policy.
B Free legal advice.
B A domestic emergency service.

Many ads manipulate this dialogic structure of discourse to their advantage. They assume shared opinions which are not shared. The Cascade ad assumes that spotted glasses cause problems with your friends (Figure 48). We have already encountered many other examples. The Subaru ad assumes that women should drive small cars (Figure 37), the Sunny Delight ad that it is difficult to be on good terms with your children while also giving them a healthy diet (Figure 41). The voice of each perspective may be associated with its own discourse type. In the Sunny Delight ad, for example, one type may be intimate family banter, another a health information booklet with a title such as 'How to Be a Good Mother'.

8.2.1 Unspoken and shared assumptions as an index of ideology

Both dialogue and monologue are structured by assumptions about shared information. Often, this shared information seems so obvious to participants that they are not even aware of the assumptions they are making. In the above dialogue all of the following is treated as already known and assumed.

- Most people have a dwelling.
- The dwelling contains property.
- The property belongs to them.
- It costs money to replace.

- Home insurance involves regular payments in return for payment when property is lost or damaged.
- Home insurance involves a legal agreement.
- Legal agreements can be complex and confusing.
- People do not like complexity and confusion.
- The terms of home insurance are described in a policy document.
- Telephone numbers are to be dialled on a telephone.
- Insurance claims involve legal knowledge which most claimants do not have.
- Home insurance is to do with accidents, losses and burglaries.
- Such events demand urgent action.
- They may happen at a time when offices are closed.

To tell a prospective purchaser these things would be both insulting and superfluous. They constitute a group of related facts, a **schema**, known to all adult members of the culture in which the ad is situated. To spell out these facts initiates a process of infinite expansion, for each statement involves further assumptions: about the law, or accidents, or homes. Yet many of these assumed facts are culture specific rather than universal. Home insurance is not commonplace in Russia, for example, and needs to be explained to Russians coming to the West, just as many aspects of Russian life need explaining to Westerners. The absence of reference to shared information has led to the observation that it is what is omitted in discourse, the **gaps** within it, which constitute the shared **ideology** of the participants (Althusser 1971: 136–69; Macherey [1966] 1978: 87; Fairclough 1989: 78–90). A parent asking for information about a particular school, for example, would not expect to be told that it is a place to which a number of children come during the daytime to be instructed and cared for by a smaller number of adults, that each of those adults specializes in one or two subjects, and that groups of children have lessons from one adult at a time. All these features of schools are taken for granted, together with the cultural beliefs about upbringing from which they stem. They are assumed to be true unless there is a statement to the contrary. It is not therefore misleading to omit mentioning teachers, or that these teachers are in charge of the children. On the other hand, in contemporary Western society, a parent might feel misled if it were not mentioned that one of the aims of the school was to teach children that their monarch is divine. In other times and places, this might be an unremarkable (and therefore unmentioned) function of the school. It is what is not said in a discourse – because everyone in the society knows it – which is most important.

Ads are a case in point. Their intention to sell is often unstated; but it is as ludicrous to criticize them for this as it would be to criticize a head-teacher for not mentioning lessons. On the other hand, when approaching ads, as with other social phenomena such as schools, it is illuminating to imagine oneself as an outsider to whom everything must be explained, for whom all gaps must be filled. Why do the children in school sit in rows, and listen to one adult at the front? Why is the city full of big pictures of happy healthy people and new objects? Why does the sender care if your glasses have spots? And who is the sender anyway?

There is a strong assumption that people who address us are saying things which are coherent. This principle is particularly important in the interpretation of poetry. We *make* sense even where there is none, using some unstated cultural assumptions to fill in the gaps. People are reluctant to suppose that the sender cannot see the sense of his or her own discourse and assume the fault must be their own. Discourse has to be conspicuously and extensively nonsensical before it is perceived as such. There is a simple experiment to demonstrate this, which usually works. Pick a short phrase at random out of another discourse and insert it into a conversation. Then ask the people you are talking to if they understood why you said it. They will usually find a connection! They want you to make sense.

Through ellipsis and assumptions of shared knowledge, ads create an atmosphere of intimacy and informality. It is a mood very well expressed in the picture accompanying the Cascade ad, showing characters in friendly interaction. This atmosphere is further reinforced by the ubiquitous use of 'you' already discussed in Chapter 7. But who is the conversation between? Often there are conversations going on between characters – sometimes we overhear them. Yet the 'you' of the ad is addressed by a voice outside these scenes with double exophora (section 7.4). The voice simultaneously addresses one character (unheard by the others) and the potential consumer, the ad's addressee.

8.3 THE WORLDS OF AN AD AND THEIR INHABITANTS

Many ads exist in four participant worlds (Figure 49): the world of the sender (in which the products are manufactured and distributed); the fictional world of the characters; the fantasy world of the receiver; and the real world of the receiver (in which the product may be purchased). A minority of ads may dispense with the second and third of these worlds.

In product ads, the aim of the sender is to push this product, via the world of fiction and fantasy, into the real world of the consumer. Movement is effected by those elements at the borders of the four quarters: the product itself, the text, the actors/characters and the addressee. In addition, some participants seem to belong to more than one world at once. Real celebrities and manufacturers appear in the fictional world, as do apparently real consumers; people speaking directly for the manufacturer appear in the fictional world too. What the ad seeks to achieve is enough contact between reality and fiction, sending and receiving, characters and consumer, fantasy and fact, for the passage of the product to be feasible.

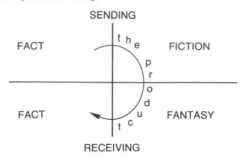

Figure 49 The four worlds of an ad

One connection between the fictional world and the real world of the addressee is the direct address or gaze of a character. (In this respect ads are like plays with asides directed to the audience, or novels in which a first person narrator apostrophizes the reader.) A further connection between worlds is the product itself, which may exist in all three, and whose purchase brings the receiver's world closer to that of the fiction. A third connecting force is the disembodied narrative voice which addresses both characters and receivers, with actual or ellipted 'you's, but does not name itself. Though in some ways like an apostrophizing narrator in literary fiction, this voice also shares features with the narrators of those novels in which authorial, narrative and characters' voices merge. The identity of the 'I' or 'we' who speaks the 'you' is unclear. Sometimes it seems to emanate from the fictional world, sometimes from the sender beyond it, sometimes from elsewhere. And we (the addressees) are distracted from this absence of identity by the compelling and attractive characters to whom the 'you' is also addressed, and into whom, if the ad is successful, we project a part of ourselves. This could also be described as a kind of ellipsis: not of words or phrases or clauses, but of the sender and addresser of the message, who, though separate from characters and receivers, can exist only through them. This omission often passes unnoticed, a gap which discloses the ideology of both manufacturer and consumer. We are not told whose voice this is, because we apparently already know.

Or do we? Ads have so many senders and addressers that it is hard to say whose voices speak in them. A tv ad such as, say, the Wrigley's ad 'Last stick' (section 3.3.2) involves at the very least a manufacturer, an agency, a copywriter, an art director, a tv producer, a director, a producer, assistants, a camera crew, musicians, actors, technicians, costume designers, a hairstylist.[4] Moreover, some of the senders described here with grammatically singular collective nouns – e.g. 'the manufacturer' – are in fact multiple. All these senders/addressees (and which is which?) are seldom mentioned – other than in trade ads for advertising agencies aimed at manufacturers, and the occasional gimmicky ad which refers to its own construction. But whose voice speaks in the ad? Arguably, the sender is not the creative team at all, but the firm; the creative team is the addresser, equivalent to the publisher in literary discourse. In this view, a comparison of participants in literary and advertising discourse might be expressed as in Figure 50.

DISCOURSE	SENDER	ADDRESSER	ADDRESSEE/RECEIVER
Advertising	client	creative team	public
Literature	author	publisher	public

Figure 50 A view of equivalent participants in literature and ads

In addition to the senders/addressees, there are the fictional characters (happily consuming or miserably lacking the product) whom the senders and addressees collaborate to create, and a third, most mysterious identity: the speaker of the voice-over, who, like the narrator of a third person novel, both is and is not the author, and cannot be identified with any one participant. The opinions expressed by this voice are unlikely to be those of the copy writer; away from work, like most other people, he or she probably considers different brands (of washing-up liquids or whatever) much the same.

8.3.1 Who is speaking thus?

In an essay on the literary narrator called 'The death of the author', Roland Barthes quoted a passage from Balzac's *Sarrasine* describing a castrato disguised as a woman

> This was woman herself, with her sudden fears, her irrational whims, her instinctive worries, her impetuous boldness, her fussings, and her delicious sensibility.

and asked

> Who is speaking thus? Is it the hero of the story bent on remaining ignorant of the castrate hidden beneath the woman? Is it Balzac the individual furnished by his personal experience with a philosophy of woman? Is it Balzac the author professing 'literary' ideas on femininity? Is it universal wisdom? Romantic psychology? We shall never know, for the good reason that writing is the destruction of every voice, of every point of origin. Writing is that neutral, composite, oblique space where our subject slips away, the negative where all identity is lost, starting with the very identity of the body writing.

(Barthes [1968] 1977)

The questions are as pertinent to ads as to novels. 'Who is speaking thus?', for example, in the Cascade ad: the manufacturer, the copy writer (out of conviction or as a job), the voice of proper behaviour, a friend of the character, the inner voice of the woman?

A clue to the nature of the voice may be found in the frequent use of 'you'. This 'you' of ads expresses two types of sender/addressee relationship at once, a conflation which is possible in English but much harder in languages with **a T/V distinction** between an intimate and formal second person pronoun (such as *tu/vous* in French). In such languages, the choice of pronoun is highly significant, and in ads will be influenced by such factors as the nature of the product or the age of the targeted addressees. Generally, the T form is both an index of intimacy and equality, and of clear superiority or subordination: used to God and parents, and to animals and servants, as well as to friends. (This dual function of the T form lends support to Wolfson's bulge theory (see section 7.2).) The V form indicates not only service and respect, but also distance. Ads, the most public of discourses, adopt the strategies of the most private. The voice of an ad must simultaneously be one of friendship, authority and respect. Ads in languages with a T/V distinction must make a choice, or seek to avoid the second person altogether.[5]

8.4 THE THEORIES OF BAKHTIN

The role of language in this complex interplay of people and worlds is best understood by examining the relation between participants and their words, rather than either in isolation. This relationship is not well dealt with by Saussurean semiotics, which treat all speakers as homogenous and take no account of how the meaning of words varies with participants. It is quite one thing to be told that 'x is the best lager' by its manufacturer, another to be told this by a celebrity one likes and respects, another by a fictional character, yet another by a close friend.

The theories of the Russian linguist and literary theorist Bakhtin (1895–1975) are helpful to an understanding of how the identity of the sender is an integral part of meaning.[6] Developed through the 1920s, 1930s and 1940s, his ideas were for a long time neglected both in Russia and the West. Their late emergence on to the academic scene from the 1960s onwards – but most spectacularly in the 1980s – distorts their importance and originality as a contribution to linguistics and literary theory. They became known after many developments which they preceded and foreshadowed.[7] I shall first give a brief outline of Bakhtin's approach to communication, and in particular his theory of **voice**, then use this to compare the voices in ads with those in the novel: a genre of particular importance in Bakhtin's theory.

8.4.1 Meaning and identity

Bakhtin observed that, despite a professed belief in the primacy of speech, semiotics is deeply affected in its view of language by the written word, which creates an illusion of linguistic meaning as something relatively fixed, existing separately from sender and receiver (Volosinov [1929] 1988: 73). In Bakhtin's view no meaning can be divorced from people: the study of a text must always be of words and participants together. To treat language as an impersonal object is to simplify and misrepresent.

This is not merely a question of a different methodology and emphasis in linguistic description, but a challenge to a view – deeply rooted in occidental philosophy[8] – of the nature of the self, society and the world. In a critique of Saussure, Bakhtin disputes the view of individual identity and thought as self-contained and separate from language (Volosinov [1929] 1988: 45–63).[9] In his view, it is not that we exist first, in isolation from each other, and then attempt to overcome that isolation through communication; but, rather, that we come into existence through our language and the social relationships it creates. What we refer to as the self, or as an individual, is not something pre-existing and independent of communication, but a projection from an intersection of discourses. Thought is internalized discourse ('I', for example, am the intersection of this book and other communications in which I am or have been involved.) The 'self', the 'individual' and the 'participant' are to be found in discourse rather than outside it. It is in this sense that I shall try to use these terms from now on.[10]

In occidental philosophy and in our day-to-day view of the world, the identity of the individual is conceived as independent, somehow locked away inside the head. Communication is the attempt to transfer thoughts from one sealed mind to another. Saussure's diagram of two talking heads (see Figure 23) and his description of language as 'the social product deposited in the brain of each individual' ([1915] 1974: 23) express this idea very simply. But there is confusion in the Saussurean view, as in occidental philosophy in general, between the physical person – a body-and-brain – and the self. Bakhtin suggests that individual identity is not within the body-and-brain, though these are essential to it, but created through interaction with another person through language. Our identities are entangled together, in discourse. In this way Bakhtin frees himself from the equally weak positions of objectivism, in which meaning is independent of people, and subjectivism, in which it is wholly within an isolated person. We cannot exist without discourse, but neither can discourse exist without us.[11]

Analysis of an act of communication must involve analysis of both the participants and their words, although – or because – the two cannot be disentangled. Meaning is not a product of a self-contained and impersonal code, but creative and fuzzy-edged.

Meaning does not reside in the word or in the soul of the speaker or in the soul of the listener. Meaning is the *effect of interaction between speaker and listener produced via the material of a particular sound complex*. It is like an electric spark that occurs only when two different terminals are hooked together. Those who . . . in attempting to define the meaning of a word, approach its lower, stable, self-identical limit, want, in effect, to turn on a light bulb after having switched off the current. Only the current of verbal intercourse endows a word with the light of meaning.

(original emphasis, Bakhtin – (Volosinov [1929] 1988: 103)

Whereas the semiotic approach tends to divorce text from both senders and receivers, viewing analyst and text as quite separate from each other, in a Bakhtinian view the identity of the receiver is so bound up with the discourse types which dominate the society through which he or she exists that this neat and secure separation is no longer possible. This has repercussions for the study of those discourse types which are prominent in the society from which the analyst comes, and with which he or she is involved. If we live in a society permeated with advertising, and receive these communications every day from childhood (as I and – I assume – you have done), then advertising is not some external curiosity which we examine, from which we are separate and superior, but something of which we are part, and which is part of us (whether we like it or not).

Bakhtin rejected dichotomies as simplifications. For this reason he attacked the Saussurean dichotomies of langue/parole, diachrony/synchrony (Volosinov [1929] 1973: 58–63), the Freudian dichotomy of conscious/unconscious (Volosinov [1927] 1973), and (less openly) the Marxist dichotomies of base/superstructure, oppressor/oppressed (Bakhtin [1940/1965] 1968).[12] Semiotics views meaning as an equivalence between one half of such a dichotomy and another, between a linguistic unit and something else (concept, an object in the world, another sign in the same or a different language) which can be dispassionately described by an observer whose own identity is somehow unaffected by his or her discoveries. Such equivalences may help understanding and create insights, but each one leads to another endlessly, altering their observers in the process. The tendency to 'interpret' ads in terms of something else (signifieds, unconscious desires, economic relations) and then rest satisfied with that finite equivalence contributes to understanding, but also simplifies. A rather different reason for interest in advertising is that, as one of the major discourse types which construct our contemporary identity, it enables us to study a part of ourselves.

8.4.2 Voices

A central concept in Bakhtin's theory of communication is that of **voice** – the presence of the speaker within a particular discourse. The role of the speaker and discourse type are often closely bound together (see section 1.1) and often imply each other. (A trial must have a judge, and a judge must have a trial.) Voices within a discourse may often be described as those of different discourse types, as well as of different people. In the Subaru ad (in section 5.3.1) the voices are those of a bar-room conversation and a cautionary tale; in the Sunny Delight ad (in section 6.3) an advisory booklet and family banter. The concept of voice forms the basis of a typology of discourse: **monologic** (with one voice); **dialogic** (with two voices); **heteroglossic** (with many voices at once). In Bakhtin's writing, this division involves a value judgement. Monologic discourse, attempting to silence all voices but one, is the hallmark of the authoritarian individual or society, which is neither open nor tolerant.

Bakhtin developed this theory by analysing dialogic and heteroglossic discourse at both the level of the single utterance (Volosinov [1929] 1973: 109–59) and at the level of discourse (Bakhtin [1940/1965] 1968; [1929/1963] 1984). For the former he concentrated upon reported speech, and for the latter upon parody and the novel.

8.4.3 Voice at sentence level: reported speech

In reported speech, by definition, the voice of one speaker is contained within the voice of another. Let us consider how this might be used in the pronouncements of a political executive, or the reporting of those pronouncements as news. Suppose the president of a country said

1 Troops will fire on rioters.

The meaning is created by the speaker's presidential power. It would have quite different meaning if uttered by a child watching tv. It will also change according to the addressee, being different when uttered in a nationwide tv presidential address, or privately to an intimate adviser. (All utterances are to somebody; even when talking to ourselves we project an imagined interlocutor.) A spokesperson[13] might then say:

2 The president said: 'Troops will fire on rioters.'

In version (2), the two voices are clearly separate. The spokesperson says: 'The president said' and the president said 'Troops will fire on the rioters'. Each voice makes its own judgements, and displays its allegiances by its lexical and grammatical choice. It was the 'president', not the 'dictator'; the people are 'rioters', not 'protesters'; the simple declarative form, used by both addresser and addressee, has possible connotations of bluntness and authority. Nevertheless the two voices and their judgements are quite distinct and clear. But it is possible to imagine this reporting of one voice by another moving off in different directions in which the two voices gradually entangle with each other to such an extent that it is quite unclear either what was originally said or whose judgements the utterance reflects. At each stage of remove the options multiply.

1 Troops will fire on rioters.
2 The president said: 'Troops will fire on rioters.'
3 The president said that troops would fire on rioters.
4 The president warned that troops would fire on rioters.
5 The president made it clear that troops would fire on rioters.
6 The president threatened that troops would fire on rioters.
7 The president gave a firm warning that he would reluctantly order troops to fire on rioters.
8 The president made another of his dictatorial announcements, callously ordering the use of violence against innocent people.

In the last of these versions, the voice of the president is submerged in that of the second reporting voice, so that the second voice, in effect, will not allow the receiver of this message to judge the president. Where there is more than one voice, either one will submerge another, or the discourse will allow tolerance of difference. There are thus a number of possible relationships of voices:

1 One voice only.
2 Two or more voices, clearly separated.
3 Two or more voices, one of which dominates and distorts the others.
4 Two or more voices, coexisting (and probably contradicting) each other.

To Bakhtin, this last preferable possibility is inherent in certain discourse types: notably the novel ([1929/1963] 1984) and the parodies of medieval carnival ([1940/1965] 1968). These have no single voice, but are a mixture of many. Bakhtin termed this **heteroglossia**. As the voices within heteroglossic discourse types are often the voices of other discourse types, as well as of individuals, there is a connection between parasite discourse (as discussed in section 2.3) and heteroglossia.

What we have to decide is whether the parasitism of ads is truly heteroglossic, or whether the apparent interplay of voices is illusory, masking a monologic discourse, in which many voices are dominated by one. To do this, we shall need to consider heteroglossia at discourse rather than utterance level. In longer extended discourse the options for the merging and submerging of many voices are multiplied, existing not only within sentences, but also in the interaction and contradiction of longer sections of discourse.

8.5 VOICES IN THE NOVEL: TWO EXAMPLES

In the novel, one of the most heteroglossic of discourse types, the entanglement of voices is particularly evident. As a way of assessing the degree of heteroglossia in ads, it may be instructive to compare them with examples of novelistic discourse. This section analyses two passages which are representative of two very different narrative techniques – one from Henry Fielding's *Joseph Andrews* (1742) and one from Jane Austen's *Persuasion* (1818) – and then makes some comparisons between their narrative voices, and those of ads.

8.5.1 From *Joseph Andrews*

In this passage, the eponymous hero, a handsome but comically naive young man, working as a servant, escapes seduction by his employer's elderly and ugly companion Mrs Slipslop, a woman whose pretensions to education lead her into frequent malapropisms. This passage spans a transition from one chapter to another.

> 'Madam,' says Joseph, 'I am sure I have always valued the Honour you did me by your conversation; for I know you are a woman of learning.' 'Yes but Joseph' said she, a little softened by the compliment to her learning, 'If you had a Value for me, you certainly would have found some method of shewing it me; for I am *convicted* you must see the Value I have for you. Yes, Joseph, my Eyes, whether I would or no, must have declared a Passion I cannot conquer, – Oh! Joseph! – '
>
> As when a hungry Tygress, who long had traversed the Woods in fruitless search, sees within the Reach of her Claws a Lamb, she prepares to leap upon her Prey; or as a voracious Pike, of immense Size, surveys through the liquid Element a Roach or Gudgeon which cannot escape her Jaws, opens them wide to swallow the little Fish; so did Mrs Slipslop prepare to lay her violent amorous Hands on the poor Joseph, when luckily her Mistress' Bell rung, and delivered the intended Martyr from her Clutches.
>
> She was obliged to leave him abruptly, and defer the Execution of her Purpose to some other Time. We shall therefore return to the Lady Booby, and give our reader some Account of her Behaviour, after she was left by Joseph in a Temper of Mind not greatly different from the inflamed Slipslop.
>
> CHAPTER VII
> *Sayings of wise Men, A Dialogue between the Lady and her Maid and a Panegyric or rather Satire on the Passion of Love, in the Sublime Style.*
>
> It is the Observation of some Ancient Sage whose name I have forgot, that Passions operate differently on the human mind as diseases on the body in proportion to the strength or weakness, soundness or rottenness of one or the other.
>
> We hope therefore a judicious reader will give himself some pains to observe. . . .

The many voices, though mixed, are yet reasonably distinct. The narrative voice speaks directly to the reader,[14] and alternates between two communicative worlds, the second of which owes its existence to the first. The first world appears as the real world in which author addresses the reader, the second as a fictional world in which character addresses character, and the two seem quite distinct. Movement between these two worlds is effected by such statements as:

> We shall therefore return to the Lady Booby, and give our reader . . .

These guide us into the fictional world, leaving us there unescorted, listening unaided to the voices of the characters, (though we know in another part of ourselves that they do not speak autonomously and that their words are as much Fielding's words as any others). There are, as it were, apparently two narrative pathways from author to reader (Figure 51).

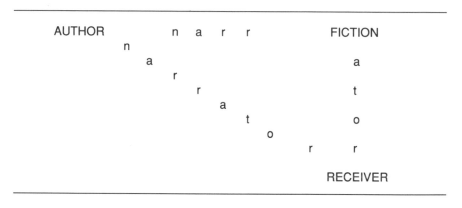

Figure 51 Narrative pathways from author to reader 1

Yet there are a number of complications. The direct, self-declaring authorial voice is itself heteroglossic. It is sometimes an unobtrusive story-teller and observer ('said she, a little softened by the compliment to her learning'); sometimes the elaborate voice of classical epic ('As when a hungry Tygress . . .'); sometimes a polite guide to the reader ('we shall therefore return . . . and give our reader some Account'); sometimes the moralist ('It is the Observation of some Ancient Sage'); sometimes colloquial and offhand ('whose name I have forgot').[15] Even within the fictional world, away from direct address to the reader, the authorial voice is still evident in such detail as the words 'poor . . . luckily . . . delivered', which convey and invite a judgement of the characters. The interweaving of voices and discourse types makes us doubt both the authenticity of the authorial voice and the autonomy of the fictional world, thus foregrounding the act of story-telling.

A further multiplication of voices can occur if characters themselves create fictional worlds in which other characters come into being, and the characters who apparently create these other characters themselves adopt narrative positions. The overall voice of the novel is the totality of all these voices. (Like the novel itself, this view ignores the intermediate role of publishers, printers, editors, binders and distributors.)

In *Joseph Andrews* worlds and voices are relatively separate. Chapters begin with direct address of author to reader, move on to report the fictional world, and in the heart of the chapter apparently abandon control, letting characters speak for themselves. This 'onion' structure is found in many other novels, either repeated in each chapter as it is here, or – as in novels presented as journals or stories within stories – in the structure of the whole work. The bulk of such novels may be enclosed in a fictional editor's or publisher's preface explaining how the journal came to light,[16] or an outer narration recounting how the story was told.[17]

Many tv ads – even within thirty or sixty seconds – manage to employ this structure too. They begin and/or end with a voice-over and/or written message in which the receiver is directly addressed, and general claims are made; in the middle, they present a fictional situation, sometimes including a conversation between characters. The device of the framing journal, which gives fantastic events a setting of sober scientific authority,[18] is echoed by toothpaste and disinfectant ads which begin and end with a scientist's report. Sometimes the white-coated boffin even appears, like the good angel of medieval drama, in the kitchen or bathroom, either invisible to all the characters, or conversing with only one of them while unseen by all the others!

Yet, while the framed narratives of novels often begin with an authoritative voice, they often finish open-ended, without further editorial comment. In ads, the reverse is true, and the voice of authority occurs or recurs at the end, to leave nothing to the receiver.

8.5.2 From *Persuasion*

As the novel developed, it tended to merge voices which were at its inception relatively distinct through the development of narrative techniques which fuse the polar opposites of first and third person narrations into one which is neither and both. An early example is Jane Austen's *Persuasion*, a novel whose suspense and power derive from rival interpretations which result from the fusion of authorial, narrative, societal and characters' voices. The plot centres upon Anne Elliot's continuing love for Frederick Wentworth, a man whose offer of marriage her family once persuaded her to reject as beneath her. He returns from the Napoleonic War, rich, successful and as attractive as ever, while Anne, though less subservient to her family, believes herself too old and plain to attract his interest again. Suspense hinges upon the fusion of narrative and characters' voices, and the ambiguity inherent in reported speech. Consider this central passage, which has given critics and students the material for lengthy debate:[19]

> On one other question, which perhaps her utmost wisdom might not have prevented, she was soon spared all suspense; for after the Miss Musgroves had returned and finished their visit at the Cottage, she had this spontaneous information from Mary:
>
> 'Captain Wentworth is not very gallant by you, Anne, though he was so attentive to me. Henrietta asked him what he thought of you, when they went away; and he said, "You were so altered he should not have known you again." '
>
> Mary had no feelings to make her respect her sister's in a common way; but she was perfectly unsuspicious of being inflicting any particular wound.
>
> 'Altered beyond his knowledge!' Anne fully submitted, in silent, deep mortification. Doubtless it was so; and she could take no revenge, for he was not altered, or not for the worse. She had already acknowledged it to herself, and she could not think differently, let him think of her as he would. No; the years which had destroyed her youth and bloom had only given him a more glowing, manly, open look, in no respect lessening his personal advantages. She had seen the same Frederick Wentworth.
>
> 'So altered that he should not have known her again!' These were words which could not but dwell with her. Yet she soon began to rejoice that she had heard them. They were of sobering tendency; they allayed agitation; they composed, and consequently must make her happier.
>
> Frederick Wentworth had used such words, or something like them, but without an idea that they would be carried round to her. He had thought her wretchedly altered, and, in the first moment of appeal, had spoken as he felt. He had not forgotten Anne Elliot. She had used him ill; deserted and disappointed him; and worse, she had shewn a feebleness of character in doing so, which his own decided, confident temper could not endure. She had given him up to oblige others. It had been the effect of over-persuasion. It had been weakness and timidity.

At every level from word to discourse, meanings are multiplied by the ambiguous identity of the voice which speaks them. Thus we do not know whether the 'spontaneous information from Mary' is judged to be 'spontaneous', perhaps wrongly, by Anne, or by the narrative voice; and, if the latter, we do not know whether the word is to be taken at face value, or as an ironic indictment of Mary's cruelty (the assumption being that spontaneity is less likely to be dishonest[20]). Crucially we do not know the extent to which Mary's rendition of Wentworth's words distorts them, and, even if these were his words, whether they were uttered in the knowledge that they would be relayed to Anne. The meaning of confidential critical remarks, even when quoted verbatim, is distorted when they are repeated to the person criticized – a fact which the reporter very often knows and calculates (Tannen 1989: 105–10). Yet even assuming that Wentworth uttered the words exactly as reported, fully aware and perhaps intending that they should be repeated to Anne, they are still not clear: 'altered' does not necessarily mean 'altered for the worse', for example. Nor can we rely, as in Fielding, upon a clear alternation between the perceptions of the characters and a detached and reliable narrative judgement. This earlier convention is now manipulated to tease. Narrative control appears to return in

Frederick Wentworth had used such words

but this is immediately followed by

or something like them.

which abdicates responsibility and denies any privileged knowledge. The passage is full of puzzles. Who says 'the years had destroyed her youth and bloom'? Austen? General opinion? Anne at her most objective? Anne when she is pessimistic and depressed? Who says Wentworth has a 'decided confident temper'? Perhaps only Wentworth, trying to cheer himself up. The strength of this novel lies in this plethora of possible interpretations, which resist reduction to a single uninteresting voice. Iconically, the ambiguity and open-endedness of this narrative mimics the uncertainty and intensity, the alternation between hope and fear, of the central characters. The voice of the author, accessible only through the voices of characters, is thus never clearly perceived, but remains both mysterious and intriguing (Figure 52).

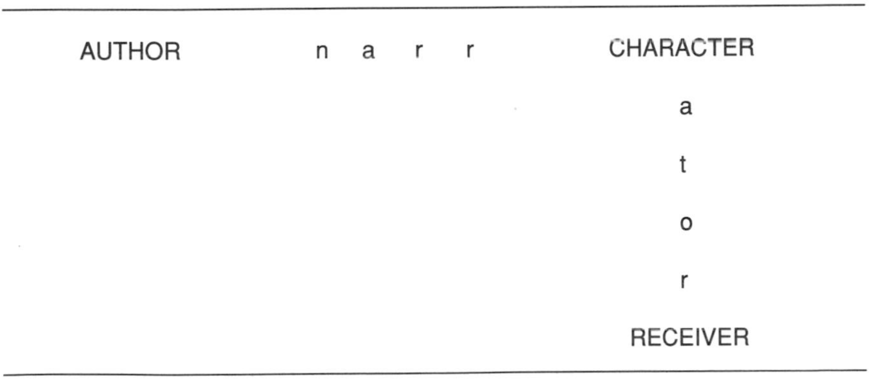

AUTHOR	n	a	r	r	CHARACTER
					a
					t
					o
					r
					RECEIVER

Figure 52 Narrative pathways from author to reader 2

If these two novels represent two poles of narrative technique, we might then ask which, if either, is closer to the narrative technique of ads.

There is no simple answer to this question, for ads, like novels, provide too many exceptions. Yet there is in ads a reluctance to leave matters open, which results, even in the most heteroglossic ads, in the assertion of a single monologic and authoritative voice at the end. This in turn leads to a clearer separation of voices. The reason for this is the constraint imposed by the client: the overall judgement must be final and closed. This perhaps will prevent ads ever developing more heteroglossic narrative techniques in the future.

8.6 INTER- AND INTRA-DISCOURSAL VOICES IN ADS

Most discourses contain the voices of other examples of the same type, or of other discourse types. The meanings deriving from these echoes are usually described as intertextual (as in 1.0). Yet, though such voices are usually attributed to the text, they rely very much on the receiver's knowledge, and are part of the interaction of sender and receiver through text, rather than of the text as a disembodied object. They are thus better described as discoursal, and divided into two types:

1 **intra-discoursal**: containing the voice of another example of the same discourse type, as when an ad assumes knowledge of another ad.
2 **inter-discoursal**: containing the voice of another discourse type, as when an ad evokes knowledge of a film or story.

The passages from Fielding and Austen contain examples of both. *Joseph Andrews*, by dealing in its ribald way with the tribulations of a young person besieged by lecherous older people, almost certainly evoked, for its contemporaries, if not for us, the presence of another, more serious novel on the same theme, Richardson's *Pamela*. The convoluted clauses and elaborate similes of the paragraph beginning 'As when the hungry Tygress . . .' parody the discourse of classical epic (and translations of it) and use this to ridicule Mrs Slipslop. Jane Austen makes a less tangible allusion to the conventions of other novels – including Fielding's – by appearing to return from characters' perceptions to authorial comment, but shying away at the last moment in mid-sentence ('or something like them').[21] Such voices, based on a correct prediction of the discourse experience of contemporaries, now need pointing out, especially when there is the strange but common phenomenon of the parody proving more durable than its target.

Ads, like novels, contain both intra- and inter-discoursal voices. These have increased as ads have grown in quantity and salience, and accumulated their own history and tradition. If there is (as suggested in the foreword), a new departure in advertising from the mid-1950s, amounting to the creation of a new discourse type, then it is not surprising that early ads are intra-discoursally uninteresting and impoverished. (The same cannot be said of early novels – but that is what makes the early novel so remarkable.) Lacking a tradition of other ads on which to draw, early ads slavishly employed the voices of other discourse types to lend credence to a straightforward act of persuasion. Favourite among evoked types were the scientific report (transmitted by a white-coated male scientist), the conversational advice of a confidante (such as a more experienced mother/housewife/woman of fashion,[22] etc.), or the sales rap (delivered by an eloquent and enthusiastic man in a suit!). All these are gifts to ridicule. They still appear in ads, though less frequently.

As the tradition of ads has grown, the nature and number of intra-discoursal voices have changed. Sometimes, ads assume and exploit knowledge of another product and its ads merely to attack a competitor. In 1991 the slogan for the Peugeot 405 'Takes Your Breath Away' is parodied without direct reference in an ad for the VW Polo whose copy reads 'It doesn't take your breath away' – a device which both attracts attention and makes the claim that the Polo's catalytic converter reduces air pollution.

Such cross-references reflect serious competition between manufacturers of similar products. The long-running war between Pepsi and Coca-Cola provides many examples. The concern is the comparison of products more than the comparison of ads. At other times, however, one ad will make use of another which is particularly well known and successful, not because it is purveying a competing product, but simply to attact attention, often through parody. If we extend the metaphor of ads as parasites, these ads are parasites on parasites. A good example can be found in ads making use of the Levi 501 ads which appeared in Britain in 1985 and 1987. The 1985 campaign comprised two ads: the first, 'Launderette', showing a young man stripping down to his boxer shorts in a launderette; the second, 'Bath', showing a young man wearing his Levis in the bath so that they would shrink to fit him (see Figure 8). Their success was spectacular. UK sales of 501s rose from 80,000 pairs to around 650,000 in one year (Sebag-Montefiore 1987). Re-releases of the 1960s pop songs which accompanied the ads became hits again. Nick Kamen, the actor in 'Launderette', became a major star in his own right. The ads were widely appreciated and discussed. The 1987 campaign continued the success. In the first ad, 'Parting', set in the 1950s, a young GI says goodbye to his girlfriend at the bus station. As he leaves, he gives her a parcel. When she later opens the parcel in her bedroom, she discovers it contains his 501s. She lies down and puts on the jeans.

The success and popularity of these ads virtually guaranteed their exploitation by others. An ad for Carling Black Label lager shows the same situation as 'Launderette' to the accompaniment of the same music, with a similar young man who strips to his boxer shorts to the appreciation of similar giggling girls. On the other side of the launderette are two older, fatter men, completely naked with their hands folded modestly across their laps. One comments: 'I bet he drinks Carling Black Label.' The other replies: 'No. He doesn't wash his underpants.' An ad for the beverage IRN BRU (=iron brew) parodied 'Parting' by showing a similar girl splattered with mud as the bus departs. This ad contains a pastiche of such parodies. When a boy inserts money into a drink-dispensing machine, as in a contemporary Coca-Cola ad, the machine does not work. When he shakes it, it responds by banging him on the head. (A later ad even parodies this parody by creating expectation of this bang on the head, but having the boy thumped in the stomach by the can emerging from the slot.) The slogo for this product

  Iron brew: brewed in Scotland from girders

is inter-discoursal, and makes a more obscure allusion to the poetry of William McGonagall, a Scots poet famous for his clumsy verse, who frequently uses the word 'girders' in his eulogies of Scottish engineering. The popularity of this ad soon warranted an extension of its market and a large growth in sales.[23]

Such cross-references can be multi-layered, for the ad to which another ad refers is itself likely to make inter-discoursal references to other discourse types. 'Parting', for example, assumes knowledge of romances in films and novels.

An ad for Nescafé Gold Blend coffee borrowed inter-discoursally from the discourse type of soap opera by taking the form of a serial, each episode of which ended with a cliffhanger. A man calling at a neighbour's door to borrow coffee is invited in by the sultry and glamorous female occupant. They seem attracted to each other. On another occasion the door is opened by another man. In the next episode . . . it turns out to be her brother . . . And so on. An ad for Sharp Lager showed a similar situation. In this case, the woman lives in a high-rise flat. She leaves the man alone with her dog, called Randy, and goes off to make her visitor a cup of tea (a drink with more mundane connotations than coffee). There is an open window. Seeking to ingratiate himself with the woman by befriending Randy, the man bounces a ball. The ball flies through the open window, closely followed by the dog, who falls, presumably to his death many storeys below. 'Time for a Sharp exit.' The man leaves immediately without explanation. We see him in the pub below. (The black humour of this ad is rather softened by the appearance of the dog, unharmed, in the pub: no doubt in deference to the British love of dogs.)

Another kind of cross-reference occurs when an ad evokes memories of older ads for the same product, thus giving the product a dimension of respectability by drawing attention to its long history. An ad for Bisto Gravy Powder shows the Bisto kids (two of the most well-known British ad characters of the 1950s) setting off in a time machine for the late 1980s. There, they walk into a modern Bisto ad, to find that – although much has

Figure 53 Sharp lager ad: 'Randy'

changed – the smell of Bisto has remained the same! In an interesting attempt to create a similar sense of the history of the advertising of one product, Hamlet cigars are marketing a video of their ads from the 1960s to the 1980s in the hope that it will be watched for pleasure (see Exercise 2.3a, p. 35).

The growth of a tradition, and the accumulation of knowledge of past ads which increases the scope for intra-discoursal references immensely, leads to a growing complexity. Inter-discoursal possibilities, though they have always been available, are constantly extended and exploited.

EXERCISES

1 An ad for Waterman fountain pens shows a fountain pen and two cherries on a black plate. The copy reads:

Envy. Desperately sinful. Wickedly Waterman. And absolutely forgivable. The Man. Waterman.

Is it possible to supply ellipted elements which convert these orthographic sentences into full grammatical sentences with main verbs? What cultural knowledge do you use to make sense of this ad?

2 In the following drink ads, consider what is ellipted, and the information which is assumed.

a (Under a nineteenth-century scene of a handsome young man pic-
nicking beside the Mississippi with two belles. See Figure 54):

Southern Comfort was often drunk neat. But rarely on its own.

b (Picture of a bottle and two glasses):

The cool crisp taste of Martini Extra Dry shines through. Once
found, never lost. It's there to be discovered.

c (Picture: a bottle with a vineyard painted on it; a bottle and a glass)

A poet, a man of the theatre, an art collector, Baron Philippe
always appreciated the finer things in life. And it was his opinion
that nothing is finer than a wine steeped in history and flowing
with quality. We therefore bring Mouton Cadet Blanc Sec to your
attention. Light, crisp, and fresh. A classic vintage Bordeaux
appellation controlée wine. A wine that's as clean as the open sky.
And Mouton Cadet Rouge. A vintage claret. Full, round, fruity
and smooth.

3 Find an advertisement with dense inter- or intra-discoursal allusions.
Discuss how these allusions are established and how successful they are
in increasing the impact of the ad.

4 Consider the following text of an ad for Citizen Watches in terms of

a its assumptions of shared knowledge and value
b its narrative technique
c its intra- and inter-discoursal allusions

Before the night was through they would reveal a lot more to
each other than just their watches.
Copacabana danced below as he came face to face with her
bewildering elegance. Her movements held him spellbound as she
slipped her immaculately manicured fingers inside her leather
handbag to emerge with a cigarette pack.
It was the same American brand of Light 100's he always
carried. Her pack was empty. 'Have one of mine.' Hesitating
slightly, she took one and lit it herself.
That's when he noticed her watch. Like his, it was a modern
Roman face, gold cased with a stitched leather strap. 'We obviously share the same excellent taste in watches, too. What's your
favourite champagne?'
She laughed and spoke at last. 'Same as yours?'
Citizen First Class
Write for our new catalogue with the full range to . . .

Figure 54 Southern Comfort bourbon ad

5 Is the density of narrative voices in a story a measure of quality? If so, how do ads compare with novels and short stories?

FURTHER READING

The Bakhtinian theories of language described in this chapter, and Bakhtin's critique of Saussure, can be found in *Marxism and the Philosophy of Language* ([1929] 1986), a book which Bakhtin published under the name of his friend Volosinov. A more easily accessible introduction to Bakhtin's theories of language and the novel are Chapters 10–11 and 13–14 of K. Clark and Holquist (1984) *Mikhail Bakhtin*. The description of narrative technique in the novel in this chapter owes a great deal to Chapters 6 and 8–10 of Leech and Short (1981) *Style in Fiction*, which provides one of the best introductions to the discourse analysis of fiction.

This chapter has stressed the many voices present within the apparently single voices of sender and addresser. An interesting approach to this phenomenon can be found in Goffman (1981), further developed in Levinson (1988).

9 Ways of hearing

9.0 SENDERS, RECEIVERS, OBSERVERS

Chapters 7 and 8 discussed the narrative voice of ads (the 'I') and the kind of reception it assumes and encourages in the receiver (the 'you'). Though both are important in the discourse, neither narrator nor receiver can be treated as identical with the person who actually writes or reads the ad. Creator(s) of an ad, quite as much as novelists, lawyers, newscasters or scientists, adopt a voice which is suitable to the discourse of these roles, and receivers also, once they have identified the discourse type, adopt a particular stance, or stances, of interpretation.

The role of the receiver in creating meaning has generally been neglected in the study of language, which usually focuses upon either the disembodied text or the sender. (Exceptions are Goffman 1981 and Levinson 1988.) Even Bakhtin's approach lacks this focus, stressing the voices in discourse, and ways of speaking. Yet voices exist only if they are heard. What is needed is an equivalent focus on the receiver, on ways of receiving, even within one person. The obvious term to balance that of voice is **hearing**.

The absence of attention to receivers leads to a considerable simplification of their roles and abilities, and in analyses of advertising receivers are often simplified, patronized and misrepresented.

Generally, it is quite naïve for a competent member of a culture to be unable to disentangle the various roles adopted or demanded by different discourse types. In the public sphere, we know that the prosecution lawyer has private feelings about a case, but accept that he or she speaks as though convinced of the defendant's guilt; that a teacher admonishes behaviour which privately he or she might find amusing; that the teller of a detective story knows who the criminal is, but withholds this information, and so on. In the private sphere, we know that people with whom we are intimate, who talk to us frankly and often emotionally in private, perhaps using 'baby talk' or taboo language to do so, do not talk like that in more public roles. Knowledge, recognition and acceptance of such conventions is part of our cultural competence. Inevitably problems arise when people interpret one discourse type as another: fiction as fact, a joke as a serious comment, political debate as a personal attack, an off-the-record remark as an official statement, and so on. Words must be interpreted within the discourse type to which they belong. 'Dear John' means one thing in conversation, something else at the beginning of a letter.

Because of its relative novelty, and its ambiguity and instability as a discourse type, advertising causes problems, and is often read by conventions imported from other situations and discourses. The voice of the advertisement is treated as the voice of the advertiser, or interpreted by the conventions of another discourse type. The purpose of this chapter is to examine this phenomenon and its results: attitudes towards advertising; ways of reading them; and some judgements of ads by their receivers.

Chapter 8 has provided a framework which will distinguish the **senders** of ads (the people who write, direct, photograph and act in them) from the **narrators** of ads (the personas, characters and voices which senders adopt). In reception we need a parallel distinction between the **recipient** (the receiver responding to an ad by entering into its conventions) and the **observer** (the receiver adopting a more detached perspective, seeing ads in the context of other discourse types).[1] Hearing as a recipient and hearing as an observer are not mutually exclusive. The borders are fuzzy, and there is an infinity of possible positions along a continuum between the two. One person may hear in both ways at once, or in different ways on different occasions.

Although the voice of the narrator is part of the wider personality of the sender, and that personality in turn expresses part of itself through the ad it creates, the senders of ads may maintain some distance from their professional role. A further complication to neat divisions is that senders are also recipients and observers (like everybody else). In reception, observation is affected by experience as a recipient and vice versa. Contrary to the conventions of the scientific approach to language, the most effective observers may also be recipients or narrators.

In the creation of an ad, there are likely to be several senders – manufacturer, photographer(s), writer(s), model(s) or actor(s) (see section 8.3). As senders, these people may either dislike the product or have no experience of it. As narrators, they adopt a voice which may be interpreted as the inner voice of the character, of a confidante, of society in general, or of the addressee. Similarly, an addressee of an ad, as a recipient entering into its spirit, may find it amusing and attractive, or silly and unconvincing; simultaneously, as an observer, he or she may stand back from it, knowing that there is no necessary connection between a good ad and a good product, and judging it according to his or her personal views on gender roles, ecology, economics, politics, aesthetics, and so on. Many analyses of ads depend upon the unproven assumption that addressees have only one impoverished way of responding to discourse, and are too simple to distinguish fact from fantasy or fiction. It is often argued that people are tricked into believing that if they buy the product they will experience the attractive lifestyle of the characters (Berger 1972: 131). As Thompson (1990) sensibly observes (commenting on the prevalence of this view among his students):

> The problem with this is that clearly anyone who *did* believe any such thing as a result of exposure to the advertising message would be gullible to the point of madness, as eccentric as those often-posited, rarely-met individuals who believe in the reality of soap-opera fictions. Students themselves never own up to any such belief, and it is not likely that advertising's power can be based on any *mass* delusional system of this sort.
>
> (original emphasis, Thompson 1990: 211)

As advertising is not a remote and specialized discourse, but a prominent discourse type in contemporary society, of which people have vast and daily experience, reactions to it are correspondingly complex, experienced and sophisticated. They involve many ways of hearing at once.

9.1 NEGATIVE HEARINGS

There are undoubtedly many reasons to dislike ads, whether individually or as a genre. Many people do so, either consistently, or from time to time. Ads usually ask only passive involvement on the part of the receiver (though so does a good deal of art). They are uninvited and intrusive, thrust upon the reader or viewer without consultation. Though print ads can be skipped, and tv ads avoided by zipping and/or zapping, it is virtually impossible to avoid ads entirely. Junk mail is particularly persistent, and often very annoying. It also infringes privacy, making use of large data-bases of personal information about individuals.

While some ads are witty, imaginative, poetic or well filmed, at least an equal number are trite, sentimental or unoriginal. Even the cleverest and most entertaining ads, though interesting at the level of detail, form and execution, can often, in quantity, become dull and trivial.

Ads glorify widely accepted values. A positive evaluation of them may reflect the degree of the observer's belief in the status quo. To the feminist opposed to patriarchy, the gay opposed to heterosexual hegemony, the socialist opposed to capitalism, ads may seem to advocate values whose end is desired.

Ads promote consumption in a world which needs to save resources, and the acquisition of personal wealth in a global society which desperately needs fairer distribution. In the case of junk mail (which threatens to increase) they waste resources even more directly. In the UK in 1986, a mere seventy items per household created a total of 1,400 million items (R. White 1988: 153). In 1990 in the USA, an estimated 500 mail shots per household (*Equinox: Junk Mail*, Channel 4 (UK) 14 October 1990) accounts for around 50 billion items.

Such criticisms as these are relatively straightforward, and no doubt shared by many people. Against them it can be said that ads are often criticized for failing to do things they never set out to do: vying with works of art, providing sustained entertainment, making radical changes to our perception of the world. If they express objectionable social trends or states, it could be argued that they are indices of the enemy, not the enemy itself; if so, they should not perhaps be the first line of attack for those who seek change.

Arguments about ads boil down to some rather straightforward matters of opinion. Are ads trivial? Are there too many of them? Are they unwanted? Do they represent unpleasant values and, if so, are they a major force in promoting those values or only peripheral? Are ads comparable to art? These are matters on which the reader must decide for himself or herself, and it is not my intention to argue for one side or the other. I could not do so even if I wanted to, for like many people I hear ads in several contradictory ways at once. It is the difficulty of finding simple answers to these questions which, in my opinion, makes ads so interesting as a discourse type. (This is not the same as saying that every individual ad is interesting.) Many analyses, however, do take sides, and seek to impose an unequivocal view, using ads as a starting point for discourses which say more about their own creators than about the ads they assault. It is to such discourses that the next two sections turn in detail.

9.2 HOW ADS ARE HEARD BY ARTISTS

In literature, song, film and painting (henceforth 'the arts' for brevity), reactions to ads, as among the general public, range from violent hostility, through indifference and amused detachment, to appreciation (see section 1.6). Though it is impossible to survey such a field in entirety, it is worth citing some representative examples.

Broadly speaking, reactions follow the rise of advertising: the occasional curiosity of the 1930s and 1940s, when ads were relatively peripheral, was replaced by a more aggressive attitude during the rapid expansion and hard selling of the 1950s and 1960s. This in turn gave way to a degree of wry tolerance during the 1970s to 1990s, when ads became both more established and more sophisticated.

Early criticisms are mild, very much in the spirit of Raymond Chandler's Philip Marlowe who, talking about chess, remarks that it is

> about as elaborate a waste of human intelligence as you could find anywhere outside an advertising agency.
>
> (quoted in E. Clark 1988)

(This is, however, the voice of a character, whose presupposition that chess is a waste of time may tell us more about himself than about the author.) Such mildness was not to last. In the early 1950s, the surrealist René

Magritte, asked what he hated most in the world, answered unequivocally: 'advertising . . . imbecilic . . . mediocre stuff for the public'.[2] Allen Ginsberg in *Howl* (1953) included among the forces which destroyed 'the best minds of my generation':

> blasts of leaden verses and the tanked up clatter of the iron regiments of fashion and the nitroglycerine shrieks of the fairies of advertising and the mustard gas of sinister intelligent editors.

Perhaps more dangerous to advertising than such furious attack is indifference, appropriation or laughter. Both ads and the arts are robust, parasitic and self-confident. When there is contact, both struggle to assimilate the other: borrowing, stealing, parodying, smothering, debunking. When the arts have not ignored advertising, they have often approached it with detachment, ridicule and a sense of absurdity – confident that ads are a peripheral and inconsequential phenomenon posing no threat to its own ascendancy.

> Oh set me down on the television floor,
> I'll flip the channel to number four.
> Out of the shower comes a grown-up man
> With a bottle of hair oil in his hand.
> (It's that greasy kids stuff.)
> Well, the funniest woman I ever seen
> Was the great granddaughter of Mr Clean.
> She takes about fifteen baths a day,
> Wants me to grow a cigar on my face.
> (Bob Dylan, *I Shall Be Free* 1965)

As advertising has preyed upon the arts, stealing many of its ideas and incorporating them into its own creations, so the arts are quite prepared to respond in kind, reincorporating ads, using them for its own purposes. In painting, ads and bits of ads have appeared in collage and background since the turn of the century.

In literature, advertising often appears as a symbol of absurdity, a realization of false values in contrast with those of the people into whose lives it intrudes, only emphasizing an absence of meaning. An early example (1926) is the giant poster which broods over the 'valley of ashes' in *The Great Gatsby*

> above the grey land and the spasms of bleak dust which drift endlessly over it, you perceive, after a moment, the eyes of Doctor T.J. Eckleberg. The eyes of Doctor T.J. Eckleberg are blue and gigantic – their retinas are one yard high. They look out of no face, but, instead, from a pair of enormous yellow spectacles which pass over a non-existent nose. Evidently some wily wag of an oculist set them there to fatten his practice in the borough of Queens, and then sank down

himself into eternal blindness, or forgot them and moved away. But his eyes, dimmed a little by many paintless days, under sun and rain, brood on over the solemn dumping ground.

The climax of the novel, a car accident bringing death and separation to the protagonists, takes place near this ad, whose superficial resemblance to a divinity – though one which is uncaring, decayed and outdated – emphasizes the absurdity and hopelessness of the drama acted out beneath it. Since *The Great Gatsby*, there have been many literary contrasts between the bright optimistic images of ads and the drabber, more painful world of everyday life. Philip Larkin's poem 'Sunny Prestatyn', for example, contrasts the advertising image of a seaside resort, showing a girl

kneeling up on the sand
in tautened white satin

with the obscene graffito ('a tuberous cock and balls') drawn between her legs.

From the late 1980s, a new tone has appeared alongside attack and ridicule, which, while maintaining the stereotypes of deceiver and deceived, is marked by a willingness to perceive advertising from inside the mind of its creators as well as through the eyes of the deceived. An example is *Bliss*, a novel by Peter Carey about an ad man who moves to a commune dedicated to environmental protection, forsaking the stressful life of the city to become a tree planter. Although there are many voices in this novel, both for and against ads, and even if both writer and many readers may prefer his second life, there is also a willingness to adopt, albeit temporarily, the voice of the creator of an ad:

Imagine this: a colour poster thirty inches long and eight inches deep. A photograph of a match, very large, occupies almost the entire length of the poster. Beneath it, in Franklin Gothic type, these words: '*All the wood you need to burn this winter*', and beneath that, the logo: Mobil LP Gas.

All this for stores in country areas, to stick on walls for flies to shit on, for mutants to stare at. But look at it there, lying against the pink wall with its cell overlay: a thing of beauty destined to take its place in the One Show in New York . . . All the client had asked for was something cheap and nasty to shut up the country dealers who were complaining about a lack of promotional support. He had not asked for this pristine piece of art lying against the pink wall.

(Peter Carey, *Bliss*, 1982: 205)

Though still critical, this book eschews the total villainization and excommunication of the advertiser.

In film a similar progression to that in literature is evident in the postwar decades. Advertising appears only comic in the films of the 1940s and 1950s such as Sturgess's *Christmas in July* (1940), or Tashlin's *Will Success Spoil Rock Hunter* (1957). Directors of the 1960s and 1970s express their disdain, by never – that I know of – making advertising a central topic, but using it only as a symbol of greed or superficiality. It is in films of this period that the device of ads as a symbol of absurdity becomes prominent. A typical – perhaps seminal – example occurs in Makavejev's *W.R. The Mysteries of the Organism* (1971), where the comment that 'The American Dream is dead' is immediately followed, as though in illustration, by a Coca-Cola jingle. (The connection is implied by proximity and exploits the tendency to create connections when none is signalled: see section 7.1.) In films, this contrast between the jolly voices and affluent images emanating from tv, radio and posters, and the poverty or anguish of characters, has become a cinematic cliché – though still an effective one. Such contrasts reflect a constant tension between the world depicted in ads and the world in which they appear. The 1980s, while still critical, have produced films which both make advertising a centre of attention and present the people who work in it as complex and creative, if also destructive and unseeing. Vigne's *A Woman or Two* (1985) is the story of a high-minded archaeologist (Gerard Depardieu) whose find is exploited by a ruthless advertising executive (Sigourney Weaver). Robinson's *How to Get Ahead in Advertising* (1989) is the story of a creative whose agonizing over a brief for pimple cream causes him to develop a pimple on his neck which grows into a talking head, takes over its host, and arranges for his death. While still anti-advertising, it yet presents the topic from inside, with understanding and consideration of the complexity of the emotional, moral and personal issues for both senders and receivers.

In addition, many film directors, as well as innumerable comedians and actors, are keen to work in ads,[3] for satisfaction as well as for money. Scorsese has directed a perfume ad, Fellini an ad for pasta, Ken Loach an ad for a chocolate bar, and Peter Greenaway an ad for Philips. Alan Parker began his career as a director in advertising (*Late Again* BBC2). The singers of the 1980s and 1990s also endorse ads by promoting and releasing songs through them.

Artistic attitudes to advertising are changing, both among artists and their audiences, though the battle between opponents and apologists continues unabated at the same time. This is clearly the case in France, where in 1983 – as reported by Cinquin (1987) – both the President and the Minister of Culture, Jacques Lang, gave their support to a conference whose objective was, in the words of the latter,

> to prevent the market mechanisms and the economic power struggle from imposing stereotyped, culturally meaningless products on the people.
>
> (Cinquin 1987: 485)

The people, however, did not agree. Cinquin continues:

Advertising has become the most popular art of our time. A French topical magazine could run as a headline: 'The Triumph of Advertising. Within Ten Years the French Have Gone from Ad-phobia to Ad-philia' (*Le Point* 1985: 48). 82% of the French from 10 to 24 years of age declare themselves unreservedly in favor of advertising. 60% of the French think that advertising is informative and entertaining rather than manipulative. 60% consider that it is close to art and 45% prefer advertising to political discourse. . . . 48% of the French less than 35 years of age would not object to the Coca-Cola corporation installing a giant Coca-Cola bottle on the Place de l'Etoile, close to the Arc de Triomphe.

(Cinquin 1987: 490, 493)

And the same Minister, Lang, seems at other times to agree:

Lang who is always in tune with public opinion, inaugurated a Museum of Advertising in Paris on 26 October 1982. On this occasion he declared that 'advertising is cultural for it is part of our universe of forms and signs . . . It is a modern culture insofar as it allows the advances of civilization and puts the newest technologies in its service.' Undoubtedly, advertising is a popular culture.

(Cinquin 1987: 490)

His ambivalence and self-contradiction typify contemporary confusion.

9.3 ACADEMIC ATTITUDES

Academic attitudes to advertising display a similar range to those in the arts. Early work in sociology, semiotics and linguistics (Williams [1960] 1980; Barthes [1964] 1977; McLuhan 1964; Leech 1966; Goffman [1976] 1979), though at times very critical, remains calm. With a new, uncharted and innovative discourse type before it, it provides equally new and suitably perceptive analyses. Much recent work, whether generally supportive (Umiker-Sebeok 1987), neutral (Vestergaard and Schroder 1985) or politically critical (Davis and Walton 1983; Fairclough 1989) is similarly stimulating, though faced with an increasingly complex and heavily analysed discourse. A middle period, however, with its heyday in the late 1970s and early 1980s, was one of ferocious and emotional attack. Though it is written at a later date, this mood is illustrated by the entry under 'advertising' in the *Fontana Dictionary of Modern Thought* (1988 edn), a scholarly, wide-ranging encyclopedia of twentieth-century ideas, whose general tone is informative, factual and non-partisan, even in entries for 'Nazism', 'Stalinism' and 'Apartheid'. In the entry for 'Advertising', however, this tone disappears:

Creativity [in ads] means instant attention-getting, resulting in a glibness or lateral cleverness, not to be confused with creativity in, say, film, literature or art. . . . Concern that such creativity has hidden shallows has resulted in a plethora of self-aggrandizing award festivals, locally and internationally, at which 'creatives' award each other glittering prizes.

(The rest of the short entry is in the same vein.) Though there are valid reasons why many people regret the advent and rapid growth of mass advertising, such all-out abuse in a publication with pretensions to scholarly detachment is intriguing. There may be other reasons than those advanced by the critics themselves why advertising arouses stronger feelings in this period than mass murder and oppression.

To examine this approach, and speculate on its causes, I shall deal with two representative works: Judith Williamson's (1978) *Decoding Advertisements* and Michael Geis's (1982) *The Language of Television Advertising*. These are longer, more detailed works than the encyclopedia entry, but their conclusions, though extended, are as sweeping in their condemnation. As they raise important issues, and typify a species of common but self-defeating criticism, I shall deal with them at some length.

The argument, and the anger, have three bases: an emphasis on text which ignores or simplifies its relation to participants; an unquestioning acceptance of 'scientific fact', 'naturalness' and 'real relationships' as centres of belief; and lastly, though not explicitly, a fear of a discourse type which the authors cannot identify with any existing well-established categories. I shall deal with each in turn: the first two in this section, the last (which raises larger issues) in the concluding sections of this chapter.

In the world of Williamson and Geis, the divisions between types of participant are distinct and unproblematic. They are dealt with swiftly, allowing attention to be centred on the text. The observers regard themselves as above the process, and in no way like the recipients. This swift disposal of participant roles rests upon a gross caricature: the senders of ads are villains, intent on deception; the recipients are uneducated, vulnerable and easily deceived; the observers are superior to both, and unaffected by the text, because they can decode it. (It is a Saussurean rather than Bakhtinian model of communication, treating meaning as a feature of the code.) Geis describes receivers as 'logically and linguistically naïve speakers' (1982: 70), lacking any insight into their own everyday lives; they are 'speakers untutored in logic' who 'do not control' the fine distinctions of his analysis (1982: 12). And they suffer accordingly.

> To some degree, viewers get the commercials they deserve, that is, commercials to which they respond.
>
> (Geis 1982: 110)

> if language scholars do not draw attention to linguistic abuses in public uses of language we leave the field open to various self-styled language experts whose critiques are usually shallow and misinformed.
>
> (Geis 1982: xiii)

It is unclear why Geis does not consider himself 'a viewer' along with everybody else, nor why other experts, but not he, are 'self-styled'!

9.3.1 Logic and fact

For Geis, decoding means transforming the text into its underlying logical and factual form. (He appeals to the formal logic of propositional calculus.) But this logical meaning is not seen as a *part* of the meaning, but its totality. This leads to consternation and outrage when language resists transformation. Of a cereal ad which begins 'Mother Nature sweetens apples for two good reasons' he writes:

> Everything claimed is false, for there is no such thing as Mother Nature.
>
> (Geis 1982: 88)

Of a margarine ad which describes its taste as 'buttery':

> if someone says something is buttery there is no objective basis for determining whether or not what is said is true.
>
> (Geis 1982: 122)

To a pet food ad with the words:

> she thinks she's still a puppy, and she looks like one too, but she's 14 years old

he objects, firstly on the grounds that dogs can't think in this way, and secondly that the simile is not apt because, although

> The older dog does look like a puppy in that she has four legs two ears a tail, a dog shaped body and head etc. . . . . it is difficult to see how a 14 year old dog could actually look like a puppy unless it had oversize paws much puppy fat etc.
>
> (Geis 1982: 123)

At the centre of this approach is the belief that the surface forms of language are mere translations of a 'deeper', hidden, but superior language – in this case a logical representation. Substance and situation (see Chapters 2–4), connotation, metonymy and metaphor (see Chapter 5), the emotive, conative, phatic and poetic function of language (see Chapter 6), the interactive potential of the text to mean different things to different people in different situations (see Chapter 7), the different stances of senders (see Chapter 8) and receivers (see this chapter) are all ignored.

In many discourses, the underlying factual or logical content is either non-existent or of secondary importance; yet this does not deprive them of value. If we return, for example, to the stanza of Oscar Wilde's *The Ballad of Reading Gaol*, cited in Chapter 6 as an example of parallelism, it is possible to translate this stanza (and the whole discourse of which it forms a part) into underlying logical and semantic representation. (Geis would presumably conclude that the stanza is nonsense, because one cannot kill with a 'bitter look' or 'flattering word'.) But such 'facts' are of little relevance to an analysis of the effect of this stanza on a receiver. This will depend more on knowledge, recognition and judgement of, on the one hand, surface linguistic phenomena such as prosody, parallelisms, the connotations of specific signifiers (e.g. 'kiss'), and, on the other hand, of facts which are not referred to in the text – about Oscar Wilde, his imprisonment, capital punishment and so on. If the aim of linguistic analysis is to account for understanding of texts, then it must take all this into account, and describe sender, text and the receiver. In certain discourse types, including poetry and ads, the underlying logical representation – if it exists at all – may not be particularly important.

9.3.2 'Natural' and 'real'

Closely wedded to the unquestioning belief in the logical and factual basis of the text as an evaluative measure is the insistence that it be 'natural' and 'real': terms which are bandied about in criticisms of ads quite as freely as they are in ads themselves! (This irony seems to have passed unnoticed.)

Despite brief lip-service to the view that the term 'fact' is not quite as straightforward as it might appear, Williamson (1978: 29) has no hesitation in presenting her own semiotic interpretations as facts, even on the same page! Each element in a picture is given a single 'meaning'. These equivalences reveal that ads are both 'unreal' and 'unnatural'. They 'violate natural human needs' (1978: 110). In them

> We are placed in reconstructed and *false* relationships to *real* phenomena. We misrepresent our relation to nature, and we avoid our real situation in time.
>
> (Williamson 1978: 102, original emphasis)

> Advertisements obscure and avoid the real issues of society. . . . Real objects are lifted out of our physical reality and absorbed into a closed system of symbols, a substitute for reality and real emotions.
>
> (Williamson 1978: 47)

> this prevents us from assessing the real relationship between sign and referent, finding out ads' real process of signification.
>
> (Williamson 1978: 73)

For Williamson, who declares herself to be (at once!) a Saussurean, Freudian and Marxist, 'reality' is the underlying meaning, the equivalence between the surface form of an ad and (respectively to the above list of allegiances) its signified, latent unconscious content, or economic relations. Like logic for Geis, this 'reality' needs to be interpreted by an authoritative figure who knows the code. All other meanings are 'unnatural' and 'unreal'.

This confidence in distinguishing the real and the unreal, and condemnation of any representation of the latter as immoral continues in the late 1980s:

> People's involvement in politics is less and less as citizens and more and more as consumers; and their bases of participation are less and less the real communities they belong to.
>
> (Fairclough 1989: 211)

> when we are surrounded by a synthetic intimacy, friendship, equality and sympathy, could that not affect our ability to confidently recognize the real article?
>
> (Fairclough 1989: 218)

I am not criticizing these writers for preferring one kind of relationship, or one system of political and economic organization to another. I agree that increased consumerism has many detrimental and socially undesirable effects. But in what sense is the production and reception of advertising not 'real'? Is the objection that the content of ads is often fiction? If so, is all fiction being condemned? It is not clear. It seems that the criticism of being 'unreal' applies both to the fictional world portrayed within ads and to the kind of producer–consumer relationships they create in the world outside. Ads, and the relations within them and around them, are contrasted with 'real emotions', 'real situations in time', 'real communities', 'real relationships', 'real meanings'. But why is one community, one kind of human relationship, one mode of existence more 'real' or 'natural' than another? Ads, the world they portray, and the world in which they exist, may indeed have replaced other kinds of discourses, situations, communities, relationships or meanings, which the observer values, and this may be a cause for regret. But that is to say that the economic, political or social system of the present is undesirable – not that it is unnatural or unreal. The relationships of manufacture and consumption, and their discourses, of which advertising is one, are as real and natural (or, if you prefer, as unreal and unnatural) as those of any other discourse. In the 1990s they may – perhaps regrettably – seem more real and natural than a utopian future or a golden past.

> The need for relationship and human meaning appropriated by advertising is one that, if only it was not diverted, could radically change the society we live in.
>
> (Williamson 1978: 14)

9.3.3 Decoding decoders

Several points may be made in deconstruction of such approaches. There is a contradiction between the professed opposition to a hierarchical, exploitative and elitist system – their supposed championing of the oppressed – and the elitist assumptions of the analyses. Despite the claim to uncover and decode hidden meanings and ideologies, they produce yet another version (in structuralist terms a 'transformation') of one of the myths underpinning the patriarchal system they attack. A hero (the academic observer/knight in armour) frees the weak victim (the 'viewer'/damsel) enslaved by the oppressive tyrant (the advertiser/wicked king). The means of enslavement is the text, which like the chains of more exciting versions is treated as a material object rather than a living communication. To effect this emancipation the observers must reveal hidden meanings of the text which the recipients (who are ignorant of the code) cannot perceive without their help. It is a simple and distorted evasion of a complex cultural phenomenon.

This is by no means to discount all opposition to ads. As I have said, there are many valid grounds for opposition. But a weakness of these approaches is that the features they highlight are not only features of advertising but of many other discourse types as well, including those of art. Williamson, for example, criticizing the notion that a possession may express the personality of the owner (1978: 47), would damn Van Gogh's painting of his chair or boots, as well as any advertisement. Likewise the insistence on the representation of reality would condemn the whole realm of fiction, myth and symbolic meaning. Demands for logic and fact exclude all phatic, emotive, connotational or metaphorical expression. If ads are to be singled out, it must be for features which they do not share with other discourse types.

9.4 THE AMBIGUITY OF ADS AS A DISCOURSE TYPE

To continue in this deconstructive vein, perhaps one unacknowledged reason for venom against ads is their failure to conform to a known discourse type. It is claimed by Lévi-Strauss ([1964] 1969) that people or entities which cannot be classified within a cultural or semantic system become taboo, and objects of hatred. In this context, the charge of 'unnaturalness', often made against ads, is revealing – for it seems to assume the order of discourses before the advent of advertising as the only possible one. Geis (1982: 150–9) criticizes the dialogue of an ad for not being like that of a conversation. It is not 'natural', 'not the sort of thing one would ever say spontaneously' (1982: 159). This criticism, which applies equally to Shakespeare's verse, denies advertising its own status and conventions as a discourse type and demands it conform to another, in comparison with which it is inevitably found lacking. Favourite discourse types for comparison are conversation, news, law and poetry. This point does not absolve ads from criticism; but it distinguishes two different lines of attack. One approach recognizes ads as a discourse type which it analyses and evaluates; the other seeks to deny them even their existence.

Critics who take this latter approach are less likely to win their case, for their criticisms do not match wiser popular perceptions. In searching for the features of other discourse types, they often write off important features in entirety. An example is humour, which for many people is one of ads' most salient characteristics. Predictably, Williamson and Geis are disapproving:

> the joke is the inadequacy of the given cause in explaining the effect.
>
> (Williamson 1978: 82)

> I suspect that some viewers will find these commercials amusing.
>
> (Geis 1982: 126)

This outcry, with its insistence that all discourse must be socially or educationally improving, still continues. Writing of Barthes's idea that a text might be a stimulus for play and pleasure, Day (1990) expresses indignation:

> if this is the case then analysis becomes self-indulgence which is hardly a good basis for political progress.
>
> (Day 1990: 3)

and continues

> Advertising promotes insecurity. It encourages consumers to believe in a state of affairs – Utopia or their own perfectibility – which can never be realized. Moreover, this intense stimulation of belief takes place in the context of a culture which believes in nothing.
>
> (Day 1990: 4)

The demand for a monologic, humourless, paternalistic authority could not be clearer.

The approach is out-of-date. Ads and their receivers have changed, and the methods of Williamson and Geis do not work on the ads of the 1980s and 1990s, which are no longer solely concerned with verifiable facts, nor with persuading the supposedly gullible masses that a particular product will transform them.

9.5 NEW FACTORS

This leaves us with two questions. How have ads changed? What is their current content and function if it is no longer to lie and seduce? The orders of discourse in a society change with its technology, especially its technology of communication. Periods of change understandably arouse insecurity and anger in those with interests in existing discourse types, because new ones disturb an existing way of classifying the world. This happens with major changes in modes and media. There have been attacks on writing, print, photography, film, television, computers. There is also antagonism towards the genres which develop from these changes. In chirographic culture, few texts were considered worth the labour of copying. With the advent of printing, when more could be produced, new genres evolved, including the novel. But the novel was criticized as mere entertainment: immoral, trivial and fictional (Watt [1957] 1963: 36–61). Similarly, film (as a genre) dependent on film (as a technology) aroused antagonism in its early days.

New technologies bring the opportunity to reproduce both greater varieties and greater quantities of discourse. Advertising as it is today (rather than in 1950) – brief, disposable, multi-modal, often quite trivial – is very much the child of television and new printing technology. In earlier decades, it would have been unthinkable to devote film and printing to such unimportant issues as the purported difference between one soap powder and another. Yet, although our society has the capability to produce on such a scale, there is also awareness of a new factor which should motivate reduction. Paper and other materials, in a world of diminishing resources, are always valuable, and there is a valid ecological argument against the quantity used. This, however, is a different issue from moral, aesthetic and political criticism. In its criticisms of ads, the artistic and academic establishment seems often to be saying that only the most serious discourse deserves paper or tv time. There is also an implication that more serious discourses are being swamped. This is without evidence, and betrays both a paternalistic and pessimistic view of humanity. There is no sign that interest in film, books or tv programmes is being replaced by interest in ads, nor any reason to suppose that people would go to the cinema, buy magazines or switch on the tv only for ads. The alarm is unjustified. Boursicot's *The Night of the Ad Watchers* (1990), a film which strung ads together for seven hours, made the audience react, as intended, with criticism and ridicule.[4]

To some extent, for this reason, the anger has subsided. Ads need not be perceived as a threat to other discourse types nor the harbingers of social disintegration. They are one among the many discourse types of contemporary society. In small doses – which is how most people take them – they are often entertaining, sometimes amusing, sometimes aesthetically pleasing, occasionally insightful and thought-stimulating; but as with other imaginative discourse types, many instances are also often trite, predictable, annoying or boring. (Precisely which ads belong to which category will vary between individuals and groups.) The same is true of the discourse types of art. Many poems are trite and predictable; many novels are full of objectionable views, or generally not worth reading – though, again, not the same ones for everyone. Advertising is a new discourse type, and as it enters the complex field of discourse types in our society it is bound to cause reactions and changes to the whole. Its use of many literary and artistic techniques provokes reappraisal of those genres which have monopolized these techniques for so long. Yet if we believe in the value of an existing canon, and the judgements of our own and earlier generations which it reflects, we should have faith in future generations too. There is no reason to suppose that they will suddenly cease to value those discourses which seem to provide insight into life and increase understanding of it, though there is reason to suppose that precisely which discourses fulfil that role will be different.

The argument is circular. Ads have no special power to demand attention, and thus, for most people, they remain of peripheral interest. If in the future they become more important, this will presumably be because they deserve attention. If they become valuable, even according to values alien to us, they will be valued. For the moment, while they remain of interest as an active part of the totality of contemporary discourse, as individual works, they often seem no more than mildly entertaining. But there is room for such discourses too.

EXERCISES

1 What is your view of ads? If you are using this book as part of a course, can you divide your class by their attitude to ads? Is your view of ads affected by consideration of any of the following?

   a Cigarette ads aim to persuade people to use a drug which causes foetal abnormalities, bronchitis, cancer and death.

   b The late 1980s saw a marked increase in condom advertising. Condoms help to prevent the spread of AIDS.

   c The weeks leading up to Christmas are marked by an increase in toy advertising during children's programmes, drawing children's attention to toys which their parents may not be able to afford.

   d The weeks leading up to Christmas are marked by an increase in advertising to stop drinking and driving. A link has been suggested between the effectiveness of these campaigns and falling casualties (*Campaign* 30 November 1990: 14). The 'better' the ad, it is claimed, the greater the effect. One hard-hitting campaign in Australia was followed by a 37 per cent fall in road deaths in the seven weeks following the campaign (*The Observer* 7 July 1991).

2 Many artists and writers have designed and written ads.

   a Several paintings by Toulouse-Lautrec were ads for the Moulin Rouge.

   b Salvador Dali wrote and appeared in an ad for Lanvin Chocolate. He bites into a bar of Lanvin with the words 'Je suis fou du chocolat Lanvin' and the ends of his long moustache vibrate and curl upwards.

   c The novelist Fay Weldon is reputed to have written the words of an ad for eggs: 'Go to work on an egg.'

   d Magritte ran an advertising agency called Dongo, and produced many ads for it.

   e Mayakovsky wrote an ad for biscuits.

Should their creations be considered part of their oeuvre? If not, why not?

3 Direct mailing operations categorize people by area. Terms used include:[5]

In the USA	*In the UK*
Blue Blood Estates	Cosmopolitan
Money and Brains	House Sharers
Furs and Station Wagons	Upwardly Mobile
Pools and Patios	Financially Active
Two More Rings	Golf Clubs and Volvos
Young Influentials	Lager, Crisps and Videos
Young Suburbia	
Urban Gold Coast	

How successful would you expect such divisions to be in predicting consumption? Would you expect different areas to like different types of ad? Do areas match more traditional divisions such as socio-economic class, personality, lifestyle, age, gender?

FURTHER READING

The best way to follow this chapter is with a series of polemical readings both for and against advertising. Particularly useful are the chapters on advertising in Alvarado and Thompson (1990) *The Media Reader*, which deliberately sets out to provide a balance between proponents and opponents. Other useful readings are:

Against

Chapter 7 of Berger (1974) *Ways of Seeing*; Chapters 10 and 13 of Bolinger (1980) *Language: The Loaded Weapon*; Knight (1990) 'Is the micro macho? A critique of the fictions of advertising'; Chapter 8 of Fairclough (1989) *Language and Power*; Raymond Williams [1960] (1980) 'Advertising: the magic system'.

For

Most essays in Umiker-Sebeok (1987) *Marketing and Semiology* are implicitly 'pro', but especially interesting in this respect is Cinquin (1987) 'Homo Coca-Colens: from marketing to semiotics and politics'; Chapter 16 of R. White (1988) *Advertising: What It Is and How to Do It* (2nd edn) is a 'common sense' defence of advertisers.

And, while in controversial mood, Susan Sontag's essay [1962] (1972) 'Against interpretation' is a stimulating iconoclastic attack on the whole business of the academic search for 'underlying meanings'.

10 Conclusion: ads as a discourse type

10.0 INTRODUCTION

This chapter reassesses the issue with which we began: the nature of ads as a discourse type. Taking account of the analyses in the preceding nine chapters, it first attempts to extract from them features which are characteristic of the materials, language and participants of ads. It then makes further suggestions about ads' social and psychological function.

Let us begin with fourteen features suggested in the analysis so far. In keeping with what has been said earlier about the indeterminacy of definitions, and the impossibility of establishing clear boundaries between one discourse type and another, features are presented as prototypical of ads rather than as definitive components (see Chaper 1).

1. ads use a variety of substances for discourse, including some which are not used elsewhere (e.g. soap, vapour)
2. ads are embedded in an accompanying discourse[1]
3. ads are presented in short bursts[2]
4. ads are multi-modal, and can use pictures, music and language, either singly or in combination, as the medium permits
5. ads, in their use of language, are multi-submodal, and can use writing, speech and song, either singly or in combination, as the medium permits
6. ads contain and foreground extensive and innovative use of para-language
7. ads foreground connotational, indeterminate and metaphorical meaning, thus effecting fusion between disparate spheres
8. ads make dense use of both intra-modal and inter-modal parallelisms
9. ads use a heteroglossic narrative
10. ads are parasitic: appropriating and existing through the voices of other discourse types
11. ads are often heard in many contradictory ways simultaneously
12. ads merge the features of public and private discourse, and the voices of authority and intimacy, exploiting the features which are common to these poles
13. ads make extensive use of intra- and inter-discoursal allusion

14 ads provoke social, moral and aesthetic judgements ranging from the most positive to the most negative ('harmful'/'beneficial', 'bad'/'good', 'not art'/'art').

As this list progresses it becomes more controversial. There is no clear dividing line between a feature which appears independent of individual or group opinion, and is thus apparently a feature of text, and one which depends upon the existing values and knowledge of the receiver, and is thus clearly open to dispute. But this is not surprising. Discoursal features arise, as we have seen, through the interaction of sender and receiver, and are therefore relative and variable. Even assuming an unlikely uniformity among the senders of ads, there is tremendous variation both within and between the people who receive them. It is impossible to be specific about discoursal features without also specifying the receiver (variation between individuals) or one way of hearing (variation within an individual). Advertising, or an individual ad, can thus be many contradictory things at once: precisely because judgement depends on factors which vary most between individuals in our[3] societies (such as attitudes to inequality of wealth, consumerism, economic growth, capitalism, patriarchy, 'high' culture), and because the receptiveness of an individual will change with mood.

This book has adopted a metaphor of discourse as levels, and moved 'upwards' from substance through form to interaction. As we 'rise' through the levels, the situation becomes more and more controversial. There is certainly nothing like daylight on the surface. Thus while features 1–5 are relatively uncontroversial and 6–8 a little less so, features 9–14 are becoming more contentious. Look, for example, at feature 9. For some people, and for some ways of hearing, the apparent heteroglossia of ads is a complete sham, masking a noxious monologic discourse. In this view, there are not many voices in ads at all, but one voice, skilled in ventriloquism and mimicry. Where differences in receivers may yield opposite results only an area can be specified. One might say, for example, that 'ads provoke moral judgements', and this might be widely accepted. Saying that 'ads are immoral' or 'ads are moral' on the other hand, will be true only for some people. Perhaps the only features of ads on which everyone might agree is

15 ads provoke controversy.

If discourse must always be linked to a particular sender, then this chapter, and this book as a whole, are no exception. Though written in an academic style, they too express the opinion of one person. By writing above about 'what this chapter does', I personified this text which you are now reading. It might be preferable to say that it is I, the writer, and you, the reader, who do things by means of this text. In the same way, it is not ads which do the things listed above, and have intentions and habits, but their senders and their receivers – although from another perspective senders and receivers gain their identity from interactions with texts. Personifications of texts are perhaps a necessary metaphor, if only because they are so deeply rooted in the language and culture of contemporary chirographic societies, with their tendency to reify or attribute human characteristics to discourse. The notion of 'objectivity' in discourse, when pursued, may mean no more than the statement of 'shared assumptions', and 'subjectivity' the statement of more personal or idiosyncratic views. Yet although 'objectivity' in discourse, in the absolute sense of representing truths independent of observers, may be a positivist myth,[4] there persists a feeling (which I share) that there are degrees of objectivity and subjectivity. Thus, though no statement about advertising is uncontroversial, the remainder of this chapter (and of the book) could be described as a more speculative view of the nature and function of advertising than earlier chapters – though its purpose is to raise rather than answer the larger questions of advertising. It focuses upon five main areas: the restlessness of ads; their disposition to change and reverse any features which become typical; their uses of time and space; their social and psychological role (in particular their code play and its relation to poetry and display); and their value. It suggests a further eleven typical features which may be added to the fifteen above. Again, these features, are proposed as prototypical, rather than definitive.

16 ads have the typical restless instability of a new discourse type
17 ads are a discourse on the periphery of attention
18 ads constantly change
19 ads follow a principle of reversal, causing them to change many features, as soon as they become established, to their opposite
20 ads seek to alter addressees' behaviour but this is understood by default, and need not occupy space or time
21 ads are identified by their position in an accompanying discourse, and do not need to use space or time to establish their identity as an ad
22 ads use their space and time in an attempt to give pleasure
23 ads use code-play
24 ads answer a need for display and repetitive language
25 ads are unsolicited by their receivers
26 ads, as verbal art, are detrimentally constrained by the need to fulfil the wishes of their clients

10.1 A RESTLESS DISCOURSE

Ads have the typical instability of a new discourse type. Alluding to their frenetic brevity, Barthes aptly referred to the images of ads as 'restless'. This restlessness not only is internal to an individual ad, but also applies to advertising in general, its effect on receivers, and its relations to society and to other discourses. The conventions of ads change fast, driven by an internal dynamic, by changes in society, and by changes in the discourse types on which they are parasitic or in which they are embedded. Virtually any statement about advertising becomes outdated as soon as it is made. Like parody and the novel, ads have no voice of their own (though this similarity does not necessarily imply that they are of equal value); they are a fluctuating and unstable mixture of the voices around them, constantly transmuting and re-combining, so that at present (1992) any lasting characterization is impossible. Synchronically, there are too many exceptions. Diachronically, the rules are in flux.

This restlessness is characteristic of new discourse types, which, like volcanic lava, erupt through the hardened cold rock of older discourses, before themselves hardening as time progresses. Before they settle and cool, their shape is indefinable.

10.1.1 The periphery of attention

Another reason for this impression of restlessness is that ads, for many people, are either not at the centre of attention or do not hold attention for long. Ads come in short bursts. While they may momentarily amuse or attract, their nature changes under scrutiny. Their brief is to gain and hold attention, fix a name with positive associations, and go. Yet many ads do not succeed in attracting attention at all. Those which do, do so only briefly. They are uninvited, embedded in another discourse such as a tv programme, newspaper article or mail delivery, which, for the recipient, is more important. For these reasons, ads often exist on the periphery of receiver attention.

To say this is not to criticize, for that is how ads are designed to be perceived. To subject them to intense analysis changes this nature (and is also very unsettling for the observer). In a sense, an ad ceases to be itself when it is scrutinized, and it is impossible to study an ad as it is usually perceived. To treat an ad as something at the centre of attention transforms it. This makes ads frustratingly resistant to dissection and criticism, which always seems to be taking ads more seriously than they were intended.

10.2 CONSTANT CHANGE

Advertising is constantly changing. This is most evident in changes at the 'lower' levels of substance, surroundings, mode and paralanguage (dealt with in Part I), and also at the level of text (dealt with in Part II). Some might say that changes only take place at these 'lower' levels, and that the readiness for innovation there is compensation for an inability to change at 'higher' level of content ('what sort of world is portrayed') and overall intention ('what advertisers aim to do'). I believe that there is some degree of change at these 'higher' levels too, as I shall argue below (section 10.3 onwards), though there are also severe constraints. But let us deal with these changes level by level, and look first at the less controversial areas.

Whereas the substances of other discourses tend to change only with the advent of major new technologies (writing, printing, the telephone) which profoundly affect society, in advertising, new uses of substance appear all the time, though their significance appears gimmicky and trivial. In their relationship to their surroundings, ads constantly raid new territory. During their short history, they have frequently moved into new media: shop fronts, magazines, posters, film, radio, tv, the telephone, the post (junk mail) and computer networks. Consequently, they have appeared in new places: the street, the cinema, the sitting room, the mailbox, the roadside and the computer screen.

The relationship of ads to their accompanying discourses changes too. Within forty years they have shifted away from attempts to merge with accompanying discourses, to a tendency to keep separate, and then back again. (On tv, the sponsored tv programmes of the 1950s gave way to the clearly delineated 'commercial break' and then moved back to sponsored tv programmes; in print, ads clearly labelled 'advertisement' in newspapers and magazines are in competition with advertorials.) Some tv ads also try to break out of their enclosed space through inter-discoursal allusion, or by creating stories which proceed from one commercial to the next (see section 8.6). Yet generally the space assigned to ads is clearly delineated. Ads are under considerable pressure to remain short, and the borders of other discourse types are well defended against encroachment.

The focus on the modes used in ads has also shifted, from print to pictures and (where possible) music; it now threatens, in the ecologically irresponsible burgeoning of junk mail, to move back to print. At the textual level, there has been ever greater foregrounding of indeterminate and emotive meaning, and parallelism.

10.3 A PRINCIPLE OF REVERSAL

But ads not only change their features, but also reverse them. This tendency is so marked and persistent that it warrants description as a **principle of reversal**. According to this principle many features, once established as typical of ads, are liable to be replaced by their opposite. This can take place at any of the levels of discourse (except perhaps that of overall intention). It is motivated, presumably, by the advertisers' constant desire to attract attention. Features considered typical of ads are often pointedly abandoned, thus defeating expectation and arresting attention. (Paradoxically, this principle, if typical of ads, will lead to its own reversal!)

Let us look at three common assumptions about ads:

- they are 'unrealistic'
- they always portray a bland and problem-free world
- they eulogize a product, stressing its advantages, while ignoring, or distracting attention from, its disadvantages.

10.3.1 'Unrealism' in ads and its reversal

Ads are no longer necessarily 'unrealistic'. In ads, as in literature, the effect of realism derives partly from the manipulation of convention rather than from correspondence to the non-linguistic world. It may be caused by the inclusion of detail which by earlier conventions is omitted (Tomashevsky [1925] 1965; Jakobson [1921] 1978). Consider, for example, a fictional description of a male character in a novel, as perceived by a female character, at a first meeting. The whole event is fictional, in the sense that these two people don't exist and never came together in this place; yet it is also measurable against reality, in that the component details may be matched against the reader's own non-fictional and non-verbal experience. By current convention, saying that the man has rippling muscles and steel-blue eyes is regarded as 'unrealistic';[5] saying that he has bad breath and a fat beer-belly may be regarded as 'realistic'. Yet both kinds of men exist in the real world. (If the latter kind occur more frequently in a reader's experience, that does not make the former unreal.) Similarly, it is convention which makes coincidence considered 'unrealistic' in literature, though it happens in life (and thus paradoxically occurs less often in 'realistic' literature than in life). The relation between 'realism' and reality, in other words, is anything but simple. In our society, 'realism' in art is generally considered to be a positive quality. This is a good example of something unsaid, a 'gap' which reveals a shared ideology (see section 8.2.1). If we say a book is 'realistic', we do not need to add 'and I think realism is a positive quality'. This reflects a widely held view that art and literature should be, as Hamlet says, 'a mirror up to nature'.[6] By such conventions, advertising has been criticized as 'unrealistic' and therefore automatically bad. And it is true that it does not generally represent the world as it is. Its portrayal of home life, for example, does not reflect the proportion of single-parent families, or of gays and lesbians.

Yet it is not just that the worlds in ads is 'unrealistic', as are the worlds of science fiction; they are also often bland and problem-free. All families are happy; all days are sunny; all meals tasty; all Christmases snowy; all grannies kind and white-haired; all countryside litter-free; all farming traditional. The conventional nature of this 'unrealism' is borne out by the fact that all of the above occur. In the real world, a granny who rolls out home-made pastry and then sits in a rocking chair by a log fire is possible; so is a bad-tempered granny who cooks tasteless meals. There are cows and chickens which roam freely in green meadows and farmyards, as well as those in factory farms. By convention, however, the former cases are regarded as less realistic.

If we criticize ads for this selectivity and avoidance of problems, we should remember that many respected art forms are open to the same criticisms. In ancient Greek sculpture, all young men are muscular, all young women shapely, all old men dignified. In pastoral poetry, just as in butter ads, all rural life is idyllic. In Jane Austen's novels, all deserving unrequited love finds fulfilment.

10.3.2 Reverses in the worlds portrayed

In the terms of current conventions, however, advertising is becoming more 'realistic', though how far the trend will go is as yet unclear. Some recent British ads are striking in their reversal of expectations. In an ad for Fuji film, the example of a good photograph is not a snapshot of a 'normal', happy, healthy family (two parents, two children) on the beach, but a photograph suggsting hope amid scenes of racial tension between parents outside an inner-city school (see Figure 55). An ad for Bisto Chicken Gravy does not show the usual happily married housewife feeding her growing son, but a divorced father in a bedsit. An Anadin ad shows a husband being unpleasantly aggressive towards his wife. A controversial ad against drinking-and-driving shows a small girl listening to her mother screaming at her father, asking how she is to explain that he murdered a little boy. An ad urging middle-aged men to eat more healthily shows a woman waking to find her husband has died in bed beside her.

Some ads are shot from a real rather than a staged scene.[7] A Wranglers jeans ad includes documentary footage of beggars and a mugging in New York.[8] An ad for Southern Comfort shows kerb crawlers and pickpockets in the red light district of New Orleans. In these ads, however, though the photographs make use of actual events, their function, in provoking an attractive aura of streetwise excitement, is closer to the idealizing 'un-realistic' ad than to those fictional but cautionary ads against anti-social behaviour like those showing the screaming mother and the dead man in bed.

The popular view that ads are uniformly anodyne and idyllic overlooks the fact that, paradoxically, some of the most shocking and disturbing pictures are found in ads. Ads for charities use images which most indict the consumers of the rich world: the emaciated legs and distended sto-machs of children on the verge of death; the homeless on the streets of rich cities; sufferers from diseases which can easily be cured. An ad for Amnesty International shows thirteen photographs of tortures, executions and beatings in thirteen different countries.[9] One photograph shows sol-diers casually carrying the parts of a child they have torn apart alive. Critics should remember that these images, as well as those of happy prosperous families, are brought to our attention by advertising agencies. They are 'realistic' in both senses: they depart from convention, and also inform us of a real situation. Against this, it may be said that opinion and behaviour in the rich world are too hardened to the plight of the poor and oppressed for such ads to have any effect. Yet, if anything might shift this entrenched complacency, it is such photographs. Of course, they appear only in a minority of ads, and only when agencies are paid to produce them. But if the credit for showing such pictures lies with the client rather than with the agency, then, by the same token, the blame for 'unrealistic' ads should surely lie with the client too. So, while the majority of ads show a world where all is well, others, albeit a minority, show the world as – for many of its inhabitants – it is. Such a reverse is typical of this restless discourse.

In describing changes within literary discourse types, it has been proposed that as each generation rejects existing values there is some coincidence with the values of the generation before (Eikhenbaum [1927] 1978: 32). For this reason, it is said, current instances of a genre resemble their grandparents rather than their parents. There is a tendency to elevate a genre which was neglected or relegated by the previous generation to the status of high art. Formalist critics regard such changes as the result of an internal dynamic quite independent of changes in the real world, and intend talk of generations only metaphorically. Changes in fictional worlds, however, are also influenced by the actions and reactions of the people in the world at large. In the case of ads, there is the further complication that, as a genre held in low esteem (at the bottom, as it were, of the artistic heap), they tend not only to respond to changes in the world at large, but also to changes in more esteemed genres such as film and poetry, and even to changes in other 'low-cultural' forms such as pop songs and soap operas. The lower the esteem for a genre, the more receptive and unpredictable it becomes. Paradoxically, low status, which makes a genre most susceptible to change, also makes it, for this very reason, interesting and innovative. This in turn leads to a rise in status, which in turn leads to rigidity.

As we have seen, the 'lower' levels of ads all change with speed. The world to which they refer – whether real or fictional – also changes. It is not only representations of the real world which respond to changes in the real world. Fictional worlds are also affected. At the simplest level, the realia of ads – clothes, cars, houses – keep pace with change. Yet as fiction can influence the behaviour of real people, so the relation between the fictional and real worlds is dynamic, with each affecting the other. This is particularly true of commodities depicted in ads, for if advertising has any success at all, then presumably the kinds of commodity found in the real world reflect those found in advertising, and vice versa. Yet in the case of commodities one may feel with some justification that this is not of profound importance. Ads show a world in which toothpaste is used more often than tooth powder, because that world was influenced by the successful marketing of toothpaste. They show a world in which men, as well as women, smoke tipped cigarettes,[10] because there was once a remarkably successful advertising campaign which persuaded men that this was not 'effeminate'. Some might ask: 'So what?' What matters is people and society; objects are interesting only for their cultural and social significance. The connection between plain cigarettes and masculinity is arbitrary. What of the people in ads and the kind of personal or social relationships between them? They too change. The obedient housewife of the 1950s and 1960s becomes the sex object of the 1970s, the power-dressed executive of the 1980s the super-fit woman of the 1990s. The patriarch of the 1950s and 1960s becomes the vain Don Juan of the 1960s and 1970s, the selfish executive of the 1980s becomes the smug family man of the 1990s.[11] The same questions arise concerning the direction and state of influence between fiction and reality. Do these changes reflect only an internal dynamic which is a law unto itself, or changes in the real world to which they refer? And, if the latter, do they follow rather than lead? (The same questions apply to pictorial art or literature.)

10.3.3 Claims, techniques and their reverses

Further evidence of a principle of reversal is provided by the way ads mock advertising conventions. If an ad departs from expectation, it will attract attention and/or convince. Take, for example, the 'blonde on the bonnet' syndrome: the gratuitous use of conventionally attractive women in advertisements aimed at men. A car ad uses the phrase 'blonde on the bonnet' but shows not a bikini-clad girl, but an elderly judge in a wig. A related tendency is the attraction of attention by internal contradiction. An ad for Anderson & Lembke with the headline 'Why people don't read long copy ads' is followed by two pages of small print copy and no pictures.

Standard claims for the product are also reversed. Sanatogen Cod Liver Oil 'tastes as awful today as it always did'. 'It's good, but not that good,' says a character in a Tennent's Pilsner lager ad, leaving his pint unfinished to accompany a beautiful girl. In the USA, Eastern Airlines, in a bid to attract attention and win sympathy, produced an ad which quoted genuine customer complaints, such as:

> Lack of professionalism
> Bags don't get there when the planes get there
> I don't feel its a first class carrier right now.
> Mechanical problems.
>
> (*Advertising Age* 23 July 1990)

The ad admits these are true but promises to try and improve! Apart from attracting attention, this strategy also skilfully manipulates the assumption that ads lie. The honesty of a part cunningly implies the honesty of the whole.

Such total reversals of expectations may make us wonder whether any feature of ads is stable other than their instability. Yet, though the method and the content may change, the desired effect remains the same: to influence behaviour in the way demanded by the advertisers' brief, by their employer. Yet even this down-to-earth feature is not as stable as it seems. Adam Lury, one of Britain's most innovative advertisers, claimed in a tv discussion[12] to exercise control over this constraint by refusing to accept ads to which he had moral objections, citing high-pressure toy ads and ads for South African goods as examples.[13] Such freedom of choice may be rare, limited, or a cynical publicity stunt, but it should also give pause to the image of the advertiser as necessarily a slave of the client.

10.4 USES OF TIME AND SPACE

The time and space of an ad are usually limited: a minute or less of tv time, the area of a screen or poster, one or two pages of a magazine. Even within that limited time and space, there are apparently further constraints of content and function. The advertiser, it seems, is obliged to serve a client and sell a particular product. The stereotypical ad is distinguished from other discourses by its obligatory reference to a product, and its intention to make that product appeal to the addressee. It might also seem that an ad must take time and a space to identify itself as an ad, and such restraints could account for the predictability, uniformity and superficiality of many ads. An ad is a time and a space whose content – already hopelessly brief – is also predetermined.

The situation is, however, more complicated. Though time and space are indeed limited, there are a number of reasons why their use is not as predictable as might at first appear.

10.4.1 Uses of time and space: seeking to change behaviour

The notion that ads must always refer to a product (or service) is limited to ads which sell something: product ads (see section 1.3). These are the majority of ads, it is true, but there is also a minority of non-product ads – warnings, health advice, political campaigns and charitable appeals – which do not fit into this category. A general characterization of ads will need to take these into account too.

If we view ads as discourse advocating a change of behaviour, rather than as just referring to a product, then both kinds of ad can be accounted for. Product ads also refer to a change of behaviour: buying the product. Non-product ads (which are often conveniently ignored by the opponents of ads) encourage such changes of behaviour as not drinking and driving, wearing a condom, voting Green, releasing a hostage, going to a concert, sending money for famine relief, helping a political prisoner, even paradoxically (in ads for advertising control) reporting ads which are untruthful. Yet even in non-product ads (including those of which we approve) the argument that the content is predetermined still applies. An Amnesty International ad must tell you about the work of Amnesty International with the purpose of getting you to join or send money. So the claim that all ads advocate a change of behaviour makes little difference to the issue of whether the content of ads, and therefore their use of time and space, is determined. Ads may not always be obliged to refer to a product, but they *are* still obliged to refer, however obliquely, to a change of behaviour.

Yet the reference to a change of behaviour need neither occupy much time or space nor preclude other elements entirely; and it is not the case that for the receiver who does not change his or her behaviour as suggested there is nothing else in the ad at all.

Ads do not always refer to the advocated behaviour directly, though in the case of ads which encourage purchase the identity of the product must be clear. Naming is often oblique, and demands some induction on the part of the receiver; but, as in riddles and lateral thinking problems, addressees derive pleasure from their own successful inferencing strategies and ability to decipher unusual ways of encoding the product name. In Britain, some recent famous and popular campaigns, such as those for Silk Cut cigarettes, are widely believed not to name their product (see section 3.5). Nothing could be further from the truth, for these ads consist entirely of an elaborate and roundabout naming. In the wordless pictures, a piece of silk iconically signifies SILK, which is the signified of the signifier 'silk'; another object or action iconically signifies a CUT, which is the signified of the signifier 'cut'; the two signifiers then combine to form a composite signifier 'silk cut' which in turn names the cigarettes. Yet in most ads the naming of the product takes very little space.

10.4.2 Uses of time and space: establishing the discourse type

Similarly, in contemporary ads, very little space is taken either establishing the text as an ad or by overt persuasion. Ads do not need to identify themselves as ads, for this is done, as it were, outside them, by their position within other discourse types. Once recognized as an ad, the intention to persuade the addressee is assumed. Product ads simply depict a scene, including the product, and/or the name of the product. Non-product ads often show only the effects of not adopting the advocated behaviour: accidents caused by drunkenness, people worried about AIDS, etc. They too do not need to say that their intention is to alter our behaviour.

10.4.3 Uses of time and space: opportunity and variety

So it takes little or none of the available time or space to refer to a product or desired behaviour; establishing the discourse type and the intention to persuade may take no space at all. Even where there is reference to one or more of these supposedly 'defining' features, they need not be at the centre of either the sender's or the receiver's attention. This frees the time or space of the ad – small as it is – for other uses. The obligatory core element – 'do this' (usually 'buy our goods') – is either external to the text or only a small proportion of it. Almost the entire time or space of the ad is left, to be used in any way which does not negate that central core.

The use of such vacant discourse time and space says a great deal about the needs of the society from which it comes. In this respect it is revealing that ads of the 1950s and early 1960s filled this space with pseudo-scientific descriptions of newly available goods, that the ads of the late 1960s and 1970s used it to present an idyllic and idealized fictional world. But no particular use is definitive of this discourse type, and it would be a mistake to assume that the features of ads in one decade are features of advertising as a whole. As the reverses cited in section 10.2 bear witness, the uses of this time and space have changed, are changing, and will probably go on changing, at least until this restless new discourse type cools down. Yet, though these uses may not be defining of the discourse type, it is they, rather than the minimal core, which attract interest.

10.4.4 Uses of time and space: giving pleasure

But how do ads actually use this vacant time and space? The traditional critical view (derived from the advertising of the 1950s–70s) has been that it is used first to attract receivers' attention, then trick them into buying the product, appealing to greed, vanity, lust and fear, and suggesting that purchase will make the receiver like the people portrayed. For many ads, this characterization is as true as ever. Yet the time and space in contemporary ads is also used in other and more complex ways as well, and the general tendency is perhaps away from simple attention-grabbing and deception.

It is worth considering that ads, despite the belief of manufacturers and advertisers that they exist solely to promote goods, may do many other things as well, and that these other activities are extremely revealing about the needs of contemporary society. Debate about the morality of ads tends to focus on the use of time and space to sell. This, however, may be only a small part of ads' function and attractiveness.

Pateman (1985) and Thompson (1990) argue that many ads aim to give pleasure, and thus create a loose association between this pleasure and the advocated behaviour.[14] If this is the case, then further questions arise about what exactly gives pleasure, and why. We might suppose that pleasure is an epiphenomenon, a side-effect of experience which, while not of immediate practical or social benefit, is yet in the long run biologically, socially or psychologically beneficial. In previous chapters we have analysed the ways in which the space of contemporary ads is used: to merge the public and private; to foreground elements of the substances and codes used in discourse through innovative use of paralanguage, parallelism, and connotational meaning. It seems that such features give pleasure and answer a need. We need to consider why.

10.4.5 Uses of time and space: code play

As we have seen in Chapters 2–6, ads indulge in **code play**: focusing attention upon the substance and means of communication, rather than using these only to refer to the world. At the textual level they play with the sounds and rhythms, meaning and grammatical patterns of language. As has often been observed, such self-reflexive use of language is a common feature of poetry. The question arises as to whether some advertising merits being described as 'poetic', and whether, more generally, it has usurped some of the social and psychological functions of poetry.

Sadly, the discourse of poetry is in practice now often confined to a social minority. Even within that minority, it is frequently considered as a private and individual activity rather than as a public and collective one. It has also become synonymous with seriousness, and is valued only if it is felt to yield some insight of social or individual significance. In these circumstances, some ads may answer a need for a light-hearted code play in the public domain, which, though once provided by poetry, is now no longer available to many people, either because they do not come into contact with poetry or because, when they do, they are encouraged to focus only upon its more serious aspects or manifestations.

'Useless' play with language – patterning and variation of no apparent meaning or purpose – is now often restricted to intimate discourse: lover talk, baby talk, grumbling, boasting, banter. Yet it is also reminiscent of public discourses of a kind associated with very different times and places in our[15] own – riddles, rituals, spells and incantations. The diminishing importance of such discourse in our societies is evidence of a dislocation of public and private. Though there are other discourse types, such as graffiti, stand-up comedy and pop songs which bring code play into the public domain, they are often marginalized. Graffiti are regarded as irresponsible and criminal; stand-up comedy and pop songs are denied the status of poetry or drama. Yet the code play of such marginalized 'low' discourses may answer a need. They fuse the public and private domains, and indulge in trivial public wordplay in a society dominated by notions of communication as the 'container' of facts or deep insights, or the performer of utilitarian practical and social functions. In literature code play is often valued only as the vehicle of psychological and social insight; in ads the means of selling and trade. Ads' apparently trivial uses of language, in other words, are given high status through their association with big business, trade and prosperity. It is as though we need a reason for the pleasure of code play, and cannot value it for itself. It reflects badly, I believe, on contemporary values, that we must give such reasons for this pleasure. Manipulation of the code, so widely enjoyed in all cultures, must in contemporary society often be justified in terms of something else. In ads, the commercial role is an excuse!

But this view, far from answering all problems, leads on to others. Why is code play so pleasurable, and why does it resurface in new discourse types when it is undervalued or marginalised in others, or denied to a section of the community? What is its function? On the psychological level, it may be that code play has cognitive benefits of which we are only vaguely aware, providing us with a readiness for complex change and innovation which is essential to human survival.[16] It may also be typical of language which functions as a means of display.

10.4.6 Uses of time and space: display and ritual boasting

As already described in Chapter 7, Goffman ([1976] 1979) has suggested that ads frequently make use of verbal and other communicative behaviour reminiscent of 'display' and ritual boasting between contestants (both animal and human). The purpose of display is to establish identity, to act out a version of the relationships which exist within society. As such, it may be, on occasion, a kind of talking-to-oneself in public, as much for the benefit of the sender as of the receiver, whose reception of it may be almost incidental. It is an aspect of behaviour neglected by functional views of language, which tend either to ignore it, conflate it with the phatic function, or regard it as an ephemeral feature in infancy. Perhaps one reason for its neglect is its association with aggression – though it is often a substitute for violence, a means of avoiding rather than initiating conflict. Though it may originate in competitiveness, this origin is often eclipsed by the intricacies of composition, which become a substitute purpose in themselves. Another reason for neglect is the incompatibilty of its apparent use*less*ness with descriptions which classify all uses of codes in terms of their social or practical use*ful*ness. Yet its ubiquity and persistence suggest that it is both an important and a needed activity, even if we cannot explain why; there is good reason to agree with Goffman that ads, in contemporary society, partly answer this need. They are an activity absorbing an amount of effort, talent and attention, far in excess of their proclaimed purpose.

Because display is in essence talking for the sake of talking, it leads to the use of language and other semiotic systems in ways which are repetitive and predictable, or – if innovative – seem to play with substance and code for no purpose other than to attract attention. It may also involve, as does talking to oneself, the dramatisation of points of view as different voices – a feature which the discourse of display shares with that of the novel.

Ads' repetition of the same texts, over and over again, is a feature which is so obvious that it is often neglected. A regular tv watcher may see the same ad tens of times or more, a magazine reader will see the same print ad again and again. Most discourse types, in contrast, are received only once.

An exception to this is favourite works of literature and art, which may be read or experienced repeatedly. Another exception are prayers and liturgies. A difference between these texts and those of ads, however, is that the repetition of ads is not sought out, but forced upon us. One reason for the dislike of ads is this unsolicited intrusiveness.

Although there is evidence to suggest that lengthy verbatim repetition is less common in pre-literate societies than commonly supposed,[17] repeated texts are a feature in literate and partly literate societies. Again, they unite the most private and the most public spheres. Prayers, for example, are said not only at children's bedsides, at deathbeds, at moments of crisis and loss, but also in public congregation. The words of songs are also repeated in the most private and public circumstances. One might speculate that repetition induces a sense of security, community, and is a means of establishing or confirming (if only to oneself) identity within the society to which the text belongs (because everyone within the society knows the same text). Repetition also allows the comfort of speech, without the burden of invention. In many contemporary societies, especially those in which rote knowledge of prayers or poetry and songs has declined,[18] such widely shared texts are hard to find. Ads, by constantly repeating themselves, seem to bid for this need. Yet participation of the receiver in these repetitions of ads is passive. Perhaps the purchase of a product is a kind of surrogate participation!

Ads are not usually regarded as poetry or art, but perhaps poetry and art, while adding much more besides, also partake of this need for display and repetition, and it is this common origin which accounts for some apparent similarities with ads.

10.5 AESTHETIC VALUE JUDGEMENTS

The rapidly changing uses of the available space in ads, and its employment for purposes other than those of the manufacturer, has dismayed and confused critics. But the problem remains as to whether the existence of the mercenary central core (even if it is unstated or only briefly mentioned) debars ads in perpetuity from achieving the status and acclaim of the arts. Are ads comparable to the uni-modal arts of literature, music, painting, photography, or to the bi-modal or multi-modal forms of art such as song, opera or film? Although they represent fictional situations and scenes, and demand the same technical skills as other arts, many people still feel that they do not have such profound importance, or give such sustained pleasure.

The reason for this cannot be explained away as arising from their short length: one page in a magazine or at most sixty seconds of television time. Many paintings and poems are as brief in space or time, and the simultaneous use of writing and pictures, in conjunction with speech and music on tv, gives ads, like opera or film, dimensions which create concentrations of meaning which the linear nature of language, or the static nature of still photography and painting, find difficult to emulate.

Neither can the relation of ads to the arts be explained away by defining different artistic genres in minimalist terms using such parameters as length, mixtures of modes and so on. (Saying, for example, that poetry is language presented in lines or making use of rhythm; that painting is coloured marks on a two-dimensional surface, etc.) By such criteria, advertising can be not only excluded from other genres, but also assigned a slot of its own, defined in terms of typical length, its combination of the modes of music, language and pictures. (This in turn allows sub-categorization of ads by medium.) But such a formal approach dodges the key issue of value. Considering the strength of a possible comparison with poetry, for example, it must be said that poetry, in the contemporary view, is not just *any* discourse in lines or rhythm but *valuable* discourse in lines or rhythm. Indeed, the sense of value outweighs all other criteria, for discourse in lines or rhythm but without value is only 'verse', whereas discourse without these formal features may still be described as poetry.

It is this emphasis on value which for many people excludes ads from admission into the cannons of art. This value, moreover, is often associated with opposition to or detachment from the dominant values of society. In comparison with literature, ads accept and glorify the dominant ideology while literature often rejects and undermines it. The fact that ads must answer to the brief of their clients may also lead to a feeling that ads are typically vehicles of deceit, while art is a vehicle of honesty.

Yet the notion that art is rebellious and honest is not universal. The kind of relationship which ads have to their patrons, and their service to their patrons' ideology, is by no means unknown in the arts, especially in music and painting. In music this is usually considered unimportant. Handel and Mozart are not considered compromised by their jobs as court musicians. In pictorial art, the situation is more complex. Take, for example, Western European portraiture and religious painting of the Renaissance. Such paintings have many of the features often detrimentally attributed to ads. The creators (often a team rather than an individual) worked under patronage, with strict instructions from their employer. They both ex-pressed and were limited by the general dominant ideology of their society. A receiver who objects to that ideology (Catholicism, hereditary privilege, inequality) might object to such paintings. They propagate those values, just as ads propagate certain political economic and social means of organization. The strength of that ideology has been softened by time and the diminution of their patrons' power, but that may also happen to ads. Yet it is not, for many people, the expression of beliefs imposed from outside (which the painter may well have shared) which is valued. As in ads, there was space in these paintings, around the central obligatory core, for other purposes, and they are not *merely* evangelical, exegetic or flattering of their patrons. Consequently, they are not *only* valued for the purposes for which they were commissioned. Yet, for some people, the ideological purpose of such creative activity overweighs all other considerations (Berger 1972). For others it is relatively unimportant. It may be that in ads the ideological content is salient because it is contemporary. Perhaps it will soften as time progresses, enabling receivers to turn to elements outside the central mercenary core – though it may also be that, when they do, they will find nothing there to value.

Yet whereas music, and to some degree the pictorial arts, may maintain its integrity under patronage, it is harder for the verbal arts to do so. It is in the nature of language to commit its user to a point of view more unequivocally than pictures and music, and whereas painters and composers may survive the constraints of patronage it is harder for the speaker or writer to do the same. Consequently, there is a stronger link between independence and the right to dissent in literature than in the other arts. For this reason, the verbal creations of advertising, though often skilful and clever, seem unable to attract the same positive evaluation which would lead them to be classed as literary. Ads may have usurped some of the functions of literature, and in particular poetry, but there is reason to regret this. Poetry, when not limited to minorities or monopolised by limited interpretations, may, being disinterested and freer, fulfil these functions more fully. If there is some need for code-play and display in our society, there is reason to regret the fulfilment of this need in a commercial arena permeated by competitive consumption.

Yet the very quantity of advertising in our society, the skill and effort which goes into its creation, the complexity of its discourse, and the impression it undoubtedly makes, are enough to make it interesting. Advertising can focus and redefine ideas about language, discourse, art and society, and in this respect its study is well worthwhile.

Figure 55 Fuji film ad

Notes

FOREWORD

1 *Collins Concise Dictionary Plus*.
2 The pronoun 'we' is often used to imply a uniformity which does not exist, to exclude outsiders, or to create a scientific impersonality. In this book it means people who belong to a society where advertising is a prominent discourse. 'I' (the writer) am such a person, and I assume that 'you' (the reader) are too.

1 INTRODUCTION: ADS AS A DISCOURSE TYPE

1 *Campaign* 21 December 1990: 33–4.
2 George Lakoff (1987: 145) argues that this view of prototype representations as an aid to recognition has since been abandoned by Rosch. Prototypes, he claims, are used in reasoning rather than recognition.
3 The fact that the slogan 'Washes whiter' was adopted for a tv history of advertising (BBC2, 1–22 April 1990) reflects its status as a prototype.
4 The study of **cohesion** (the formal relationships between clauses and sentences in texts) is what some people mean by 'discourse analysis'; but the **coherence** of texts (their overall sense and unity) cannot be described with reference to language alone (see Cook 1989a: 14 44).

2 SUBSTANCE AND SURROUNDINGS

1 A slogo is a short phrase or clause regularly accompanying the name of the product.
2 Ads even occur without comment in programmes about ads, and an ad used in the programme may immediately precede or follow an ad in the advertising break.
3 The Gulf War of January 1991 witnessed a mass defection of advertisers in the USA from programming dominated by coverage of the fighting. Opinion polls, however, revealed that such programmes were widely regarded as fulfilling a public service, and advertisers who used them as 'doing their patriotic duty' (*Media Guardian* 15 April 1991).
4 A logo is a name or initial in a distinctive typeface.

3 PICTURES, MUSIC, SPEECH AND WRITING

1 This differs from the usual use in linguistics, where it is limited to language and used to refer to the choice of speech or writing – and various subdivisions of these such as reading aloud.
2 An exception is the work of Holbrook (described in Holbrook 1987).

3 'Sprite' is a registered trademark of the Coca-Cola Company.
4 There is a paradox here, as though music extended infinity. In theory the number of acceptable combinations which a language can produce is infinite (as Chomsky has often remarked, e.g. 1965: 19–37; 1988: 21–8) although in practice most possible combinations are not produced (Hymes 1972; Pawley and Syder 1983). Music has a similar potential to produce an infinity of linear (i.e. syntactic) combinations, yet any one of these can also be infinitely varied through the addition of other notes at any point in time (i.e. paradigmatically). (This comparison talks only in terms of morphemes and notes, and says nothing about voice quality, paralanguage, instruments, etc.)
5 In the very early days of film and tv advertising, Vance Packard's (1956) *The Hidden Persuaders*, based on very flimsy evidence, raised a quite unwarranted alarm about the dangers of 'subliminal advertising'.
6 Wrigley's controlled 88 per cent of the UK market in 1991 (*Campaign* 23 November 1991) and similar proportions elsewhere.
7 In the longer of two versions.
8 *The Thirty Second Seduction* (HBO (USA) 1989). (See under tv programmes in references.)
9 The Dada creation 'the gift' (by Man Ray, 1921) is also an iron with spikes.
10 **Homophones** are words with the same pronunciation but different meanings, e.g. herd, heard.

4 LANGUAGE AND PARALANGUAGE

1 This is not necessarily the order of the psychological processing of language.
2 Many words which seem onomatopoeic to speakers of one language do not seem so to speakers of another, even when those languages belong to the same family (e.g. Russian '*ga*' and English 'honk' for the noise of a goose). On the other hand, there are sometimes striking similarities between distant languages (the Japanese for 'miaow' is '*nyao*'). Although Saussure believed in the phenomenon of onomatopoeia, he marginalized its importance; for discussion, see Derrida [1967] (1976); (1974: 106–10); Culler (1983: 189).
3 This, at least, is the traditional view of metaphor. For a discussion of alternatives, see G. Lakoff and Johnson (1980: 106–10).
4 Peirce (see 4.1.3) uses the term 'symbol' in a more general sense to mean an arbitrary signifier.
5 'Rat' may even be realized without sounds or letters – as it is in shorthand or Chinese ideograms – and still be the same word.
6 For a critical discussion of this finding see Ellis and Beattie 1986: 165–72.
7 Quite independently, Steiner (1975: 99–114) describes the roots of Chomsky's theory in the exegesis of written texts.
8 Peirce uses the term 'symbol' more broadly for any arbitrary sign.
9 Both mean 'fart': the first a short, explosive fart, the second a long and loud one.
10 Ontogenetic is to do with the development of the individual; phylogenetic is to do with the development of the species.
11 This is perhaps changing: see, for example, Billen (1990).
12 In a lengthy court case between Elizabeth Taylor and her 'ex-lover' Henry Wynberg over who branded the perfume, one of its features was said to be its 'distinctive heart-shaped bottle' (*The Independent*, December 1990).
13 For further analyses of this advert, see Cook 1990b; forthcoming.
14 I am informed, however, by dunhill that the logo predates its use on cigarette packets by a quarter of a century.
15 This method of revealing repetition is influenced by Tannen (1989) who sets

out her transcriptions of spoken discourse so that repeated words and phrases occur next to each other or in columns.

5 WORDS AND PHRASES

1 The opening line of Kafka's *Metamorphosis*.
2 The opening line of a poem by Robert Frost.
3 The view of indeterminate meaning in this section is based on Cook 1991.
4 A collocation is a frequent occurrence of one or more words together, e.g. 'natural goodness'.
5 A homonym is a word with the same form but different meanings, e.g. 'bank' (of a river) and 'bank' (for money).
6 In *Voices*, broadcast by Channel 4 (UK, 1988). Searle's arguments against Artificial Intelligence are also in Searle [1980] (1987).
7 I do not imply that average perfume prices are negligible; but perfumes are one of that category of goods carefully – and presumably arbitrarily – priced just high enough to be perceived as indulgently extravagant for oneself, or lovingly generous as a gift.
8 Belk (1987) reports that in a survey of 248 American adults asked to grade items on a continuum between 'self' and 'not self', cars (for men) and perfumes (for women) ranked higher than any other products, with the former ranking higher for the subjects than their own bodily organs and religion!
9 A hunch confirmed by informal enquiries in the perfume departments of large stores.
10 An excellent fictional illustration of this is Patrick Suskind's novel *Perfume* [1985], set in eighteenth-century France.
11 For the meaning of these terms see section 4.1.1.
12 The celebrity being in semiotic terms a kind of sign (though much more besides).
13 Ford, as is well known, takes its name from its manufacturer Henry Ford. The Buick is called after David D. Buick, a Detroit plumber who entered the automobile business in 1899 and ended up bankrupt.
14 I assume the ad is aimed at the man of the couple.
15 The same forty young adults questioned about *White Linen*.

6 PROSODY, PARALLELISM, POETRY

1 In Old and Middle English verse the **caesura**, a break in the middle of the line, is the norm rather than an innovation.
2 Significantly, Thomas Sebeok, the editor of the Indiana conference papers (Sebeok 1960), has recently been a key figure in another cross-disciplinary conference on marketing and semiotics (Umiker-Sebeok 1987).
3 I have altered Jakobson's original terminology to bring it into line with that in Chapter 1.
4 An exception is Hopkins's 'sprung rhythm'.
5 Both nouns and adjectives can function as complements.
6 A device also used in an ad for the perfume *Beautiful*.
7 Computer corpora (providing both larger quantities of examples and the means to search and retrieve them) are a partial answer to this problem. They cannot, however, provide information about a new utterance other than to say that it has not occurred before. They are thus of little help in assessing deviant language, and saying how a new combination 'feels' to an expert speaker.
8 Leech (1966: 4) suggests that the proof of a norm is the existence of parodies.

9 They are sometimes distinguished by the terms 'deviance' and 'deviation' respectively (Leech and Short 1981: 55–7). For an excellent discussion of the phenomenon and its terminology see Wales (1989: 116).

10 Jakobson (1960) himself had written: 'Any attempt to reduce the sphere of the poetic function to poetry or to confine poetry to the poetic function would be delusive oversimplification. The poetic function is not the sole function of verbal art but only its dominant, determining function, whereas in all other verbal activities it acts as a subsidiary, accessory constituent.'

11 Television advertising began in the UK in 1956.

7 CONNECTED TEXT

1 This does not imply that people in pre-literate cultures remember discourse verbatim. Contrary to popular belief, they do not (Lord 1960; Buchan 1972; Ong 1982: 59–61). But their discourse does make extensive use of parallelism of many kinds, including plot structures, verse forms and sentence structure.

2 'Hidden' by being left in the most obvious place.

3 Though written as a separate sentence, 'creating . . .' is a non-finite relative clause which is part of the noun phrase in the preceding orthographic sentence.

4 For ease of reference I shall use the pronoun 'she' generically in this paragraph. Clearly identifications are affected by the gender of singer and receiver.

5 This and the following claims about pronoun interpretation in songs and ads are based on an informal survey of forty-seven (thirty-one female, sixteen male) young British adults.

6 A fuller version of this analysis can be found in Cook 1988.

7 I first encountered this ad on the London Underground – a situation where people are likely to pay more attention to the words of ads than usual.

8 *Shorter Oxford English Dictionary*.

8 NARRATIVE VOICES

1 Note how the connotation of 'bears' raises this plastic card to the level of heraldry!

2 In many ritual 'dialogues', neither voice is independent.

3 Writing is not necessarily non-reciprocal, nor speech reciprocal, but there is an affinity between speech and reciprocity, writing and non-reciprocity.

4 See *Marketing* 7 February 1991: 21–4. The numbers of people involved is one reason for high costs. 'Last stick', for example, cost $5.5 million to make (*Campaign* 23 November 1990).

5 There are of course considerable differences between the uses of T/V in different languages. Correspondingly, motives for choice may vary. Western-style ads now appearing in Russian invariably use the V form '*vy*', in reaction against the '*ty*' of communist slogans.

6 I do not make use here of the customary distinction in linguistics between the semantic meaning of an utterance (its encoded denotation which is not context dependent) and its pragmatic **force** (what it is intended or taken to do by particular people in a particular context). In keeping with Bakhtin's belief that the former cannot be divorced from the latter, I use the term 'meaning' to encompass both.

7 They have elements in common with Firthian linguistics (see e.g. Firth 1957), Vygotsky's theories of language acquisition (Vygotsky [1934] 1962), pragmatics, reader response theory and deconstruction.

8 'Occidental' includes Russian philosophy and is opposed to 'Oriental'; I use this

term to avoid confusion with the more recent political division of East and West.

9 I follow the view of Bakhtin's most authoritative translators and biographers, K. Clark and Holquist (1984), that this book, and Volosinov [1927] (1973), published under the name of Bakhtin's friend Volosinov, are by Bakhtin.

10 The idea of the self as separate from discourse and society is so deeply 'written into' our way of speaking that it is very difficult not to fall back on it.

11 This view of the self as primarily social has a long tradition in Russian thought (Cook 1990d). It is also evident in the work of the psychologist Vygotsky (1886–1934) who, in developing a theory of child development, suggested that the child first enters into and participates in communicative behaviour without understanding, then gradually internalizes this behaviour, to create his or her 'self'.

12 For a discussion of Bakhtin's attitudes to Marxism see K. Clark and Holquist 1984: 295–341.

13 This political use of a messenger, though justified by busy schedules, is also a confusion tactic, introducing another voice, giving the sender a later option of withdrawal and dissociation. Secretaries are often employed to the same effect.

14 Even two hundred and fifty years later, when readers are very different from those originally envisaged.

15 A clause which draws attention to the convention of suspended disbelief in the fictional world, treating names within it as though they existed independently and were not invented by the author.

16 An example is Swift's *Gulliver's Travels*.

17 An example is Henry James's *The Turn of the Screw*.

18 An example is Poe's *The Facts in the Case of M. Valdemar*.

19 For a summary of the critical debate see Leech and Short 1981: 339.

20 In the pre-Romantic moral code of Jane Austen's novels, it also signifies superficiality.

21 In an earlier novel, *Northanger Abbey*, she had made a much more explicit use of the voice of one particular Gothic novel, Anne Radcliffe's *The Mysteries of Udolpho*.

22 Significantly, though women frequently correct other women in ads, very few ads show a man being corrected by another man.

23 *Marketing* (7 March 1991).

9 WAYS OF HEARING

1 These terms reflect attitudes of receivers; the term 'addressee', by contrast, reflects the intentions of the sender.

2 *France-Soir* Expos Special: 'Art Pub', November 1990: 3.

3 According to *Private Eye* one famous actor was so keen to appear in a coffee ad that he shaved off the beard he had grown to play King Lear.

4 *The Independent* 30 November 1990.

5 *Equinox: Junk Mail*, Channel 4 (UK) 14 October 1990.

10 CONCLUSION: ADS AS A DISCOURSE TYPE

1 Apparent exceptions to this are junk mail and hoardings. But junk mail is embedded in the post it accompanies, and the hoardings are embedded (although they also often dominate) in road signs and other information.

2 The term 'short bursts', though derived from tv, is applicable to magazines and posters too; for, though it is possible for attention to linger on them as on any printed text, we flick or drive past them, creating the effect of short burst.

3 See Note 2 in the Foreword for comment on this use of 'our' and 'us'.

4 For discussion of this point see, for example, Hudson (1972); Chalmers (1982).

5 The cliché derives as much from the set phrases 'rippling muscles' and 'steel blue eyes' as from the person – factual or fictional – to whom they refer.

6 *Hamlet* III: ii: 27

7 The distinction between pictures of real and fictional scenes is, as many have commented, more complex than popularly supposed. A real scene may be used as fiction, or a fictional scene presented as real. For discussion of this, see Goffman (1976: 10–23) and Barthes ([1961] 1977: 15–32).

8 *The Observer* 25 March 1990.

9 *The Observer* 26 May 1991.

10 In the USA and elsewhere, but not in Britain, where the effect of legislation leads to ads which do not show anyone smoking at all.

11 For an excellent analysis of these changes in gender portrayal see the tv programme *Washes Whiter* (BBC2 1–22 April 1990); also Frances (1989).

12 *Behind the Headlines* BBC2 12 December 1990.

13 A similar claim is made in a Reebok ad which refers to the company's refusal to invest in South Africa.

14 The doubtful sales psychology of this does not invalidate the point. Advertisers may simply be wrong in assuming that an ad which gives pleasure also sells the product. One of the great popular fallacies about advertisers is that they possess psychological insights which give them uncontrollable power. This fear is similar to that of the security services (CIA KGB MI5, etc.) who are also imagined to have similar insights. In reality, the psychology of both may often be questionable, clumsy and unsuccessful.

15 I use the term 'our' in the belief that the decline in such discourses, though it may vary from society to society, is a general feature of most societies in the contemporary world. See also Note 2 in the Foreword.

16 This view is further developed in Cook (1990) and Cook (forthcoming).

17 See Note 1 of Chapter 7.

18 Though the words of songs are widely known, those of a particular song are often known by a section of society rather than by the society as a whole.

References

(Where a later edition or translation is cited, dates in square brackets indicate date of first publication or the original-language version.)

Althusser, L. (1971) *Lenin and Philosophy and Other Essays* (translated by B. Brewster), London: New Left Books.

Alvarado, M. and Thompson, J. (1990) (eds) *The Media Reader*, London: British Film Institute.

Argyle, M., Salter, V., Nicholson, H., Williams, M. and Burgess, P. (1970) 'The communication of inferior and superior attitudes by verbal and non-verbal signals', *British Journal of Social and Clinical Psychology* 9: 222–31.

Argyle, M., Alkema, F. and Gilmour, R. (1971) 'The communication of friendly and hostile attitudes by verbal and non-verbal signals', *European Journal of Social Psychology* 1: 385–402.

Attridge, D. (1989) 'Closing statement: linguistics and poetics in retrospect', in N. Fabb, D. Attridge, A. Durant and C. MacCabe (eds) *The Linguistics of Writing*, Manchester: Manchester University Press.

Bakhtin, M.M. [1929] (1988) see Volosinov, V.N.

Bakhtin, M.M. [1929/1963] (1984) *Problems of Dostoevsky's Poetics* (translated by C. Emerson), Manchester: Manchester University Press.

Bakhtin, M.M. [1940/1965] (1968) *Rabelais and His World* (translated by H. Iswolsky), Cambridge, Massachusetts: MIT Press.

Barthes, R. [1957] (1973) *Mythologies* (translated by A. Lavers), London: Paladin.

Barthes, R. [1961] (1977) 'The photographic message', in Barthes 1977: 15–32.

Barthes, R. [1964] (1977) 'The rhetoric of the image', in Barthes 1977: 32–51.

Barthes, R. [1967] (1985) *The Fashion System* (translated by M. Ward and R. Howard), London: Cape.

Barthes, R. [1968] (1977) 'The death of the author', in Barthes 1977: 142–9.

Barthes, R. [1972] (1977) 'The grain of the voice', in Barthes 1977: 179–90.

Barthes, R. (1977) *Image, Music, Text* (translated by S. Heath), London: Fontana.

Beezer, A., Grimshaw, J. and Barker, M. (1986) 'Methods for cultural studies students', in D. Punter (ed.) *Introduction to Contemporary Cultural Studies*, London: Longman.

Belk, R. W. (1987) 'Identity and the relevance of market, personal and community objects', in J. Umiker-Sebeok (ed.) *Marketing and Semiotics*, Amsterdam: Mouton de Gruyter.

Berger, J. (1972) *Ways of Seeing*, London: BBC and Penguin.

Bernstein, D. (1974) *Creative Advertising*, London: Longman.

Bernstein, L. (1976) *The Unanswered Question*, Cambridge, Massachusetts: Harvard University Press.

Billen, A. (1990) 'The trouble with Trot', *Observer*, 18 November.
Bolinger, D. (1975) *Aspects of Language* (2nd edn), New York and Chicago: Harcourt Brace Jovanovich.
Bolinger, D. (1980) *Language: The Loaded Weapon*, London: Longman.
Bonney, B. and Wilson, H. [1983] (1990) 'Advertising and the manufacture of difference', in M. Alvarado and J. Thompson (eds) *The Media Reader*, London: British Film Institute.
British Code of Advertising Practice (1988) (8th edn), London: Committee of Advertising Practice.
Brooks, R. (1990) 'Added value', *Radio Times*, 31 March.
Brown, G. and Yule, G. (1983) *Discourse Analysis*, Cambridge: Cambridge University Press.
Brown, P. and Levinson, S. (1978) 'Universals in language usage: politeness phenomena', in E. Goody (ed.) *Questions and Politeness: Strategies in Social Interaction*, Cambridge: Cambridge University Press.
Brown, P. and Levinson, S. (1987) *Politeness: Some Universals in Language Usage*, Cambridge: Cambridge University Press.
Buchan, D. (1972) *The Ballad and the Folk*, London: Routledge & Kegan Paul.
Cameron, L. (1991) 'Off the beaten track: a consideration of the implications for teachers of recent developments in the study of metaphor' *English in Education* 25(2): 4–15.
Carey, P. (1982) *Bliss*, London: Pan (Picador).
Carter, R. (1989) 'Introduction', in R. Carter and P. Simpson (eds) *Language, Discourse and Literature*, London: Unwin Hyman.
Chalmers, A.F. (1982) *What Is This Thing Called Science?*, Milton Keynes: Open University Press.
Chaplin, R. (1990) 'Henry's paperweight: the banks and tv advertising', in G. Day (ed.) (1990) *Readings in Popular Culture: Trivial Pursuits?*, London: Macmillan.
Chapman, S. and Egger, G. (1983) 'Myth in cigarette advertising and health promotion', in H. Davis and P. Walton (eds) *Language, Image, Media*, Oxford: Basil Blackwell.
Chomsky, N. (1965) *Aspects of the Theory of Syntax*, Cambridge, Massachusetts: MIT Press.
Chomsky, N. (1988) *Language and the Problems of Knowledge: The Managua Lectures*, Cambridge, Massachusetts: MIT Press
Cinquin, C. (1987) 'Homo Coca-Colens: from marketing to semiotics and politics', in J. Umiker-Sebeok (ed.) *Marketing and Semiotics*, Amsterdam: Mouton de Gruyter.
Clark, E. (1988) *The Want Makers: Lifting the Lid off the World Advertising Industry*, London: Hodder & Stoughton.
Clark, K. and Holquist, M. (1984) *Mikhail Bakhtin*, Cambridge, Massachusetts: Harvard University Press.
Collins Concise Dictionary Plus (1989) London and Glasgow: Collins.
Cook, G. (1986) 'Text, extract and stylistic texture', in C. Brumfit and R. Carter (eds) *Literature and Language Teaching*, Oxford: Oxford University Press.
Cook, G. (1988) 'Stylistics with a dash of advertising', *Language and Style* **21** (2): 151–61
Cook, G. (1989a) *Discourse*, Oxford: Oxford University Press.
Cook, G. (1989b) 'Adverts, songs, jokes and graffiti: approaching literary through "sub-literary" writing', in D. Hill and S. Holden (eds) *Effective Teaching and Learning*, Basingstoke: Macmillan for Modern English Publications in association with the British Council.
Cook, G. (1990a) 'Transcribing infinity: problems of context presentation', *Journal*

of Pragmatics **14** (1): 1–24

Cook, G. (1990b) 'Goals and plans in advertising and literary discourse', *Parlance: Journal of the Poetics and Linguistic Association*, Lancaster University Linguistics Dept, **2** (2): 48–72.

Cook, G. (1990c) 'A theory of discourse deviation: the application of schema theory to the analysis of literary discourse', unpublished PhD thesis, University of Leeds.

Cook, G. (1990d) 'Contradictory voices', paper given at the annual Conference of the Poetics and Linguistics Association (PALA), University of Amsterdam, September.

Cook, G. (1991) 'Indeterminacy, translation and the expert speaker', in *The Role of Translation in Foreign Language Teaching*, Proceedings of the British Council, Goethe Institute, Ens-Credif *Triangle 10*, Paris: Diffusion Didier Erudition.

Cook, G. (forthcoming) *Discourse Deviation: Learning, Literature and Schema Theory* (provisional title), Oxford: Oxford University Press

Cubitt, S. (1991) *Timeshift: On Video Culture*, London and New York: Routledge.

Culler, J. (1975) *Structuralist Poetics*, London: Routledge & Kegan Paul.

Culler, J. (1983) *On Deconstruction*, London: Routledge & Kegan Paul.

Davis, H. and Walton, P. (eds) (1983) *Language, Image, Media*, Oxford: Basil Blackwell.

Day, G. (ed.) (1990a) *Readings in Popular Culture: Trivial Pursuits?*, London: Macmillan.

Day, G. (1990b) 'Introduction: popular culture – the conditions of control', in Day 1990a: 1–13.

Derrida, J. [1967] (1976) *Of Grammatology* (translated by G. Spivak), Baltimore, Maryland: Johns Hopkins University Press.

Derrida, J. (1974) *Glas*, Paris: Galilee.

Dimter, M. (1985) *On Text Classification*, in T. van Dijk (ed.) *Discourse and Literature*, Amsterdam: Benjamins.

Douglas, T. (1984) *The Complete Guide to Advertising*, London: Macmillan.

Dreyfus, H.L. (1987) 'Misrepresenting human intelligence', in R. Born (ed.) *Artificial Intelligence: The Case Against*, Beckenham: Croom Helm.

Durand, J. (1987) 'Rhetorical figures in the advertising image', in J. Umiker-Sebeok (ed.) *Marketing and Semiotics*, Amsterdam: Mouton de Gruyter.

Dyer, G. (1988) *Advertising as Communication*, London: Routledge.

Eikhenbaum, B.M. [1927] (1978) 'The theory of the formal method', in L. Matejka and K. Pomorska (eds) *Readings in Russian Poetics*, Ann Arbor, Michigan: Michigan University Press.

Eliot, T.S. (1919) *Hamlet and His Problems*, London: Faber & Faber.

Ellis, A. and Beattie, G. (1986) *The Psychology of Language and Communication*, London: Weidenfeld & Nicolson.

Fairclough, N. (1989) *Language and Power*, London: Longman.

Federal Trade Commission Staff Report on Advertising for Over-the-Counter Drugs, Washington, DC: US Government Printing Office.

Firth, J.R. (1957) *Papers in Linguistics 1934–51*, Oxford: Oxford University Press.

Fish, S. (1980) *Is There a Text in this Class?*, Cambridge, Massachusetts: Harvard University Press.

Fitzgerald, F. Scott [1926] (1967) *The Great Gatsby*, London: Heinemann.

Fontana Dictionary of Modern Thought (1988) edited by A. Bullock, O. Stallybrass, et al., London: Fontana.

Forceville, C. (1991) 'Verbo-pictorial metaphor in advertisements', in *Parlance, Journal of the Poetics and Linguistics Association*, Lancaster University

Linguistics Department **3** (1), Spring 1991: 7–20.

Forceville, C. (1991) 'Pictorial metaphor in advertising: relevance perspectives', paper given at the annual conference of the Poetics and Linguistics Association (PALA), University of Lancaster, September.

Foucault, M. [1969] (1979) 'What is an author?' (translated by J.V. Harari), in J.V. Harari (ed.) *Textual Strategies: Perspectives in Post-Structuralism* (reprinted in D. Lodge (ed.) (1988) *Modern Criticism and Theory: A Reader*, London: Longman).

Foucault, M. (1971) *L'Ordre du discours*, Paris: Gallimard.

Frances, M. (1989) 'Women in advertising', *Woman*, November: 56–9.

Fuentes, C. [1985] (1987) *The Old Gringo* (translated by M. Sayers Peden and the author), London: Pan (Picador).

Geis, M.L. (1982) *The Language of Television Advertising*, New York: Academic.

Gell, A. (1977) 'Magic, perfume, dream', in I.M. Lewis (ed.) *Symbols and Sentiments: Cross-Cultural Studies in Symbolism*, London.

Ginsberg, A. (1956) *'Howl' and Other Poems*, San Francisco, California: City Lights.

Goddard, J. [1985] (1990) 'Editorial', *International Journal of Advertising* **4** (4) (reprinted in M. Alvarado and J. Thompson (eds) *The Media Reader*, London: British Film Institute.

Goffman, E. [1976] (1979) *Gender Advertisements*, London: Macmillan.

Goffman, E. (1981) *Forms of Talk*, Oxford: Basil Blackwell.

Gombrich, E.H. (1977) *Art and Illusion* (5th edn), London: Phaidon.

Grice, H.P. [1967] (1975) 'Logic and conversation', in P. Cole and J.L. Morgan (eds) *Syntax and Semantics*, Vol. 3, *Speech Acts*, New York: Academic Press.

Halle, M. (1989) 'On theory and interpretation', in N. Fabb, D. Attridge, A. Durant and C. MacCabe (eds) *The Linguistics of Writing*, Manchester: Manchester University Press.

Halliday, M.A.K. (1975) *Learning How to Mean*, London: Arnold.

Halliday, M.A.K. (1978) *Language as a Social Semiotic*, London: Arnold

Halliday, M.A.K. (1985) *An Introduction to Functional Grammar*, London: Arnold.

Halliday, M.A.K. and Hasan, R. (1976) *Cohesion in English*, London: Longman.

Hodge, R. (1985) 'Song', in T. van Dijk (ed.) *Discourse and Literature*, Amsterdam: Benjamins.

Holbrook, M.B. (1987) 'The study of signs in consumer esthetics: an egocentric review', in J. Umiker-Sebeok (ed.) *Marketing and Semiotics*, Amsterdam: Mouton de Gruyter.

Hoshino, K. (1987) 'Semiotic marketing and product conceptualization', in J. Umiker-Sebeok (ed.) *Marketing and Semiotics*, Amsterdam: Mouton de Gruyter.

Hudson, L. (1972) *The Cult of the Fact*, London: Jonathan Cape.

Hymes, D. [1971] (1972) 'On communicative competence', in J.J. Gumperz and D. Hymes (eds) *Directions in Sociolinguistics: The Ethnography of Communication*, New York: Holt, Rinehart & Winston.

Jakobson, R. [1921] (1978) 'On realism in art' (translated by K. Magassy), in L. Matejka and K. Pomorska (eds) *Readings in Russian Poetics*, Ann Arbor, Michigan: Michigan University Press.

Jakobson, R. (1960) 'Concluding statement: linguistics and poetics', in T.A. Sebeok, (ed.) *Style in Language*, Cambridge, Massachusetts: MIT Press.

Jefferson, A. and Robey, D. (1986) *Modern Literary Theory: A Comparative Introduction* (2nd edn), London: Batsford.

Jhalley, S. [1987] (1990) 'The valorisation of consciousness: the political economy of symbolism', in M. Alvarado and J. Thompson (eds) *The Media Reader*, London: British Film Institute.

Joyce, J. [1914] (1956) *Dubliners*, Harmondsworth: Penguin.

Kafka, F. [1933] (1961) *Metamorphosis and Other Stories* (translated by W. Muir and E. Muir), Harmondsworth: Penguin.

Kanehisa, M. (1985) 'Orthography in Japanese advertising', unpublished MA dissertation, University of Leeds Department of Linguistics and Phonetics.

Kaplan, E.A. (1985) 'A postmodern play of the signifier: advertising, pastiche and schizophrenia in music television', in P. Drummond and R. Patterson (eds) *Television in Transition*, London: British Film Institute.

Kehret-Ward, T. (1987) 'Combining products in use; how the syntax of product use affects marketing decisions', in J. Umiker-Sebeok (ed.) *Marketing and Semiotics*, Amsterdam: Mouton de Gruyter.

Knight, M. (1990) 'Is the micro macho? A critique of the fictions of advertising', in G. Day (ed.) *Readings in Popular Culture: Trivial Pursuits?*, London: Macmillan.

Kress, G. (1990) *Reading Images*, Geelong, Australia: Deaking University Press.

Lakoff, G. (1987) *Women, Fire and Dangerous Things: What Categories Reveal about the Mind*, Chicago, Illinois: Chicago University Press.

Lakoff, G. and Johnson, M. (1980) *Metaphors We Live By*, London and Chicago, Illinois: University of Chicago Press.

Lakoff, R. (1973) 'The logic of politeness: on minding your p's and q's', in *Proceedings of the Ninth Regional Meeting of the Chicago Linguistic Society* 292–305.

Langer, S. (1967) *Mind: An Essay on Human Feeling*, vol. 1, Baltimore, Maryland and London: Johns Hopkins University Press.

Lawrence, D.H. [1915] (1949) *The Rainbow*, Harmondsworth: Penguin.

Lawrence, D.H. (1922) (1960) *England My England*, Harmondsworth: Penguin.

Leech, G.N. (1966) *English in Advertising*, London: Longman.

Leech, G.N. (1969) *A Linguistic Guide to English Poetry*, London: Longman.

Leech, G.N. (1981) *Semantics* (2nd edn), Harmondsworth: Penguin.

Leech, G.N. (1990) 'What is a text: the case of Kentucky Fried Chicken', paper given at the annual Conference of the Poetics and Linguistics Association (PALA), University of Amsterdam, September.

Leech, G.N. and Short, M.H. (1981) *Style in Fiction*, London: Longman.

Leith, W. (1990) 'Pump it up', *The Independent on Sunday*, 8 July.

Levinson, S.C. (1983) *Pragmatics*, Cambridge: Cambridge University Press.

Levinson, S.C. (1988) 'Putting linguistics on a proper footing: explorations in Goffman's concept of participation', in P. Drew and A. Wooton (eds) *Erving Goffman: Exploring the Interaction Order*, Cambridge: Polity Press.

Lévi-Strauss, C. [1964] (1969) *The Raw and the Cooked* (translated by J. Weightman and D. Weightman), New York: Harper & Row.

Lord, A. (1960) *The Singer of Tales*, Cambridge, Massachusetts: Harvard University Press.

Lyons, J. (1977) *Semantics* (2 vols), Cambridge: Cambridge University Press.

MacCannell, D. (1987) "Sex sells": comment on gender images and myth in advertising', in J. Umiker-Sebeok (ed.) *Marketing and Semiotics*, Amsterdam: Mouton de Gruyter.

Macherey, P. [1966] (1978) *A Theory of Literary Production*, London: Routledge & Kegan Paul.

McLuhan, M. (1964) 'Keeping upset with the Joneses', in *Understanding Media*, London: Routledge & Kegan Paul.

Morris, D. (1977) *Manwatching: A Field Guide to Human Behaviour*, London: Cape.

Morris, D. et al. (1979) *Gestures: Their Origins and Distribution*, London: Cape.

Myers, J. and Simms, M. (1989) *The Longman Dictionary of Poetic Terms*, London: Longman.

Myers, K. (1983) 'Understanding advertisers', in H. Davis and P. Walton (eds) *Language, Image, Media*, Oxford: Basil Blackwell.

Myers, K. (1986) *Understains . . . the Sense and Seduction of Advertising*, London: Commedia.

Newman, N. (1986) 'Poetry processing', *Byte* February: 221–8.

Noth, W. (1987) 'Advertising: the frame message', in J. Umiker-Sebeok (ed.) *Marketing and Semiotics*, Amsterdam: Mouton de Gruyter.

Olson, C. (1950) 'Poetry New York', in D. Allen (ed.) *The New American Poetry*, New York: Grove Press.

Ong, W.J. (1982) *Orality and Literacy*, London: Routledge.

Packard, V. (1956) *The Hidden Persuaders*, Harmondsworth: Penguin.

Pateman, T. (1985) 'How is understanding an advertisement possible', in H. Davis and P. Walton (eds) *Language, Image, Media*, Oxford: Basil Blackwell.

Pawley, A. and Syder, F. (1983) 'Two puzzles for linguistic theory: nativelike selection and nativelike fluency', in J. Richards and R. Schmidt (eds) *Language and Communication*, London: Longman.

Peirce, C.S. [1931–58] *Collected Papers 1931–1958* (8 vols), Cambridge, Massachusetts: Harvard University Press.

Reddy, M. (1978) 'The conduit metaphor', in A. Ortony (ed.) *Metaphor and Thought*, Cambridge: Cambridge University Press.

Rosch, E. (1977) 'Human categorization', in N. Warren (ed.) *Advances in Cross-Cultural Psychology*, vol. 1, New York: Academic Press.

Saussure, F. de [1915] (1974) *Course in General Linguistics* (translated by W. Baskin), London: Fontana.

Searle, J. (1969) *Speech Acts: An Essay in the Philosophy of Language*, Cambridge: Cambridge University Press.

Searle, J. (1975a) 'Indirect speech acts' in P. Cole, and J.L. Morgan (eds) *Syntax and Semantics*, Vol. 3, *Speech Acts*, New York: Academic Press.

Searle, J. (1975b) 'A taxonomy of illocutionary acts', in K. Gunderson (ed.) *Language, Mind and Knowledge*, Minnesota Studies in the Philosophy of Science vol. 7, Minneapolis, Minnesota: University of Minnesota Press.

Searle, J. [1980] (1987) 'Minds, brains and programmes', in R. Born (ed.) *Artificial Intelligence: The Case Against*, Beckenham: Croom Helm.

Sebag-Montefiore, H. (1987) 'The bottom line', *Sunday Times* 1 February.

Sebeok, T.A. (ed.) (1960) *Style in Language*, Cambridge, Massachusetts: MIT Press.

Shklovsky, V. [1940] (1974) *Mayakovsky and His Circle* (translated by L. Feiler), London: Pluto.

Shorter Oxford English Dictionary (1944) (3rd edn) Oxford: Oxford University Press.

Sinclair, J. McH. (1966) 'Taking a poem to pieces', in R. Fowler (ed.) (1966) *Essays on Style and Language*, London: Routledge & Kegan Paul.

Solomon, M.R. and Assael, H. (1987) 'The forest or the trees? A gestalt approach to symbolic consumption', in J. Umiker-Sebeok (ed.) *Marketing and Semiotics*, Amsterdam: Mouton de Gruyter.

Sontag, S. [1962] (1972) 'Against interpretation', in *Against Interpretation and Other Essays*, Octogon (reprinted in D. Lodge (ed.) *20th Century Literary Criticism*, London: Longman.

Steiner, G. (1975) *After Babel*, Oxford: Oxford University Press.

Sterne, L. [1759–67] (1986)*Tristram Shandy*, Harmondsworth: Penguin.

Stetson, R.H. (1951) *Motor Phonetics*, Amsterdam: North Holland.

Stubbs, M. (1983) *Discourse Analysis*, Oxford: Basil Blackwell.

Suskind, P. [1985] (1987) *Perfume* (translated by J. Woods), Harmondsworth: Penguin.

Swales, J. (1990) *Genre Analysis*, Cambridge: Cambridge University Press.

Tannen, D. (1984) *Conversational Style: Analyzing Talk among Friends*, Norwood,

New Jersey: Ablex.

Tannen, D. (1989) *Talking Voices: Repetition, Dialogue and Imagery in Conversational Discourse*, Cambridge: Cambridge University Press.

Tauroza, S. and Allison, D. (1990) 'Speech rates in British English', *Applied Linguistics* **11** (1): 190–205.

Thompson, J.O. (1990) 'Advertising's rationality', in M. Alvarado and J. Thompson (eds) *The Media Reader*, London: British Film Institute.

Tomashevsky, B.V. [1925] (1965) 'Thematics', in L.T. Lemon and M.J. Reis (eds) *Russian Formalist Criticism: Four Essays*, Lincoln, Nebraska: University of Nebraska Press.

Umiker-Sebeok, J. (ed.) (1987) *Marketing and Semiotics*, Amsterdam: Mouton de Gruyter.

Vestergaard, T. and Schroder, K. (1985) *The Language of Advertising*, Oxford: Basil Blackwell.

Volosinov, V.N. (name used by M.M. Bakhtin) [1927] (1973) 'Freudianism: a critical sketch' (translated by I. Titunik), in *Freudianism: A Marxist Critique*, New York: Academic Press.

Volosinov, V.N. (name used by M.M. Bakhtin) [1929] (1988) *Marxism and the Philosophy of Language* (translated by L. Matejka and R. Titunik), Cambridge, Massachusetts: Harvard University Press.

Vorlat, E. (1985) 'Metaphors and their aptness in trade names for perfumes', in W. Paprotte and R. Dirven (eds) *The Ubiquity of Metaphor*, Amsterdam: Benjamins.

Vygotsky, L.S. [1934] (1962) *Thought and Language* (translated by E. Haufmann and G. Vakar), Cambridge, Massachusetts: MIT Press.

Wales, K. (1989) *A Dicitonary of Stylistics*, London: Longman.

Walsh, R. (1987) 'The language of perfume advertising', unpublished MA dissertation, University of Leeds Department of Linguistics and Phonetics.

Watt, I. [1957] (1963) *The Rise of the Novel*, London: Peregrine.

Werth, P.W. (1976) 'Roman Jakobson's verbal analysis of poetry', *Journal of Linguistics* **12**: 21–73.

White, D. (1988) Entry on advertising, in A. Bullock, O. Stallybrass, et al., *Fontana Dictionary of Modern Thought*, London: Fontana.

White, R. (1988) *Advertising: What It Is and How to Do It* (2nd cdn), London: McGraw Hill.

Widdowson, H.G. (1972) 'On the deviance of literary discourse', *Style* **6**: 292–308.

Widdowson, H.G. (1975) *Stylistics and the Teaching of Literature*, London: Longman.

Widdowson, H.G. (1978) *Explorations in Applied Linguistics*, Oxford: Oxford University Press.

Widdowson, H.G. (1984a) *Explorations in Applied Linguistics 2*, Oxford: Oxford University Press.

Widdowson, H.G. (1984b) 'Reference and representation as modes of meaning', in Widdowson 1984a: 150–9.

Widdowson, H.G. (1992) *Practical Stylistics*, Oxford: Oxford University Press.

Williams, R. [1960] (1980) 'Advertising: the magic system', in *Problems in Materialism and Culture*, London: Verso.

Williams, R. (1983) *Keywords* (2nd edn), London: Collins Fontana.

Williamson, J. (1978) *Decoding Advertisements*, London and Boston, Massachusetts: Marion Boyars.

Williamson, J. (1990) *Ads Nauseam*, in *Cosmopolitan*, January.

Wittgenstein, L. [1953] (1968) *Philosophical Investigations* (translated by G.E.M. Anscombe), Oxford: Basil Blackwell.

Wolfson, N. (1988) 'The bulge: a theory of speech behaviour and social distance', in J. Fine (ed.) *Second Language Discourse: A Textbook of Current Research*, Norwood, New Jersey: Ablex.

FILMS

Boursicot: *The Night of the Ad Watchers* (1990)
Makavejev: *W.R. The Mysteries of the Organism* (1971)
Robinson: *How to Get Ahead in Advertising* (1989)
Sturgess: *Christmas in July* (1940)
Tashlin: *Will Success Spoil Rock Hunter?* (1957)
Vigne: *A Woman or Two* (1985)
Welles: *Citizen Kane* (1941)

JOURNALS

Advertising Age
Campaign
Marketing

TELEVISION PROGRAMMES

Behind the Headlines, BBC2 (UK) 12 December 1990
Buy Me That!, HBO (USA) Consumer Reports Special 1989
Equinox: Junk Mail, Channel 4 (UK) 14 October 1990
Equinox: A Brush with the Greens, Channel 4 (UK) 4 November 1990
Lifestyles, Channel 4 (UK) 23 March 1989
The Marketing Mix, Yorkshire TV and Channel 4 (UK) Spring 1986
The Thirty Second Seduction, HBO (USA) Consumer Reports Special 1989
Washes Whiter, BBC2 (UK) 1–22 April 1990

Index

5542